DATE DUE

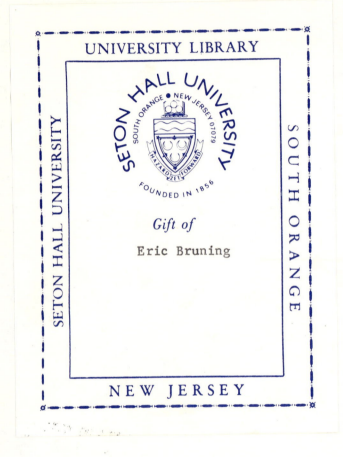

Introductory Statistics for Psychology

B. Michael Thorne
Mississippi State University

DUXBURY PRESS
North Scituate, Massachusetts

Introductory Statistics for Psychology was edited and prepared for composition by Margaret E. Hill. Interior design was provided by Jack Casteel. The cover was designed by Edward Aho.

Duxbury Press
A Division of Wadsworth Inc.

Library of Congress Cataloging in Publication Data

Thorne, Billy Michael, 1942–
  Introductory statistics for psychology.
  Includes index.
  1. Psychometrics. I. Title.
BF39.T477   150′.1′82   79-10613
ISBN 0-87872-222-X

Printed in the United States of America
1 2 3 4 5 6 7 8 9—83 82 81 80 79

Contents

Preface

A number of years ago I was using what I considered to be an adequate, if somewhat basic, text in my introductory psychological statistics class. After class one day a student happened to remark: "I can't understand why the authors named this book *Elementary Statistics*. It sure doesn't seem elementary to me." The student who made this comment was *not* one of the weaker students in the class.

Many statistics texts have the word "elementary" in their titles and quite a few at least pay lip service to the idea of a student who is not well prepared for a first course in statistics. However, I contend that at some point virtually all of the elementary texts currently available lose sight of the intended audience and include material and explanations guaranteed to traumatize the weaker student. The avoidance of "math shock" is a goal often expressed in the preface and introduction of "elementary" statistics texts but one that is ignored or forgotten in later sections of the book.

Many students entering psychology are not well versed in mathematics and, indeed, are somewhat frightened at the prospect of taking a course such as statistics. In fact, it has been my experience over the past ten years that a sizable minority of students in any introductory statistics class are very poorly prepared for any sort of math course and have great difficulty understanding the basic principles behind any of the tests and procedures covered. Of the many different levels on which an appreciation of statistics may be based, the two that this book aims at are: (1) an ability to utilize the various tests and methods presented, that is, a practical, applied approach, and (2) an intuitive feel for the principles underlying the various procedures.

My aim has been to write a simplified text without sacrificing the necessary content in an introduction to statistics in psychology.

At all times I have endeavored to keep the less well-prepared student in mind. For example, all definitions are stated as simply as possible; symbols have been simplified without compromising compatibility with other texts; complicated derivations and proofs have been omitted. Other omissions include two-way analysis of variance, complex analysis of variance designs, geometric means, and the discussion of sophisticated probability theory.

Emphasis has been placed on teaching the student to use the various tests and procedures discussed. At least two completely solved examples illustrate each new statistic or procedure. The sections labeled "Checking Your Progress," which follow the solved examples, give the student feedback concerning his or her ability to utilize the previously discussed technique. And, several additional exercises provided at the end of each chapter strengthen the student's computational skills.

To aid the student further in developing computational skills, each chapter (from chapter 4 on) contains a section entitled "Troubleshooting Your Computations." Here I discuss some of the more common errors that can be made in applying the techniques covered in the chapter. In many cases, these sections try to give the student a "feel" for correct and incorrect answers.

Where appropriate, discussions of the use of the simple pocket calculator are presented. This should enable interested students to maximize the potential benefit from their calculator.

I would like to gratefully acknowledge the continued advice and encouragement of Dr. D.A.R. Peyman. In addition, I would like to thank Dr. Bob Hudson for reading and constructively criticizing an early version of my manuscript. Finally, I would like to add a special word of thanks to Dr. Sol Schwartz, Kean College of New Jersey and Professor William Sawrey, California State University, Hayward and to all the anonymous reviewers who have added immeasurably to the final product.

I am grateful to the literary executor of the late Sir Ronald A. Fisher, F.R.S., to Dr. Frank Yates, F.R.S. and to Longman Group Ltd., London, for permission to reprint portions of Tables IV and VII from their book *Statistical Tables for Biological, Agricultural and Medical Research* (6th edition, 1974).

Introductory Statistics
for Psychology

1

Introduction

What Is Statistics?

Although a number of definitions of statistics might be given, for the purposes of this text *statistics* is defined as a set of tools concerned with the collection, organization, and analysis of numerical facts or observations. That is, statistics is a set of methods for dealing with data. By *data* I mean numbers, measurements of some kind. Herein lies the crux of the problem encountered by so many students with a course in elementary statistics. As the old saying goes, if I had a nickel for every time I have heard some student say, "I've always been weak in math" or "My weakest area is math," I would be a rich man. statistics data

I don't aim to make all of you statistical scholars; rather my goal is to enable you to apply the various tests and methods I present. Thus, my primary purpose is to supply the basic statistical procedures you'll need as you study psychology. Secondarily, I would like to impart an intuitive feel for the principles underlying the various procedures.

To make your learning task as easy as possible, I have been extremely careful both in what I have included in the text and in what I have omitted. That is, I have tried to incorporate only the most essential material for an introductory course and have not included techniques and theoretical material that might more properly be covered in a higher level course.

At the outset, I would like you to develop a positive attitude concerning your ability to learn the material covered in this text. Tell yourself repeatedly that the mathematics required to perform the various tests and manipulations in the text are very simple and that the algebraic knowledge required is minimal. By the way, you won't be lying to yourself.

Why Does a Psychologist Need to Know Anything about Statistics?

One of the first questions that any student taking a course in statistics might ask is: "Why do I need to take this course? Will I ever use this stuff or is it just another tradition that all students must suffer through?" These are reasonable questions to ask of any course you might take and if I can't give you satisfactory answers, I'm in trouble.

There are several possible answers to this question, some more profound than others. One not so profound answer is that most schools require it as a prelude to a course in experimental psychology. Another answer that is often given is that it is necessary for an appreciation of the literature in psychology. This answer usually doesn't carry much weight with students since on an undergraduate level students rarely encounter any of the source material in the field.

However, even though many of you are probably not terribly concerned with reading original journal articles containing all manner of statistical jargon and manipulations, as young people about to enter the "real world" you need to have a certain amount of appreciation for statistics. Why? The answer is simply because we are bombarded with it constantly whether we are willing consumers or not.

Some examples should make the importance of a knowledge of statistics clear. First of all, how many of you keep up with the average number of yards gained by the star running back on your favorite football team, or points scored, or batting averages of baseball players, or freethrow percentage in basketball, and so forth, *ad infinitum?* All of the things I have just mentioned involve the use of statistics.

How many of you watch the nightly news to hear the next day's weather forecast? What does it mean when the forecaster predicts a 70% chance of rain the next day or says that the temperature for the month of January was above average? When the newscaster reports that a new study has found that mother's milk or apple pie or fried bacon or whatever results in a significant increase in cancer in laboratory mice, what does this really mean? A rudimentary understanding of some of the techniques in statistics would give a better appreciation of much of the information to which we are exposed.

It would be nice to know, for example, that a relationship between two variables (correlation) doesn't necessarily mean that one causes the other. When the newscaster says there is a correlation between taking birth control pills and cancer in women, he is not necessarily saying that birth control pills *cause* cancer. Thus, when we try to interpret the information we receive, it would help to know that a very small relationship between two variables may be significant (in a statistical sense) if the samples under study are large enough.

The point is that a survey of elementary statistical techniques will aid us immensely in the interpretation of our environment. Isn't this one of the main concerns of education?

Although I have given you one pretty good reason to study statistics, I haven't really addressed the question of why it is of special interest to psychology. The answer lies in the nature of psychology and in what psychologists study. Thus, a typical definition of *psychology* that is given to introductory students is: Psychology is the scientific study of behavior. By scientific we mean that we perform experiments, manipulate things, quantify, make objective observations, and so on. However, the key to the definition is the last word—behavior. Examples of behavior studied by psychologists include such things as the barpressing behavior of the rat, language production of humans, food intake in a free feeding situation, or heart rate as a response to threatening stimulation.

psychology

What is there about behavior that requires the use of statistical procedures? The answer is that behavior is ordinarily quite variable. An example will illustrate this point. Suppose that a professor enters his statistics classroom, draws a ruler from his briefcase, and uses it to give each student in the class a simple reaction time test. Specifically, the professor asks each student in the class to hold the thumb and forefinger of his or her preferred hand approximately one inch apart. The lower end of the vertical ruler is placed between the student's fingers, and without warning the professor releases the upper end. The point on the ruler at which the student catches it constitutes a measure of ability to react to suddenly presented stimuli.

What typically happens in such a test is that a few students catch the ruler after a fall of three or four inches, some miss it entirely, and the rest of the class measure somewhere in between. What are some of the factors that might account for this diversity? First of all, sex differences could perhaps play a role in this test with either males or females reacting more rapidly. Age might be a relevant factor with older persons reacting more slowly. It is possible that a few students ingested either licit or illicit drugs prior to coming to class and this is affecting their performance. Some of the students might be much more anxious about having to perform the task than others, and this anxiety might affect their performance. With a little effort, you can probably think of several more factors that might account for the diversity.

In addition to the variability in the subjects, further variability is introduced in the measurement procedure itself. Thus, in our example the professor may not always drop the ruler in the same manner, he may be distracted when testing one student so that he drops the ruler before the person is ready, he may not always read the markings on the ruler in the same fashion, and so forth. What we have, then, is variability within and between the organisms we are studying as well as variability introduced by the procedures we use to measure organisms. This variability that is in the very nature of living things is one of the main reasons we need statistics.

If we could measure some object or phenomenon with great precision and under rigidly controlled conditions, we would have little need for statistics. We could report our results in one or a few numbers that anyone could appreciate. Unfortunately, things are not so precise in the field of psychology as the example above illustrates. Our instruments of measurement are often very crude; we frequently do not have the control over extraneous conditions that we might wish; and often we aren't aware of all the variables that could affect the performance of our subjects. We need ways to describe our data and methods that will help us relate our results to the "real world."

Uses of the Statistical Method

There are two major functions of statistics and correspondingly two major divisions of any course in statistics: descriptive statistics and descriptive statistics   inferential statistics. By *descriptive statistics* we mean techniques used basically to describe and/or illustrate the data or raw numbers we have collected. Examples of descriptive statistics are such things as graphs, averages, measures of the spread or variability in the data, measures of the relationship between two variables (correlation), and so on. When we have a large group of vastly different numbers, we need some means to summarize them, a shorthand code to represent a lot of otherwise unmanageable data. For this reason, we have descriptive statistics.

After we have calculated some numbers or have drawn a curve inferential statistics   to illustrate the data, the techniques of *inferential statistics* help us determine what our experiment has told us about the phenomenon we were trying to measure. To illustrate, suppose we have measured something based on a very limited number of individuals from some larger group. To what extent can we generalize our results from the sample to the larger group from which it was taken? If we have noted a difference in the effects upon our subjects of two different treatments, would we note a similar difference if we had observed the entire population from which our subjects were drawn? The purpose of inferential statistics is to enable us to make decisions about the larger group based on limited observation. Examples of inferential procedures that will be frequently encountered include the *t*-test, the one-way analysis of variance or *F*-test, and the chi-square test.

Some Basic Terms

There are some terms that have already been used and will be used throughout the book that should be defined. The ones I will define here are: variable (dependent and independent), sample, population, statistic, and parameter. As you will see, statistics, like most of the courses you will encounter, has its own peculiar language.

A variable is, of course, anything that varies, but, more specific to our purposes, a *variable* is anything that may take on different values or amounts. Common examples are such things as height, weight, sex, time, speed, or dosages. Some of the variables mentioned may take on an infinite range of values (for example, time) whereas others may take on as few as two values (such as, sex).

variable

In performing experiments in psychology, we often speak of two major types of variables, independent and dependent. The *independent variable* is defined as the *variable* over which the experimenter has control, the one he manipulates. The *dependent variable* in psychology is the measurement of behavior of the organism studied.

independent variable

dependent variable

We hope that the values taken by the dependent variable will reflect the manipulation of the independent variable. For example, in a typical experiment we might be interested in the effect of various drugs on the driving ability of people. The independent variable in this case would be the type of drug administered to the subjects or perhaps the amount of one particular drug of interest. The dependent variable would be some measure of driving ability, such as, reaction time (how long it takes you to react to some brief or suddenly presented stimulus) or perhaps the number of small adjustments of the steering wheel in a simulated driving test.

Perhaps another example might help to clarify the definitions. Suppose that a statistics professor wants to determine whether or not the assigning of homework affects the performance of students in the class. Further, let's suppose that in one particular semester there are three sections of the course. At the beginning of the semester the professor decides to give no homework assignments to the students in Section 1, approximately weekly assignments to the students in Section 2, and daily homework to the students in Section 3. The average grade on the final examination becomes the desired response measure. Thus, the independent variable is the amount of homework assigned, and in this case the professor has manipulated three different levels: zero homework, once weekly homework, and daily homework. The dependent variable is the average score for each section on the final exam.

Population is certainly a word with which all of us are familiar. We tend to think of it as pertaining to large numbers of people or of some species of animal. For example, we often hear (and perhaps worry) about the population explosion, referring to the fact that the birth rate in many areas of the world is much higher than the death rate. Or, we might hear that the total world population of the whale is shrinking and that many species are in danger of becoming extinct.

population

If I asked for a formal definition, most of you would say that a *population* consists of a *large* number of objects or organisms having some common characteristic. And I would say that you are right except for one minor point—a population may be any size at all. Thus, a population may be very small (for example, the population of aardvarks at the San Diego Zoo or the population of dimes minted in San Francisco in 1894); or a population may be very large (for example, the population of Catholics in Latin America or the population of rats in psychological laboratories); or any size in between. In practice, however, most of the populations that interest us are too large to measure economically.

Despite the fact that some populations of interest may be quite small, often we are faced with populations that are so large that to measure any characteristic for the entire group would be most uneconomical. What do we do in a situation like this? We select some smaller, more manageable group from the population. This smaller

sample

group or subset of the population is called a *sample*. Having selected our sample, we then measure whatever we want to measure and try to relate our result to the original population from which it was drawn.

The way we select the sample from the population is relevant to our ability to generalize from it. For example, if our sample is biased (that is, contains too many individuals with unusual characteristics relative to the rest of the population), then our results will also be biased and will not be a fair representation of the population. To illustrate, suppose that we want to know the average age of the students at some university. By chance we have chosen for our sample a preponderance of graduate students with the result that the average age we determine is 24.7 years. Will this average have any relevance for the population in which we are interested? Probably not, since in most schools the average age is lower than that.

There are at least two ways to get around the problem of a biased sample. One is by selecting a truly random sample in which each person in the population has an equal chance of being selected. Another way is to select individuals for our sample in proportion to their representation in the population. In our specific example, we would want to be sure that our sample contained approximately the same percentage of students from each of the different classes (freshman, sophomore, and so on) as are contained in the population. In addition, we would want to be sure that we had the appropriate ratio of males to females, approximately the correct proportion of minority students, and so forth. Thus, our sample would be, hopefully, a miniature representation of the population.

Continuing with the definitions, a *parameter* designates any measurable characteristic of a population. For example, suppose we are interested in the average grade point average for the population of some university. Once we have determined the average GPA, we would say that this was a parameter of the population of students. There are other parameters of this population that we could determine in addition to the average GPA. For example, we might determine the variability in the group's GPA, the number of female students, the average age of the population of students, or any of a myriad of things. Thus, a population parameter is a measurable characteristic of the population. `parameter`

Similarly, a *statistic* is any measurable characteristic of a sample. We often refer to the average of a sample or to the range of the sample as sample statistics. In inferential statistics we will often be interested in estimating population parameters with sample statistics. `statistic`

A Word of Advice

As you read through the various chapters in the text, you will find headings entitled "Checking Your Progress." Under these headings I have provided a problem for you to work which illustrates a technique that is being discussed. I have also provided the correct answer, but I have not provided the actual computations. For your own benefit I hope that you will put forth the effort required to solve the problem rather than making the facile assumption of understanding based on reading the solved examples.

Statistics is *not* a course in which you can sit back, relax, and accept passively the knowledge that is required. There must be an active effort on your part to obtain the knowledge. You must work the sample problems provided in order to gain facility in utilizing the techniques. For most of you it will not come naturally. Only after some effort on your part will facility be gained.

At this point I would like to emphasize something that is probably obvious, but, if not recognized, can lead to great difficulties in working any kind of mathematical exercise. That is, you must be *organized*. For example, if the problem requires the solution of formulas, these should be carefully written in their entirety. After the formula is written, it should be checked for accuracy and then studied to see what it tells you to do. Then, an effort should be made to see what information you have been given and what additional information is required for the solution. The point is that you should have a plan of attack in mind at all times and endeavor to carry out this plan step by step. Disorganization results in (and stems from) confusion and almost invariably leads to incorrect answers.

Recommended Materials for This Course

In keeping with my stated belief that organization is very important for performance in a course in statistics, I have listed some items here that I consider to be essential for your performance.

1. A good, simplified textbook in elementary statistics and an accompanying workbook.
2. A supply of well-sharpened pencils. I know that ballpoint pens are ubiquitous, but I recommend pencils primarily because mistakes are often made and pencil is easier to erase than pen.
3. An enormous supply of scratch paper. The only way to gain facility in the use of the techniques presented in this text is to work problems, and for this you need paper.
4. A simple, inexpensive pocket calculator with four basic functions (add, subtract, multiply, divide), floating decimal, square root key, and one memory function. I have seen students bring to class calculators that they borrowed from engineering students that have logarithmic functions, trigonometric functions, and the like. These are not only unnecessary for this course but are quite

likely to cause confusion. In several chapters I have placed sections on how to apply the pocket calculator in the computation of different statistics. In doing these sections I have assumed that your calculator is a simple one with the functions mentioned above.

Summary

The chapter has been devoted basically to defining several important terms and to providing both a rationale for the study of statistics and a look at the goals of the author. The approach of the author is basically a problem-solving, practical one, although an attempt will be made to provide an intuitive feel for the techniques presented. The study of statistics is necessary because: (1) it is normally a prerequisite to a course in experimental psychology, (2) it helps the student to appreciate more fully the literature in psychology and the world we live in, and (3) psychology deals with living organisms with inherent variability.

The following terms were defined:

1. *Statistics* is a set of tools concerned with the collection, organization, and analysis of numerical facts and observations.
2. *Data* are numbers, measurements, the results of experimentation.
3. *Descriptive statistics* are tools concerned with describing, illustrating data.
4. *Inferential statistics* are techniques aimed at permitting us to make decisions based on our data; to draw conclusions about the population from which our sample was drawn.
5. A *population* consists of all objects or organisms having some characteristic in common. The size of a population may be any number from very small to infinitely large.
6. A *sample* is some subset of the population.
7. A *parameter* is a measurable characteristic of the population.
8. A *statistic* is a measurable characteristic of a sample.
9. A *variable* is anything that may take on different values.
10. The *independent variable* is the variable manipulated and controlled by the experimenter.
11. The *dependent variable* is the measured response of the organism. In psychology, the dependent variable is the measurement of behavior.

The Frequency Distribution

Introduction

In chapter 1 I talked about the use of the statistical method to describe data. In this chapter I will develop one of the basic methods for this purpose—the frequency distribution.

Suppose that we have measured some behavioral characteristic of a sample of people. For example, imagine that 54 students volunteer to take part in a psychology experiment. They are asked to go into a room individually and learn a list of nonsense syllables (two consonants with a vowel between, for example, TAK or XUQ). For each student, the experimenter records the number of repetitions of the list the student requires before the list can be correctly recalled. The record kept by the experimenter might look like the following: 33, 24, 27, 20, 22, 26, 17, 26, 31, 17, 16, 32, 24, 22, 15, 27, 20, 23, 23, 11, 27, 25, 24, 30, 20, 25, 28, 23, 21, 24, 23, 18, 29, 19, 26, 25, 14, 21, 25, 10, 25, 19, 26, 22, 13, 22, 24, 18, 28, 21, 9, 9, 8, 7.

About all that can be said for the data at this point is that they are a bunch of numbers. Obviously, we need to do something to organize them. A first step would be to arrange them in ascending or descending order. In other words, it would be helpful to arrange them into a hierarchy of numbers, a ranking from the highest to the lowest. It would make just as much sense to rank them from lowest to highest, but by convention it is done the other way around. At any rate, after ranking the scores we would have the following:

X (Score)	X	X	X	X	X
33	27	25	23	20	15
32	26	24	22	20	14
31	26	24	22	19	13
30	26	24	22	19	11
29	26	24	22	18	10
28	25	24	21	18	9
28	25	23	21	17	9
27	25	23	21	17	8
27	25	23	20	16	7

One thing that you should note is that at the top of each column of numbers there is the letter X. The reason for this is that X is used in statistics to stand for (symbolize) a score. In this particular example we have 54 X's or scores, the highest being 33 and the lowest 7. This arrangement of scores is definitely more informative than we had previously.

However, one problem with this hierarchical arrangement of the 54 scores is that it is too bulky; it takes up too much space. How might we condense the data?

The Frequency Distribution

Looking at the scores we see that 2 students required 28 repetitions of the list before obtaining an errorless recall. Additionally, 3 persons required 27 repetitions, 4 required 26, and so on. Instead of listing each score of 28 and each score of 27 and each score of 26, we can save space without losing information if we only list each different score once and make a note of how many times it occurred. This new arrangement in which the scores are listed in order from highest to lowest and the number of times each score occurs is placed beside it is known as a *frequency distribution*. It is called a frequency distribution because the number of times each score occurs is called the frequency and is symbolized by f. Using the data that have been introduced, we would have the following:

frequency distribution

X (Score)	f (Frequency)	X	f
33	1	20	3
32	1	19	2
31	1	18	2
30	1	17	2
29	1	16	1
28	2	15	1
27	3	14	1
26	4	13	1
25	5	12	0
24	5	11	1
23	4	10	1
22	4	9	2
21	3	8	1
		7	1

The frequency distribution is much superior to our original array of scores in that we can tell at a glance the highest and lowest scores. In addition, we can readily see which scores occurred most frequently by referring to the numbers in the frequency column. At this point another example may help to clarify the construction of the frequency distribution.

Over a one-week period, 23 monkeys in a laboratory have been observed, and the number of times each engaged in threatening behavior toward another monkey has been noted. Thus, the scores indicate the number of incidents of threat for each monkey in the colony. The monkeys were observed for thirty minutes each day. The scores are: 22, 0, 3, 5, 45, 21, 18, 10, 10, 12, 3, 5, 8, 20, 18, 15, 25, 2, 12, 15, 10, 10, 9.

Using the definition of the frequency distribution, we first arrange the scores into a hierarchy and then put the number of times each score occurred beside it. The result is as follows:

X	f	X	f
45	1	22	1
44	0	21	1
43	0	20	1
42	0	19	0
41	0	18	2
40	0	17	0
39	0	16	0
38	0	15	2
37	0	14	0
36	0	13	0
35	0	12	2
34	0	11	0
33	0	10	4
32	0	9	1
31	0	8	1
30	0	7	0
29	0	6	0
28	0	5	2
27	0	4	0
26	0	3	2
25	1	2	1
24	0	1	0
23	0	0	1

In the monkey example, the highest incidence of aggression was a score of 45 and the lowest was a score of 0. In constructing the frequency distribution, the scores occurring with a frequency of zero have been included.

Checking Your Progress

For an additional exercise in the construction of the frequency distribution, assume that the numbers listed below represent the number of trials required by each of fifty graduate students to learn a list of nonsense syllables.

22, 27, 9, 18, 9, 10, 21, 10, 19, 20, 7, 15, 8, 19, 25, 26, 20, 26, 18, 18, 12, 11, 26, 19, 23, 25, 19, 24, 17, 16, 24, 8, 23, 14, 14, 24, 18, 20, 17, 17, 20, 17, 21, 13, 16, 24, 13, 16, 21, 19.

Construct a frequency distribution.

The Grouped Frequency Distribution

One of the main purposes for constructing a frequency distribution is to get a clearer idea of what form the distribution actually assumes. That is, we can look at the frequency column and tell which scores occur with the highest frequency and where the scores tail off; that is, have low frequencies. If we have a fairly large range of scores, however, it may be hard to discern any trend in the frequencies of the scores and the listing of each different score may require an inordinately lengthy column. The answer to these problems requires a further condensation of the data into what is known as a *grouped frequency distribution.*

Grouping the data involves dividing the total range of scores into a number of mutually exclusive (nonoverlapping) intervals each containing the same number of score units. To see how this is done, let's consider a frequency distribution of the test scores made by a large number of students in an introductory psychology class. The frequency distribution is reproduced below.

Suppose that we wanted to condense this frequency distribution into approximately 10 mutually exclusive intervals. How would we go about it? The first step is to determine how wide each interval would have to be in order for us to have about 10 of them. We can determine the intervals' width, defined as the member of score units

X	f	X	f	X	f
99	1	74	5	49	2
98	1	73	7	48	0
97	2	72	7	47	0
96	3	71	7	46	0
95	2	70	6	45	0
94	2	69	2	44	0
93	3	68	2	43	1
92	2	67	3	42	0
91	4	66	4	41	0
90	3	65	3	40	1
89	2	64	2	39	1
88	3	63	0	38	0
87	4	62	0	37	0
86	5	61	0	36	0
85	4	60	1	35	0
84	4	59	0	34	0
83	3	58	1	33	0
82	3	57	0	32	0
81	5	56	0	31	0
80	2	55	1	30	1
79	7	54	0	29	0
78	5	53	0	28	0
77	4	52	0	27	0
76	6	51	0	26	0
75	8	50	1	25	1

in the interval, by dividing the range of the distribution by the number of intervals wanted.

In this particular case, the number of desired intervals is 10. Since the range of the distribution is 74 (highest score minus the lowest score, or $99 - 25 = 74$), the width of each interval should be $74 \div 10 = 7.4$ or, rounding to the nearest odd integer, the width will be 7 units.

We can put what we have just done into an equation as follows: the width of the class interval (indicated by i) is equal to the range of scores (R) divided by the number of class intervals (CI) desired or $i = R/(\text{no. of CI})$. Once we have determined i, we are ready to construct our grouped frequency distribution.

To begin, we take the lowest score, 25, and add to it $i - 1$. Adding $i - 1$ to the lowest score results in an interval with the desired number of units, while adding i would result in an interval containing one too many units. In this case the result would be 25 + (7 − 1) = 25 + 6 = 31 and the interval contains 7 units; 25, 26, 27, 28, 29, 30, and 31. The scores 25 and 31 are the limits of the lowest class interval. In order to find the limits of the second lowest class interval, we add i − 1 to 32 resulting in 38. This procedure is continued until we have determined the limits of the interval containing the highest score in our original frequency distribution or 99. The resulting grouped distribution is shown below.

CI (Class Interval)	f
95–101	9
88–94	19
81–87	28
74–80	37
67–73	34
60–66	10
53–59	2
46–52	3
39–45	3
32–38	0
25–31	2

Once the class intervals have been determined, we refer back to the frequency distribution to find the frequency for each interval. Thus, in the class interval containing the scores 25–31, there was one score of 25 and one score of 30 giving a total frequency of 2 for the interval. This has been done for all the intervals and is shown in the f column.

In comparison with the original frequency distribution from which the grouped distribution was constructed, the trends in the distribution are more clearly defined. We can see, for example, that over half of the students scored between 67 and 87 and that the scores tail off more toward the low end of the distribution than toward the high end. Despite the clearer picture of the distribution and despite the compactness of the grouped distribution, we have lost something by constructing it. We no longer know the exact location of each score! In fact, in future problems involving the grouped frequency distribution, we will make the assumption that all the scores in an interval are evenly distributed across the interval.

At this point in the discussion, you undoubtedly have some questions that you want to ask. For example, you probably noticed that, although I said that we would condense the frequency distribution into 10 class intervals, I wound up with 11. What happened? Well, when the width (i) of the interval was determined, the result was the number 7.4, which was rounded to the nearest odd integer or 7. If the grouped distribution had been constructed using 7.4 as the width of the class interval, the result would have been 10 class intervals. However, 7.4 would have been an awkward width for any further manipulations.

You may also have noted that I specified that the fractional width that was calculated should be rounded to the nearest *odd* integer. Thus, if we computed an i for a particular distribution and found it to be 4.4, I would still say to round it to the nearest odd integer or 5 even though according to the rules of rounding this would be improper. Why do I insist on rounding to the nearest odd integer? The reason is that this makes the midpoints of the resulting class intervals whole numbers. In our example, the midpoint of the first interval (25–31) is 28. If we had used 8 as width of the interval (25–32), the midpoint would have been 28.5 which is not nearly as handy a number as 28.

A third question might be: Why did I choose to divide the distribution into 10 class intervals? Why not 5 or 20 or some other number? Well, we would not want an extremely large number of CI in a grouped frequency distribution since condensation was one of our original goals. For this reason a number of CI as large as 20 usually defeats one of the main purposes in the use of the grouped frequency distribution. If we use a very small number of CI (for example, 5 or less), the resulting grouped frequency distribution may be so compact that trends in the data are obscured.

For example, let's take another look at the frequency distribution we have been considering and this time divide it into 5 CI instead of 10. The width of each CI will be $i = R/$(no. of CI) = 74/5 = 14.8 or rounding to the nearest odd integer, 15. Adding $i - 1$ or $15 - 1 = 14$ to the lowest score, we have $25 + 14 = 39$ as the upper limit of the lowest interval. Continuing this procedure, our new grouped frequency distribution is:

CI	f
85–99	41
70–84	79
55–69	19
40–54	5
25–39	3

While the new distribution is undoubtedly more compact, it is also much more inaccurate and much less informative. In general, a useful rule of thumb is that a grouped frequency distribution should consist of between 10 and 15 class intervals.

Finally, some of you may have noticed that there are actually gaps between each of the class intervals. Although in the particular example we have been considering it wouldn't be very meaningful, what would we do with a score of 94.3 or 59.8 or any other fractional values that fall into the gaps between intervals? The answer lies in the consideration of real limits.

Real Limits Versus Apparent Limits

apparent limits

A grouped frequency distribution constructed from a frequency distribution in which the scores are whole numbers results in gaps between the limits of each CI. Limits of class intervals with gaps between them are called *apparent limits*. Thus, in our preceding example we were considering apparent limits rather than "real" ones.

real limits

What is a grouped frequency distribution with *real limits*? It is one in which there are *no* gaps between the class intervals. In practice, real limits are constructed by subtracting a half unit from the lower apparent limit of CI and adding a half unit to the upper apparent limit of the same interval. For the example we have been considering, the interval with apparent limits of 25–31 would have real limits of 24.5–31.5 ($25 - 0.5$, $31 + 0.5$). Continuing this procedure for the entire distribution would result in the following:

CI	f
94.5–101.5	9
87.5–94.5	19
80.5–87.5	28
73.5–80.5	37
66.5–73.5	34
59.5–66.5	10
52.5–59.5	2
45.5–52.5	3
38.5–45.5	3
31.5–38.5	0
24.5–31.5	2

continuous variable

Real limits are discussed because many of the variables in which we might be interested are continuous variables. A *continu-*

ous variable is one whose measurement can take an infinite number
of values. For example, time is a continuous variable. Thus, the
passage of time may be broken into an infinite number of units.
Between one minute and the next we could subdivide the seconds
into milliseconds (thousandths of a second) or even microseconds
(millionths of a second). The point is that, in the measurement of a
continuous variable, gaps are caused by the crudeness of our measurement and are apparent rather than real. The use of real limits
rather than apparent limits will be considered further when we discuss certain types of graphs and the location of the median from
grouped data.

Another Example to Illustrate the Construction of the Grouped Frequency Distribution

At the end of the term, students in a large general psychology
class are given a test consisting of a list of 50 commonly encountered
terms in psychology to match with a list of definitions. Each student
receives a score indicating the number of correctly matched items.
The resulting frequency distribution is:

X	f	X	f
45	2	29	11
44	3	28	13
43	2	27	8
42	4	26	7
41	3	25	3
40	5	24	6
39	6	23	1
38	3	22	0
37	5	21	2
36	6	20	3
35	4	19	0
34	7	18	1
33	7	17	1
32	8	16	0
31	10	15	2
30	9	14	1

For illustrative purposes, let's construct a grouped frequency
distribution. To begin, we need to determine $i,$ the width of each

class interval. Again, suppose that we want to have approximately 10 CI.

$$i = \frac{R}{\text{no. of CI}} = \frac{45 - 14}{10} = \frac{31}{10} = 3.1 \text{ or 3 score units}$$

Starting with the lowest score, 14, we add $i - 1$ to it giving us 16 [14 + $(i - 1) = 14 + (3 - 1) = 14 + 2 = 16$]. Thus, the apparent limits of the lowest interval are from 14 to 16.

Continuing, we have 17 as the lower apparent limit of the second lowest interval. Adding $i - 1$ or 2 to 17 gives the upper apparent limit of the second interval or 19. The completed grouped frequency distribution is shown below.

CI	f
44–46	5
41–43	9
38–40	14
35–37	15
32–34	22
29–31	30
26–28	28
23–25	10
20–22	5
17–19	2
14–16	3

Checking Your Progress

As part of an experiment on the brain's control of learning, an experimenter trains a large number of rats on a visual discrimination task. Each animal receives a score indicating the number of errors it makes prior to an errorless session. The frequency distribution of the scores is:

X	f	X	f	X	f
55	1	39	3	33	1
50	1	38	2	32	4
45	3	37	5	31	6
42	2	36	6	30	5
41	1	35	3	29	1
40	2	34	2	28	9

X	f	X	f	X	f
27	8	21	10	15	1
26	10	20	8	14	1
25	10	19	7	12	2
24	9	18	5	10	1
23	8	17	2	9	1
22	11	16	3	8	1

Construct a grouped frequency distribution with approximately 10 class intervals.

Summary

In this chapter we have considered two preliminary techniques used for describing data. The first method discussed was the *frequency distribution* in which the scores (symbolized by the letter X) are ranked from highest to lowest with the number of times each score occurs listed beside it. The number of times each score occurs is known as the frequency (symbolized by the letter f).

In situations where we have a frequency distribution with a large range of scores (differences between the highest and lowest scores), a further condensation of the data contained in the frequency distribution may be in order. The *grouped frequency distribution* is used for this purpose. To construct a grouped frequency distribution, we divide the range of scores into a number of mutually exclusive intervals containing several score units. The size of each *class interval* (CI) is determined by dividing the range of scores by the number of intervals desired. There is no set rule for determining the number of intervals wanted, rather it depends on the range of scores. However, for many purposes 10 to 15 CI is a reasonable division.

The width or size of the CI (symbolized by the letter i) can be determined by the formula:

$$i = \frac{\text{range of scores}}{\text{no. of CI desired}}$$

The resulting answer is rounded to the nearest odd integer so that the midpoint of the resulting CI will be a whole number. Construction of the grouped frequency distribution then consists of adding $i - 1$ to the lowest score to find the upper limit of the lowest interval, adding $i - 1$ to the next score unit in the frequency distribution to determine the limits of the second lowest interval, and so forth.

A grouped frequency distribtion constructed from a frequency distribution in which the scores are whole numbers will have gaps between the intervals. In this situation the limits of the class intervals are called *apparent limits* rather than *real limits*. Real limits simply close the gaps between the CI to accommodate continuous variables in which gaps in measurement exist only because of the crudeness of our instruments of measurement. In order to determine the real limits in a grouped frequency distribution we subtract a half unit from the lower apparent limit of each CI and add a half unit to the upper apparent limit.

Exercises

1. In an experiment in social psychology, 35 soldiers were ordered by an unpopular officer to eat some grasshoppers. The number of grasshoppers provided was 50 and each soldier received a score indicating the actual number of grasshoppers eaten. The scores were:

37	48	29	50	13
34	47	29	40	16
27	45	25	38	18
28	33	20	35	14
23	15	18	33	38
50	11	16	25	40
44	12	13	20	14

   Describe the data using techniques discussed in this chapter. Construct a grouped frequency distribution with 8 class intervals.

2. In a study of the effects of hunger on the barpressing behavior of rats, one group of 20 rats was tested after 24 hours of food deprivation. Their response rates during a 20-minute session were as follows:

233	255	328	300
122	115	155	183
187	255	243	273
275	282	305	300
263	266	168	179

   Make a frequency distribution of the scores.

3. In the study cited in question 2, 20 rats were tested after zero hours of deprivation. Their response rates during a 20-minute session were:

98	100	105	97
128	155	152	107
123	135	141	145
133	125	107	103
95	148	140	127

Arrange the data into a grouped frequency distribution with approximately 8 class intervals.

4. What are the real limits of each of the following:

   (a) 8

   (b) 10.5–12.5

   (c) 133.7

   Hint: Remember that real limits are constructed by subtracting ½ unit from the lower apparent limit and by adding ½ unit to the upper apparent limit. You must recognize what the basic unit is. In a) it is 1 but in b) it is 0.1.

5. Thirty-seven people got off a bus and were going into a diner when a car rounded a corner at a high rate of speed and smashed into the rear of the bus. As part of the accident report, each witness was asked to independently estimate the speed of the car before it struck the bus. Seven persons claimed that they did not see the incident, and thirty people gave the following estimates:

35	40	28	40	60
25	45	30	40	55
55	37	45	35	50
40	50	40	38	45
65	30	40	30	48
25	30	35	32	37

   Construct a frequency distribution and a grouped frequency distribution with 8 CI. Give both the apparent and real limits for the grouped distribution and include the midpoints of the CI.

6. A simple reaction time test was described in chapter 1 in which a person tries to catch a ruler that is suddenly released between the person's thumb and forefinger. The following are actual scores generated with the test in a statistics class.

Females			Males		
5	13	7	5	5	9
9	9	9	6	6	6
2	5	6	8	8	6
9	7	10	4	6	6
7	11		7	3	

   Construct a separate frequency distribution for the females and males. Combine the scores and construct a frequency distribution for the class. Why is it unnecessary to make a grouped frequency distribution with these data?

7. In an experiment on sexual attraction, the pulse rate of 30 male students is recorded before they are shown a centerfold from *Playboy* magazine. The pulse rates in beats per minute are:

75	68	77	69	90	70
72	102	78	67	83	77
83	75	81	68	80	72
95	73	80	110	88	65
65	74	75	95	75	87

Construct a grouped frequency distribution with 10 CI. Give the real limits.

8. After viewing the centerfold, the pulse rates are:

85	97	110	85	128
85	95	135	80	135
91	93	125	93	120
110	100	110	97	117
125	105	115	97	118
130	75	107	110	110

Construct a grouped distribution as in problem 7 and compare the distributions in problems 7 and 8.

3

The Graph in Psychology

Introduction

In chapter 2 we considered one preliminary way to describe data, the frequency distribution. In this chapter we acknowledge the old adage that a picture is worth a thousand words and discuss graphing as a descriptive technique. Although there are many different types of graphs, in this text we consider only those most commonly used by psychologists: the frequency polygon, the cumulative frequency curve, the line graph, and the bar graph. We will also consider a "rule" for graphing and examine the shapes of frequency polygons that are commonly encountered.

The Frequency Polygon

The frequency distribution discussed in the last chapter was a very useful way to organize data and to get an impression of the overall distribution. From it we could get an idea of where the scores were concentrated, we could readily see the highest and lowest scores, and we could tell where the scores were very sparsely represented. A graph of the frequency distribution is even more useful in a descriptive sense.

The *frequency polygon* is constructed by plotting the scores (or the midpoints of the class intervals in the case of the grouped frequency distribution) on the baseline or *x*-axis and the frequency of each score (or of each CI) along the *y*-axis. The *x*-axis is also known as the abscissa and is the horizontal axis, while the *y*-axis is the vertical line or ordinate. To illustrate, let's consider the frequency distribution from chapter 2 that consists of the number of repetitions required by 54 students to learn a list of nonsense syllables. The distribution was:

frequency polygon

X	f	X	f	X	f
33	1	24	5	15	1
32	1	23	4	14	1
31	1	22	4	13	1
30	1	21	3	12	0
29	1	20	3	11	1
28	2	19	2	10	1
27	3	18	2	9	2
26	4	17	2	8	1
25	5	16	1	7	1

The frequency polygon based on this distribution is shown in figure 3–1.

Examining the polygon, we can see the trends in the data clearly with the majority of scores piling up in the region of the scores 24 and 25 and a longer tail of scores to the left side of the figure than to the right.

You will note that the axes of the graph have been labeled with the word "Scores" appearing below the x-axis and the word "Fre-

Figure 3–1: Frequency polygon based on the number of repetitions required to learn a list of nonsense syllables.

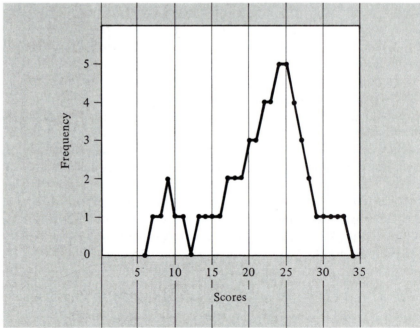

quency" appearing to the left of the *y*-axis. It is not necessary to denote each possible score and for this reason only selected ones have been labeled on the *x*-axis. It is very important that the axes be labeled appropriately, since otherwise the graph is meaningless. Before considering further examples of graphing, let's briefly discuss a general rule for the lengths of the axes.

Rule for Graphing

To help prevent misrepresentations of data, a convention has been adopted for determining the relative length of the axes. The rule is that the distance between the points on the axes should be chosen so that the *y*-axis is approximately three-fourths as long as the *x*-axis. This convention is necessary in order to prevent different impressions from being created with the same data by appropriate manipulation of the relative lengths of the axes. For example, suppose that we have a frequency distribution such as:

X	f
10	1
9	2
8	3
7	4
6	5
5	4
4	3
3	2
2	1

Let's make three frequency polygons from the data, keeping the *x*-axis the same length while varying the length of the *y*-axis. The results are shown in figure 3–2.

It is apparent that each of these frequency polygons creates a different impression. Only the middle one corresponds to the rule.

Frequency Polygon from a Grouped Frequency Distribution

The only difference between the frequency polygon described in the first section and one based on a grouped frequency distribution is that we plot the frequencies over the *midpoints* (MP) of the class intervals rather than over the scores themselves. For our example, let's consider one of the grouped distributions from chapter 2. The data are test scores made by students from a large section of introductory psychology.

CI	MP	f
95–101	98	9
88–94	91	19
81–87	84	28
74–80	77	37
67–73	70	34
60–66	63	10
53–59	56	2
46–52	49	3
39–45	42	3
32–38	35	0
25–31	28	2

As you can see, the midpoint of each CI is listed under the heading MP. The midpoint for any CI can be found by adding $(i - 1)/2$ to the lower limit of the CI. For example, consider the interval from 25–31. The interval width we used was $i = 7$, so $(i - 1)/2 = (7 - 1)/2 = 6/2 = 3$. Adding 3 to the lower limit of the interval we have $25 + 3 = 28$, and this is the value shown.

The frequency polygon based on the grouped frequency distribution we have been considering is shown in figure 3–3. As you can see, the primary difference is that the baseline of the graph is labeled

Figure 3–2: Three graphs to illustrate distortion resulting from manipulation of the relative lengths of the x and y axes. The middle graph conforms to the rule.

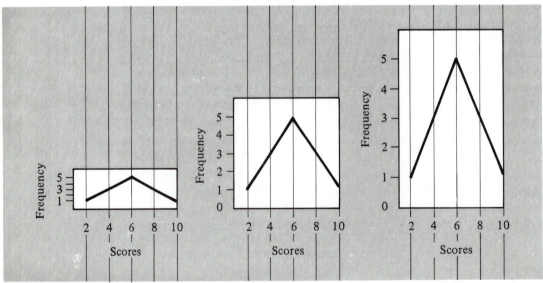

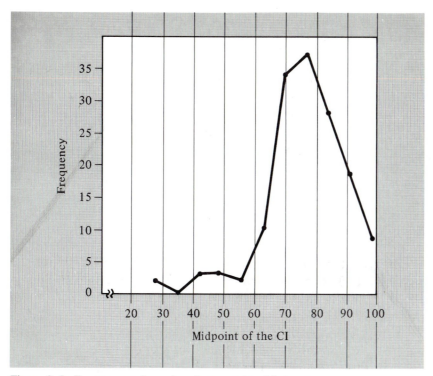

Figure 3–3: Frequency polygon based on a grouped frequency distribution.

"Midpoint of the CI" instead of "Scores." Otherwise the graph is plotted in precisely the same manner as before.

Before continuing our survey of graphing techniques commonly used by psychologists, let's look at some possible shapes of frequency polygons.

Shapes of Frequency Polygons

A frequency polygon can assume many shapes, but some are more common and therefore more interesting to us than others. One of the most interesting curves, both because of its properties and because so much of the data in the real world approximates it, is known as the normal curve. Data we often assume to be almost normally distributed include IQ scores, heights, and weights.

The shape of the *normal curve* is symmetrical (one half would   normal curve
fit precisely over the other), and it is often referred to as the bell-shaped curve. Of course, many curves can be symmetrical without having the properties of the normal curve. Examples of symmetrical, nonnormal curves and of the normal curve are shown below in figure 3–4.

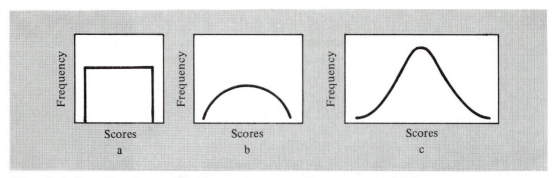

Figure 3–4: Examples of symmetrical curves. Curves a and b are nonnormal while curve c is normal.

skewed curves

Some curves that are not symmetrical are called skewed curves. *Skewed curves* are curves in which a large number of scores are piled up at one end or the other with a tail at the opposite end. If we consider the right side of the *x*-axis to be positive and the left side to be negative,

then a positively skewed curve is one that has its tail to the right, and a negatively skewed curve has its tail to the left or negative side of the *x*-axis. Examples of positively and negatively skewed curves are shown in figure 3–5.

One example of a distribution that is negatively skewed, at least from my experience, is that based on the student ratings of faculty teaching performance. That is, most professors are given rather high

Figure 3–5: Examples of negatively and positively skewed curves.

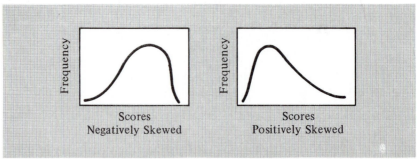

evaluations while only a select few are rated as being terrible. I have also found that test scores in my statistics classes tend to be negatively skewed with the vast majority of students making rather high grades while only a few make low grades.

A common example of a positively skewed distribution is that of personal income in the United States. That is, the majority of people make some amount below say $20,000, but a few individuals make six- or seven-digit incomes. Similarly, the distribution of aggressive behavior in certain strains of domestic rat would be positively skewed. Thus, most animals would display little aggressiveness while only a few would be hyperirritable.

A Comparison of Distributions Using the Frequency Polygon

One of the most important uses of the frequency polygon is to compare the performance of different groups of individuals (or perhaps different treatments on the same group of subjects). For example, suppose that we have administered a scrambled sentences test to a large number of students. The test consists of a list of twenty well-known statements in which the words have been rearranged so that they are no longer meaningful. For example, "The best things in life are free" might read "things free are in the best life." The students are given ten minutes to rearrange correctly as many sentences as possible and their score consists of the number of sentences correctly identified. The frequency distributions for females and males are:

Females		Males	
X	f	X	f
19	3	14	3
18	4	13	5
17	4	12	7
16	6	11	9
15	7	10	9
14	15	9	10
13	14	8	8
12	10	7	8
11	10	6	5
10	9	5	4
9	5	4	4
	$N = 87$	3	2
		2	3
			$N = 77$

Since there is a difference in the total N for the males and females, we must use *percentage* frequency instead of the actual frequencies. This is done whenever we have unequal N's in order to put each group on an equivalent basis. To convert each frequency into a percentage frequency, we first divide it by the total N and then multiply by 100. Expressed in terms of a formula, this procedure would be:

$$\text{percentage frequency} = \frac{f}{N} \times 100$$

For example, 5 females had scores of 9. To convert the frequency 5 into a percentage frequency we divide it by 87 and multiply by 100.

$$\% f = \frac{5}{87} \times 100 = 0.057 \times 100 = 5.7$$

An equivalent but somewhat simpler procedure for converting frequencies into percentage frequencies involves first dividing 100 by the total N and then using this result as a multiplier for each of the frequencies. In the case of the females, the multiplier would be $100 \div 87 = 1.149$. Multiplying this times the frequency 5 gives 5.7 ($5 \times 1.149 = 5.7$) when rounded to the nearest tenth. The multiplier 1.149 could then be used to determine the rest of the percentage frequencies for the females.

At any rate, each of the frequencies has been converted to percentage frequency and the result is shown below. Using the per-

Females				*Males*		
X	f	$\% f$		X	f	$\% f$
19	3	3.4		14	3	3.9
18	4	4.6		13	5	6.5
17	4	4.6		12	7	9.1
16	6	6.9		11	9	11.7
15	7	8.0		10	9	11.7
14	15	17.2		9	10	13.0
13	14	16.1		8	8	10.4
12	10	11.5		7	8	10.4
11	10	11.5		6	5	6.5
10	9	10.3		5	4	5.2
9	5	5.7		4	4	5.2
				3	2	2.6
				2	3	3.9

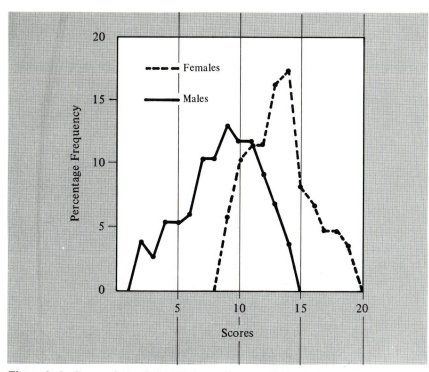

Figure 3–6: Comparison of distributions using the frequency polygon.

centage frequencies instead of the frequencies, the frequency polygons for each distribution are plotted on the same axes for comparison.

Figure 3–6 gives us a clear picture of the difference in the performance of the males and females. The entire distribution of scores for the males is shifted to the left of that for the females. The largest percentage of male scores falls between 7 and 11, while the distribution of female scores peaks at 14.

The Cumulative Frequency (or Cumulative Percentage) Polygon

Another type of graph we can plot from the frequency distribution is the cumulative frequency polygon. The *cumulative frequency curve* shows the relative position of individuals in a distribution. For example, suppose that 23 students in an honor's class are given an IQ test and the resulting frequency distribution of their scores is:

cumulative frequency
curve

X	f	X	f
170	1	144	1
163	1	143	1
160	1	142	1
158	2	140	2
157	1	138	1
153	3	129	1
150	3	127	1
145	2	120	1

The cumulative polygon is constructed by plotting the cumulative frequencies (or percentages) over the *upper real limits* of class intervals. Therefore, the first thing we must do is convert the ungrouped frequency distribution into a grouped one. Using 10 as the desired number of class intervals, we find that the width of the CI should be;

$$i = \frac{\text{range of scores}}{\text{no. of CI desired}} = \frac{170 - 120}{10} = \frac{50}{10} = 5$$

The limits of the lowest interval are 120–124 [$120 + (i - 1) = 120 + (5 - 1) = 120 + 4 = 124$]. The rest of the grouped distribution is shown below, including the real limits of the class intervals as well as a cumulative frequency column.

Class Intervals			Cum f
Apparent Limits	Real Limits	f	(Cumulative Frequency)
170–174	169.5–174.5	1	23
165–169	164.5–169.5	0	22
160–164	159.5–164.5	2	22
155–159	154.5–159.5	3	20
150–154	149.5–154.5	6	17
145–149	144.5–149.5	2	11
140–144	139.5–144.5	5	9
135–139	134.5–139.5	1	4
130–134	129.5–134.5	0	3
125–129	124.5–129.5	2	3
120–124	119.5–124.5	1	1

To construct the cumulative frequency column, we start with the frequency in the lowest interval, add to it the frequency contained in the next lowest interval, add to that total the frequency in the third interval from the bottom, and so on. For any interval, the cumulative frequency tells us the number of scores contained in that interval plus the number of scores in intervals below the one we are considering. For example, if we look at the interval whose upper real limit is 154.5, reference to the cum f column tells us that 17 individuals scored 154.5 or less on the IQ test. Similarly, there were 3 scores of 129.5 or less and 20 scores of 159.5 or less. The cumulative frequency polygon is shown in figure 3–7.

To appreciate the relative performance of any individual on the IQ test, draw a vertical line from the baseline to the curve and a horizontal line from the curve out to the y-axis. Where the horizontal line crosses the y-axis gives us an approximate idea of the number of individuals scoring at or below the score we are considering. For example, suppose we want to know the relative performance of a student scoring 151 on the IQ test. After drawing a vertical line from 151 on the baseline to the point at which it intersects the curve and then drawing a horizontal line from the point on the curve to the

Figure 3–7: Cumulative frequency curve.

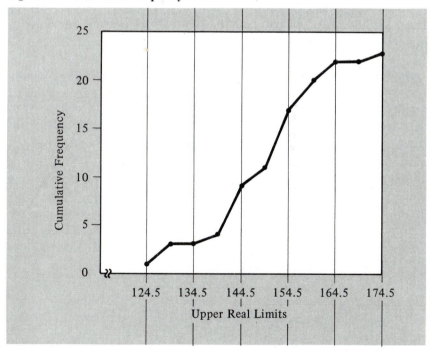

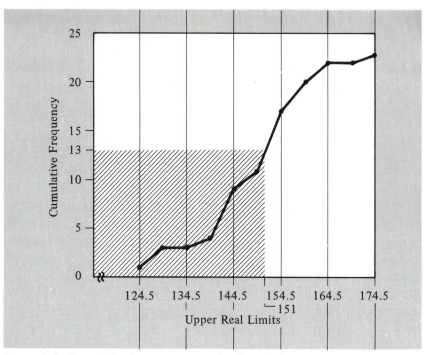

Figure 3–8: Cumulative frequency curve showing relative location of an individual scoring 151.

y-axis, we could note that approximately 13 persons had scores of 151 or lower, and correspondingly 10 persons scored this much or more. This procedure is shown in figure 3–8.

As noted in the title of this section, we may use the cumulative polygon to plot cumulative percentages as well as cumulative frequencies. But, first we have to convert the cumulative frequencies into cumulative percentages by simply dividing 100 by *N* and using this result as a multiplier for each of the cumulative percentages. In the example we have been using, the multiplier is $100 \div 23 = 4.35$. Multiplying this value by each of the cumulative frequencies gives us 4.35 for the first interval (since the cumulative frequency for this interval is 1), 13.05 for the second and third intervals, and so on, until we reach 100% of the scores at or below the upper real limit of the highest CI. An abbreviated table containing the cumulative percentages is shown below. The cumulative percentage curve is shown in figure 3–9.

Class Intervals Real Limits	f	Cum f	Cum %
169.5–174.5	1	23	100.05
164.5–169.5	0	22	95.70
159.5–164.5	2	22	95.70
154.5–159.5	3	20	87.00
149.5–154.5	6	17	73.95
144.5–149.5	2	11	47.85
139.5–144.5	5	9	39.15
134.5–139.5	1	4	17.40
129.5–134.5	0	3	13.05
124.5–129.5	2	3	13.05
119.5–124.5	1	1	4.35

The procedure for determining the relative location of a score in terms of the percentage of scores either above or below is precisely the same as illustrated with the cumulative frequency polygon. We could easily determine, for example, that someone with an

Figure 3–9: Cumulative percentage polygon.

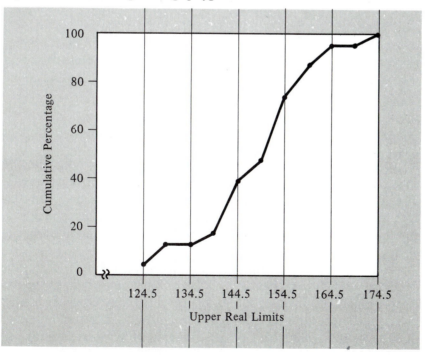

IQ score of 151 is in approximately the fiftieth percentile of this particular distribution.

Checking Your Progress

At a smoking clinic, each person fills out a questionnaire concerning smoking habits. The average number of cigarettes smoked per day for 60 people is shown in the frequency distribution below.

X	f	X	f
60	1	26	3
55	2	25	5
53	2	24	2
50	3	23	5
47	1	20	10
45	2	18	3
40	3	15	2
35	4	12	1
30	5	11	1
28	3	10	2

Using the data construct a frequency polygon, a cumulative frequency curve, and a cumulative percentage curve. If this is a representative sample, approximately what percentage of smokers smoke a pack or less per day?

The Line Graph

line graph

All of the graphs discussed to this point have been based on the frequency distribution. Although frequency polygons and cumulative frequency curves are very useful in a descriptive sense, they are certainly not the only types of graphs employed by psychologists. Another type of graph that is often encountered in the literature in psychology is the *line graph*.

One of the most common uses of the line graph is to depict the development of learned behavior. The primary reason that psychologists emphasize the study of learning is that many consider human behavior to be largely a function of interaction with the environment (in other words, learned). The development of learning in an organism is often shown by a *line graph* in which a measure of the amount of practice (time, trials, etc.) is plotted on the baseline, while a measure of performance or behavior is shown on the *x*-axis (number correct, percentage of correct responses, number of errors, speed of performance, and so on).

To illustrate, in a recent experiment I trained rats to press a lever in order to receive a food reward. After the animals had reached a stable rate of responding, they were shifted to a type of reward schedule in which long pauses between barpresses are rewarded. This type of schedule is called a DRL or differential reinforcement of low rates schedule. The purpose of training on this type of schedule is so that we can see how efficiently the animal is able to withhold a previously rewarded response. At any rate, in this particular case the rats were rewarded if they waited at least 20 seconds before making a response. If they responded after a shorter period of time, the reward was delayed. The development of their performance is shown in figure 3–10 in which the number of rewards is plotted on the *y*-axis while the testing session (day) is shown on the *x*-axis.

Figure 3–10: Line graph showing average number of reinforcements per day of testing on a DRL schedule.

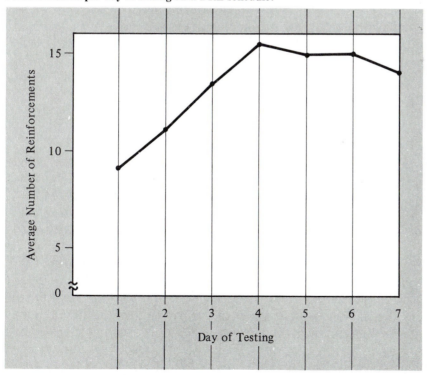

Another example of the use of the line graph concerns the learning of a list of nonsense syllables by a group of students. Suppose that 5 students have learned a list of 10 syllables to a criterion of one errorless repetition. The average number of errors per repetition has been determined and is shown below.

Repetition	Average Errors
1	9.6
2	7.2
3	6.1
4	5.8
5	5.2
6	4.4
7	3.5
8	2.1
9	2.3
10	1.3
11	1.1
12	0.6
13	0.0

A line graph showing the average number of errors per repetition has been plotted in figure 3–11. In this case the course of learn-

Figure 3–11: Line graph showing the average number of errors per repetition of a list of nonsense syllables.

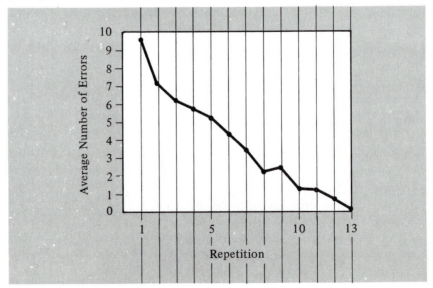

ing is illustrated by the decrease in the number of errors with repeated practice.

Checking Your Progress

In order to study experimenter bias, two groups of 10 students each are given 20 rats; that is, one per student. One group of students is told that their rats are very bright while the other group is informed of the stupidity of the animals. Each of the 20 students then trains his or her rat on a simple task and records the number of errors made daily. The results are:

Day No.	*"Smart Rats"* Average No. of Errors	*"Stupid Rats"* Average No. of Errors
1	6.2	6.5
2	5.1	6.1
3	4.1	5.5
4	2.5	5.3
5	1.5	4.8
6	0	3.9
7	0	3.5
8	0	2.9
9	0	1.8
10	0	1.3
11	0	0

Use the line graph to compare the average number of daily errors for the two groups. Incidentally, there was no difference in the intelligence of the rats. The only difference was in the instructions given to the students.

The Bar Graph

In contrast to the line graph which is used to plot continuous variables, the *bar graph* plots performance of individuals or groups that cannot be ordered along any continuum. For example, suppose a traffic planner has determined the number of vehicles passing through 5 different intersections at a particular time of the day. Although for identification purposes the planner may label the intersections 1, 2, 3, 4, and 5, the number assigned to any particular intersection is purely arbitrary. The data generated might be: Inter-

bar graph

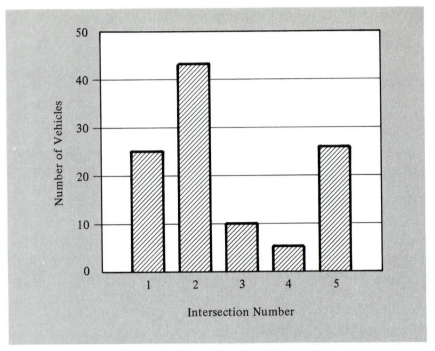

Figure 3–12: **Bar graph showing the number of vehicles passing through a particular intersection.**

section 1, 25; Intersection 2, 43; Intersection 3, 10; Intersection 4, 5; Intersection 5, 26.

The bar graph of these data is plotted in figure 3–12. As you can see, the intersection number is shown on the x-axis while the number of vehicles (frequency) is shown on the y-axis. Instead of connecting points into a line and giving an impression of continuity, a rectangle or bar has been drawn over each number on the x-axis with the height of the bar indicating the frequency of occurrence at the intersection. The spacing between the bars is arbitrary.

As a second example we might use a bar graph to depict the performance of students exposed to several different teaching methods. For example, suppose we have recorded the percentage of students passing, failing, or withdrawing from an introductory psychology course when two different teaching methods are used by the same professor. Thus, when the professor teaches the course in the traditional lecture manner, the percentages are 75, 18, and 7, respectively, while in his self-paced section the percentages are 63, 7, and 30, respectively. The data are shown graphically in figure 3–13.

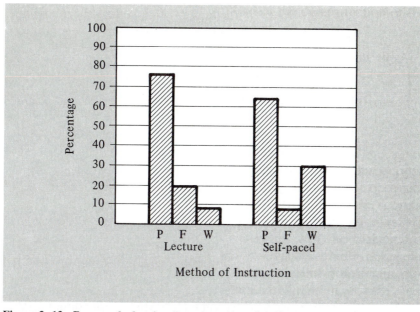

Figure 3–13: Bar graph showing the percentage of students passing (P), failing (F), or withdrawing (W) as a function of the method of instruction.

Checking Your Progress

In a large introductory psychology class, the instructor asks the following question: ''If I tilt a half-filled (or half-empty if he is a pessimist) glass of water through an angle of 30°, what angle will the surface of the water make with respect to horizontal?'' Each student identifies his or her sex on a sheet of paper and answers the question. Typical results are that 30% of the females will have the correct answer while 70% of the males will get it right. Use a bar graph to show this result.

Summary

Chapter 3 covered some commonly used graphing techniques in psychology. The first type of graph introduced was the *frequency polygon*. To construct a frequency polygon from a frequency distribution, the scores are plotted on the *x*-axis while the frequencies appear on the *y*-axis. The frequency polygon based on a grouped frequency distribution is the same except that the midpoints of the class intervals are plotted on the *x*-axis rather than the scores themselves.

A *rule for graphing* was presented which states that the lengths of the *x*- and *y*-axes should be chosen so that the *y*-axis is approximately three-fourths as long as the *x*-axis. The purpose of this convention is to help prevent misrepresentation of the data.

Some commonly encountered shapes of frequency polygons were described. One very important curve is the *normal* or bell-shaped curve. Nonnormal curves with a tail pulled either toward the right side of the *x*-axis or toward the left side are called *skewed curves*. Positively skewed curves have a tail (relatively few scores) toward the positive or right side of the *x*-axis, while negatively skewed curves have a tail toward the negative or left side of the *x*-axis.

The *cumulative frequency* or *cumulative percentage polygon* was described. It was constructed by plotting the cumulative frequencies or percentages over the upper real limits of the class intervals in a grouped frequency distribution.

Two other commonly encountered graphs in psychology are the *line graph* and the *bar graph*. In each type, the independent variable is plotted on the *x*-axis, while some measure of the dependent variable is plotted on the *y*-axis. In the line graph the independent variable is assumed to be continuous, and for this reason a line is used to connect the plotted points. The bar graph shows performance on a discrete or discontinuous variable. Instead of connecting points into a line, a rectangle or bar is drawn over each value of the independent variable to represent its frequency or percentage of occurrence.

Exercises

1. Construct a frequency polygon from the following scores:
   14, 12, 10, 10, 11, 15, 13, 13, 14, 12, 12, 11, 11, 13, 12, 14, 12, 13
2. Some students in an English class have been asked to unscramble twenty sentences in ten minutes. From the grouped frequency distribution of their scores, construct a frequency polygon and a cumulative frequency polygon.

CI	f
19–21	2
16–18	3
13–15	5
10–12	12
7–9	9
4–6	5
1–3	4

3. Over a two-semester period 49 students have taken a course in statistics. The frequency distribution of their final averages is as follows:

X	f		X	f
95	6		84	1
94	6		81	2
93	5		80	1
92	5		78	1
91	4		77	1
90	4		76	1
89	3		73	1
88	2		68	1
86	2		55	1
85	1		54	1

Using approximately 8 class intervals, construct a grouped frequency distribution and from it plot a frequency polygon and a cumulative frequency polygon. Tell whether the frequency polygon is skewed in appearance, and, if so, in which direction?

4. An experiment has been performed in which three groups of 10 rats each were subjected to brain damage and tested to see whether or not they would exhibit aggression toward the experimenter. The type of damage and the number of aggressive rats were: operated control, 0; olfactory bulb removal, 2; and septal damage, 9. Construct a bar graph from these data.

5. Ten students have been tested on a pursuit-rotor task. This task requires the person to keep a stylus on a spot on a moving turntable. The average time-in-contact was determined for each minute of a 10-minute practice session. The times were as follows:

Minute	Time-in-Contact (Seconds)
1	23
2	27
3	28
4	27
5	30
6	31
7	33
8	35
9	40
10	43

Plot a line graph.

6. A thirty-nine-year-old housewife is suffering from *anorexia nervosa* (a neurotic disorder characterized by extreme loss of appetite) and weighs only 87 pounds. She is treated by being monetarily rewarded for each pound gained. From the

following data, plot a line graph showing weight per unit of time (in this case at the end of each week).

Week	Weight (Pounds)
0	87
1	91
2	96
3	107
4	121
5	122
6	125

7. In a study of book-carrying style of schoolchildren, at least four different styles were noted and the percentages of each sex using a particular style recorded. The percentages were as follows:

Style	Male	Female
1 (side carry)	80%	15%
2 (front carry)	20%	35%
3 (both hands)	0%	15%
4 (balanced on hip)	0%	35%

Use the bar graph to illustrate these data.

8. Briefly define the following terms:
   (a) positively skewed distribution
   (b) continuous variable
   (c) symmetrical distribution
   (d) negatively skewed distribution

9. What is the rule for graphing?

4

Measures of Central Tendency

Introduction

In chapters 2 and 3 we discussed some very useful ways to describe data, first by arranging our numbers into a frequency distribution and then later by graphing them. This chapter discusses three methods for arriving at a single number to help describe a distribution of scores.

If you wanted a single number to convey as much information as possible about a distribution of scores, what number would you choose? Would you pick the highest score or the lowest score or some score point between the extremes? The title of the chapter should give you a hint: we will look for a value in the middle or near the middle of the distribution. In other words, we will locate a measure of central tendency in the data.

The measures that will be discussed in this chapter are the mean, the median, and the mode. Both the mean (or arithmetic average) and the mode are frequently encountered in our everyday lives. For example, we might hear a weather report stating that the average maximum daily temperature for the month of July was 91° or predicting that rainfall in August will be below average. Similarly, you are no doubt interested in your average test score in a class and know how to compute it to many decimal places.

We may learn from a television program that the most common annual income in a particular country is $650 or that more adults in a given state have 10.5 years of formal education than any other amount. These and other examples of the modal score are often encountered.

The median, although less often encountered than the mean and mode (or perhaps more often misidentified and confused with the mean), is nonetheless of importance. While watching an athletic event such as a gymnastics meet, you might hear that the median rating obtained by a particular gymnast for a sterling performance was 9.6 on a 10-point scale. Or, we might find that the median income in a particular state is $10,000.

Because of its importance for further statistical manipulations, we will begin the discussion of the measures of central tendency with the mean. Beginning with this chapter, sections on how to use the pocket calculator will appear where relevant.

Mean

mean

The mean or arithmetic average is a value to which most people have been exposed since elementary school. The *mean* is simply determined and defined as the sum of the scores in a distribution divided by the number of scores. The symbol for the mean of a sample is $\overline{X}$ (pronounced ex-bar) and the formula is:

$$\overline{X} = \frac{\Sigma X}{N}$$

where Σ (capital sigma) means to sum or add everything following it, in this case all the X's or scores. For example, if $X_1 = 5$, $X_2 = 3$, and $X_3 = 2$, ΣX or the sum of the X's would be $X_1 + X_2 + X_3 = 5 + 3 + 2$ $\Sigma X = 10$. (The subscripts simply tell us which score we are talking about; for example, X_1 is the first score, X_2 is the second, and so on.)

If the mean is to be determined from a frequency distribution in which some or all of the frequencies are different from 1, this must be taken into account in the formula for the mean. Thus, the formula for the mean when you are dealing with a frequency distribution is:

$$\overline{X} = \frac{\Sigma fX}{N}$$

The defining formula I presented earlier, $\overline{X} = \Sigma X/N$ assumes a distribution in which each frequency is 1.

Before considering the use of the formula for $\overline{X}$, it may be useful to compute a single average based on a small number of scores to refresh your memory about such determinations. For example, suppose you are asked to find the mean of the scores 3, 3, 0, −2. Remember, to find the average you first add the scores [3 + 3 + 0 + (−2) = 4] and then divide by the number of scores, or 4. Thus, the mean is ⁴⁄₄ = 1. Let's consider the use of the formulas.

Suppose we are asked to calculate the mean for a distribution of IQ scores in an honor's class. The distribution is shown below.

X	f
163	3
160	1
158	4
155	3
147	2
140	2
138	3
129	1
	19

The first step should always be to write the formula and look at it for a moment to see what it tells us to compute. Mathematics is a language, you see, and if you can learn to read it, you will have little difficulty with the computations. Since we are dealing with a frequency distribution, the formula is $\overline{X} = \Sigma fX/N$. There are only two things we need to know in order to apply the formula: ΣfX and N. N is the total number of students in the class or the total number of scores, which, in the case of the frequency distribution, is the sum of the numbers in the f column. Adding these numbers, we find that the Σf is 19.

The other value that we need to determine is ΣfX. In order to sum fX we need a column labeled fX. The values in this column are determined by multiplying each score by its frequency. Adding the fX column we get 2863. This procedure is shown below.

X	f	fX
163	3	489
160	1	160
158	4	632
155	3	465
147	2	294
140	2	280
138	3	414
129	1	129
	19	2863

The final step is to plug the values we have determined for N and ΣfX into the formula for the mean:

$$\overline{X} = \frac{\Sigma fX}{N} = \frac{2863}{19} = 150.7$$

The mean may also be determined from a grouped frequency distribution. In the case of the grouped distribution, we use the midpoint of each class interval for X. To illustrate, let's look at an actual grouped frequency distribution.

As part of an experiment on obesity, 64 overweight people are placed in a room containing a malfunctioning clock and a plate of 100 cheese crackers. The clock functions in such a fashion that after a person has been in the room for 30 minutes it appears that an hour has passed and that mealtime has arrived. A grouped frequency distribution of the number of crackers eaten is shown below.

CI	Midpoint	f	fX (f times the midpoint)
63–69	66	5	330
56–62	59	6	354
49–55	52	8	416
42–48	45	7	315
35–41	38	8	304
28–34	31	10	310
21–27	24	9	216
14–20	17	5	85
7–13	10	4	40
0–6	3	2	6
		64	2376

As you can see, the sum of the f column is 64 and ΣfX is the sum of each frequency multiplied by the midpoint of its class interval. In this case, ΣfX is 2376 and the mean of the distribution is:

$$\overline{X} = \frac{\Sigma fX}{N} = \frac{2376}{64} = 37.125$$

Checking Your Progress

Suppose that we have determined the digit-span (number of digits that can be held in memory for a brief time period; for example, for ten seconds) in 37 four-year olds. What is the mean digit-span for our sample?

X	f	
6	2	12
5	7	35
4	17	68
3	5	15
2	3	6
1	2	2
0	1	0
	37	138

(The correct answer is 3.73.)

A Note on Rounding

One point that will crop up throughout the remainder of the text concerns rounding. How should one round off decimal fractions? The *rounding convention* that I suggest states that when the last digit (the one you want to round) is more than 5, round the preceding digit up. If the last digit is less than 5, drop it. If it is equal to 5, round the preceding number to the nearest even number.

For example, consider the following values that we want to round to tenths:

1. 1.68 rounds to 1.7 since the number in the hundredths place (8) is larger than 5, requiring that the preceding digit (6) be rounded up to 7.
2. 1.63 rounds to 1.6 since the number in the hundredths place (3) is less than 5, and, as such, is dropped.
3. 1.65 rounds to 1.6 since the number in the hundredths place is 5 and the preceding digit (6) is even.
4. 1.75 rounds to 1.8 since the number in the hundredths place is 5 and the preceding digit is odd (7). In this case we round up to the nearest even digit (8).

The convention about what to do if the number you want to round is equal to 5 is very explicit. However, you must take care to be sure that the number to be rounded is *exactly* 5. For example, if you wanted to round 3.7850001 to the nearest hundredth, what would you do? You should round to 3.79 since there is slightly more than 5 following the 8.

Figure 4–1: Generalized keyboard for an inexpensive pocket calculator. **M** = memory storage (sometimes labeled STO); **%** = percent key: **C/CE** = combination clear and clear last entry key.

Using the Pocket Calculator to Compute the Mean

Although there is a great deal of variability in the keyboards of pocket calculators, if you have one with the functions listed in chapter 1 (add, subtract, multiply, divide, square root, memory) the layout may look something like that shown in figure 4–1.

You may have separate buttons for using the memory function such as M+, M–, MR. If so, the following discussion would be slightly simpler, but I will assume that your keyboard is like the one shown in figure 4–1.

Let's take a specific example to illustrate the procedure. A test was given to 19 students to assess their attitudes toward risk taking. The test consisted of 13 pairs of statements (for example, I would not like to be hypnotized or I would like to have the experience of being hypnotized) one of which the student circled as being more appropriate to his or her true feelings. The number of items circled indicating a desire to take risks constituted the student's score. The frequency distribution was:

X	f
11	2
9	4
8	5
7	5
5	1
2	2
	19

To find the mean we must compute $\overline{X} = \Sigma fX/N$. The first step is to sum the frequency column, giving us an N of 19. Here is where the pocket calculator is so useful. To compute the mean, use the following sequence of operations:

11 ⊗ 2 ⊜ Ⓜ⊕ 9 ⊗ 4 ⊜ Ⓜ⊕ 8 ⊗ 5
⊜ Ⓜ⊕ 7 ⊗ 5 ⊜ⓂⒺ ⊕ 5 ⊗ 1
⊜ Ⓜ⊕ 2 ⊗ 2 ⊜ Ⓜ⊕ Ⓜ⊜ ⊘ 19
⊜ 7.47

I suspect that this sequence of operations appears tedious when written out, but it really isn't in practice. What we are doing is multiplying each score by its frequency (for example, 11 ⊗ 2 ⊜) and then adding these products into the memory (Ⓜ⊕). At the end of this sequence, the memory is recalled (Ⓜ⊜) and divided by N. The final readout is the mean. Using the memory function of the calculator to sum fX saves time since it is not necessary to write down each separate product and then later to go back and sum them.

For practice, rework any of the solved examples of $\overline{X}$ using the memory function of your calculator.

A Property of the Mean

The mean is often called the balancing point in the distribution. In a distribution of scores, some scores have values greater than the mean (average), while others are below the mean. That is, some of the scores in the distribution deviate from the mean either positively or negatively. Of course, some may be equal to it. If we sum all the positive and negative deviations from the mean (the difference between each score and the mean symbolized by $X - \overline{X}$), the result will be zero. The reason for this and the reason why the mean is called the balancing point in the distribution is that the sum of the positive deviations is exactly equal to the sum of the negative deviations. Symbolically this property of the mean is expressed as $\Sigma(X - \bar{X}) = 0$.

To illustrate the property, let's consider the following example. Nine students have been given 10 problems to solve, each requiring some creative ability. The number of problems solved in a twenty-minute period is recorded, and the frequency distribution of the scores is shown below.

X	f	fX
10	1	10
8	2	16
7	1	7
6	1	6
5	1	5
4	1	4
3	2	6
	9	54

To begin, we need to determine the mean:

$$\bar{X} = \frac{\Sigma fX}{N} = \frac{54}{9} = 6$$

Imagine that the problems solved are objects placed on a see-saw. Their weights are determined by how far away from the mean they are placed. To help your imagination, this has been drawn in figure 4–2.

As you can see, the score of 7 is one unit above the mean and has been given the weight of +1. There are 2 scores of 8 which are located two units above the mean and are therefore given the combined weight of +4. Also, above the mean is the score of 10 which is four units above the mean and has been given the weight of +4. The 4 scores above the mean have a combined weight of $1 + 2 + 2 + 4 = +9$.

Since the score of 5 is one unit to the left (below) the mean, it has been assigned a weight of -1; 4 is two units below the mean and has the weight of -2; and the 2 scores of 3 are three units below the mean and have been assigned a weight of -6. The sum of the weights below the mean is $(-1) + (-2) + (-6) = -9$. Algebraically adding the weights above and below the mean yields $(+9) + (-9) = 0$. Thus, we see that the weights above the mean exactly equal

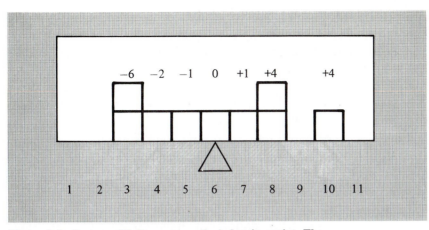

Figure 4–2: Seesaw with the mean as the balancing point. The weights above the mean exactly balance the weights below the mean.

the weights below the mean, and the mean is the balancing point for the distribution.

Earlier I said that the property of the mean could be expressed symbolically as $\Sigma(X - \overline{X}) = 0$ [or $\Sigma f(X - \overline{X}) = 0$ for a frequency distribution in which the frequencies are different from 1]. The demonstration of this without resort to the seesaw illustration is shown below.

X	f	$(X - \overline{X})$	$f(X - \overline{X})$
10	1	+4	+4
8	2	+2	+4
7	1	+1	+1
6	1	0	0
5	1	−1	−1
4	1	−2	−2
3	2	−6	−6
			0

The mean is still 6 and in the column labeled $X - \overline{X}$ the mean has been subtracted from each score and the appropriate sign has been retained. In the next column, labeled $f(X - \overline{X})$, the frequency has been multiplied by each deviation. Summing this last column we see that the sum of the deviations about the mean is indeed equal to zero. It is important to keep this property of the mean in mind when we talk about ways to determine the amount of variability (or deviation) in a distribution. We will discuss such techniques in the next chapter.

Uses of the Mean

The mean is the most useful of the three measures of central tendency because many important statistical procedures are based on it. In addition, the mean has merit because it is based on *all* of the data in the distribution and not just a limited portion of it like the median and the mode. Also, the mean is a more reliable (stable) measure than either the median or the mode, since successive sample means from some population will have greater similarity than will the median and mode of successive samples.

One of the most important properties of the mean of a sample is that it is neither always above the population mean nor always below it. Instead, if we took successive samples from a population, the mean of the sample means would equal the population mean. For this reason we say that the sample mean is an unbiased estimate of the population mean, which is symbolized by μ (pronounced mū). This property of the sample mean as an unbiased estimator of μ will be especially important in chapters 7 and 8.

There are some situations in which the mean will not be the best measure of central tendency to report. For example, in small samples with only one or a few extreme scores, the mean may poorly represent the distribution. In general, when the distribution is badly skewed, the mean may not be very representative. For example, suppose that we have a distribution of scores, such as, 3, 5, 5, 7, 17. The mean of the distribution is $\overline{X} = \Sigma X/N = 37/5 = 7.4$, which is not a very representative value since 4 out of 5 of the scores are below it.

Likewise, when we have missing scores for some reason or arbitrarily determined cutoff scores, the mean should not be reported—the reason being that the mean is a value based on the actual amount of each of the scores in a distribution. If there are some scores that we have not determined, we cannot legitimately compute the mean.

I obtained some data that illustrate this point in an experiment I performed recently. Nine rats that had had their olfactory bulbs removed were first trained to press a bar for a tiny reward and then the reward was omitted so that their barpressing eventually ceased (extinguished). The response measure that I wanted to analyze was the number of days that it took the animals to stop responding. Since I expected that some animals would continue to respond much longer than normal, I arbitrarily decided to terminate any animal that continued to respond beyond 15 days. Thus, if an animal was still responding at 15 days, I would no longer continue its training but I wouldn't actually know how long it would have taken the rat to extinguish if it had been allowed to continue. This sort of arbitrary cutoff point is often necessary in learning experiments because of the minority of subjects that just never comprehend the task requirements. It is even more necessary when working with brain-damaged subjects. At any rate, a score of 15 indicates that an animal was arbitrarily terminated. The scores were 15, 15, 15, 15, 12, 6, 5, 4, 3. Since the first four scores were arbitrarily determined, the mean should not be computed. Both for this situation and the case with a badly skewed distribution, the median is the preferred measure of central tendency.

Median

The *median* is formally defined as a point along the score scale separating the top 50% of the scores from the bottom 50%. It is a point above which half the scores lie and below which half lie and is often reported to be easier to calculate than the mean or arithmetic average. Although not as useful for further statistical procedures as the mean, the median is at times the best descriptive measure of central tendency. Elaboration of this last statement will await a discussion of computational procedures.

Locating the Median in a Frequency Distribution or Simple Array of Numbers

A simplified method for finding the median from a frequency distribution requires the use of a somewhat modified definition. Thus, we might redefine the *median* as the score in the middle of the distribution, the one above which half the scores lie and below which half lie. Using this definition, in a frequency distribution with an even number of scores the median (Md) will be a number halfway between the two scores in the middle of the distribution. For example, if there are 10 scores, the median will be halfway between the 5th and 6th scores; there are 4 scores above the 6th score and 4 scores below the 5th score.

The position of the median in a frequency distribution with an even number of scores may be determined by considering the following. The median will be halfway between the $(N/2)$th and the $(N/2)$th + 1 scores. To illustrate, if you have 26 scores, the median will be between the $(N/2)$th or $26 \div 2 = 13$th score and the $(N/2)$th + 1 or $13 + 1 = 14$th score. The location of the median in an array of 10 scores is diagrammed below.

Score No. | 1 2 3 4 | 5 | 6 | 7 8 9 10 |

4 Scores   Md   4 Scores

Let's look at some data and actually determine the median. Suppose that we measure the IQ scores of 10 mentally retarded children and find them to be as follows: 63, 37, 35, 42, 55, 13, 27, 34, 10, 25. The first step will be to arrange the scores into a frequency distribution.

X	f	Cum f
63	1	10
55	1	9
42	1	8
37	1	7
35	1	6
34	1	5
27	1	4
25	1	3
13	1	2
10	1	1

$$Md = \frac{34 + 35}{2} = \frac{69}{2} = 34.5$$

Since there are 10 scores in the distribution, the median will be halfway between the 5th and 6th scores. Reference to the Cum f column tells us that the 5th score is a 34 and the 6th score is a 35. To find the score that is halfway between them we can take the arithmetic average of them which is 34.5 as shown above. Thus, the median IQ score of our sample of 10 retardates is 34.5.

Another example of the median from an even number of scores may offer further clarification. Suppose that we have recorded the high temperature each day during the month of February in the town of Way Outback, Maine, as incidental information in a study of the mating behavior of the snow goose. The data are as follows:

X	f	Cum f
48°	1	28
42°	1	27
40°	1	26
36°	1	25
35°	1	24
33°	4	23
25°	1	19
22°	1	18
18°	3	17
15°	5	14
0°	1	9
−2°	1	8
−8°	2	7
−10°	1	5
−16°	1	4
−20°	1	3
−25°	1	2
−37°	1	1

Since there are 28 scores, we know that we need to find the 14th and 15th scores: $(N/2) = 28 \div 2 = 14$, and $(N/2) + 1 = 14 + 1 = 15$. Looking at the Cum f column we find that the 14th score is 15°. The 15th score (as well as the 16th and the 17th) is 18°. Thus, the median is $(15° + 18°) \div 2 = 33 \div 2 = 16.5°$.

Checking Your Progress

Suppose that you have taken 36 rats and trained them to make a simple brightness discrimination. To do this you have placed each rat into a small piece of apparatus known as a two-choice discrimination box. The box is divided into two compartments or chambers called the start box and the goal box. To get from the start area into the goal box the animal must pass through two doors that are blocked by movable cards one of which is painted black while the other is white. If the animal chooses the card that you have arbitrarily designated as incorrect, it receives a slight footshock and finds the card locked. The position of the cards is alternated from trial to trial so that the animal can't solve the problem by going to the same position every time. Each time the animal makes an incorrect choice of cards an error is recorded and the animal is trained until it makes 9 correct choices in a block of 10 trials. The data (number of errors) for your group of 36 rats might be as follows:

X	f
33	1
32	1
31	1
29	2
27	3
26	5
24	5
22	4
21	2
20	3
19	2
18	3
17	1
16	1
15	1
14	1

Your task is to find the median. (The correct answer is 23.)

So much for the situation where there is an even number of scores. What happens when N is an odd number? Actually this is even easier than the situation where we had an even number of scores since all that is necessary is to locate the one score in the middle of the distribution. Thus, if there are 9 scores we would locate the 5th score (4 below it and 4 above) and report this as the median. Or if we have 49 scores, the median would be the 25th score (24 scores below it and 24 above it).

The median may also be determined by finding the $[(N + 1)/2]$th score. For example, if we have 65 scores, the median will be the $(65 + 1)/2 = 66 \div 2 = 33$rd score.

Let's look at an example. Suppose that 25 students have rated their psychology professor on a 10-point scale in terms of how well prepared the lectures are. The results are as follows:

X	f	Cum f
10	3	25
9	4	22
8	6	18
7	5	12
6	3	7
5	2	4
4	1	2
3	1	1

Since there are 25 scores, the median will be the $(25 + 1)/2 = 26 \div 2 = 13$th score. Looking at the Cum f column we see that there are 12 scores of 7 or less and 18 scores of 8 or less. This tells us that the 13th through the 18th scores are all 8 and the median is 8.

For another example of the determination of the median from a frequency distribution with an odd number of scores, let's reconsider the digit-span data introduced in the section on the mean. The distribution of scores was as follows:

X	f	Cum f
6	2	37
5	7	35
4	17	28
3	5	11
2	3	6
1	2	3
0	1	1

The mean was found to be 3.73. What is the median?

Again, our first step is to determine the position of the score that we want. Since N is 37, $(N + 1)/2 = (37 + 1)/2 = 38 \div 2 = 19$. From the Cum f column, we determine that the 19th score (actually the 12th through the 28th) is a 4, and we conclude that the median digit-span for the four-year olds we measured is 4.

Checking Your Progress

A type of clinician known as a behavior therapist has used a technique called systematic desensitization to treat 23 patients for removal of phobic symptoms. In systematic desensitization, the patient is first taught relaxation techniques, i.e., he or she is taught how to relax. Then, a fear hierarchy is constructed in which the patient ranks fearful situations relevant to the phobia. For example, if the patient has a snake phobia, the most feared situation might be handling a live snake. The second most fearful situation might be handling a dead snake, and the least feared situation might be encountering a garden hose coiled in the grass. After the fear hierarchy is developed and the patient learns relaxation techniques, the two things are combined. That is, the patient is asked to imagine each of the feared situations beginning with the least feared while maintaining relaxation.

In our hypothetical situation the therapist has recorded the number of sessions required by each patient to achieve symptomatic relief. Unfortunately, 4 patients showed no progress after 20 sessions and were assigned an arbitrary score of 25. The data are as follows:

Number of Sessions	f	
25	4	23
14	1	17
12	2	16
11	3	16
10	3	13
9	4	10
8	2	6
6	1	4
5	1	3
4	1	2
3	1	1

Determine the median. (The correct answer is 10.)

In summary, the procedure for determining the median from an array of scores or from a frequency distribution is:

1. When confronted with a group of scores that is not arranged into a frequency distribution, you must arrange them before trying to locate the median.
2. Determine whether the total number of scores is odd or even.
3. If the number of scores is even, the median will be halfway between the two scores in the middle which we determine by

looking at the Cum f column. The location of the median will be halfway between the $(N/2)$th score and the $(N/2)$th + 1 score.

4. If there is an odd number of scores, the median is the one in the middle determined again by reference to the Cum f column. The position of the median is determined by finding the $[(N + 1)/2]$th score.

Locating the Median from a Grouped Frequency Distribution

To determine the median from a grouped frequency distribution, we first locate the class interval containing the median and then interpolate to find the exact location. To aid in the description of the procedure, let's consider a specific example.

Earlier in the chapter, we considered a grouped distribution based on the number of crackers eaten by a group of overweight people when faced with a malfunctioning clock. The distribution is again shown below.

CI	f	Cum f
63–69	5	64
56–62	6	59
49–55	8	53
42–48	7	45
35–41	8	38
28–34	10	30
21–27	9	20
14–20	5	11
7–13	4	6
0–6	2	2

According to the definition presented earlier in the chapter, we know that we want to find the case at the 50th percentile. Since there are 64 scores, we need to find the 32nd score (50% of 64 = 64 × .5 = 32). Looking at the Cum f column we see that the 32nd case is in the interval with apparent limits from 35 to 41 or with real limits from 34.5 to 41.5. That is, there are 30 scores of 34.5 or less (34.5 is the upper real limit of the interval from 28 to 34 or it is the lower real limit of the next higher interval) and 38 scores of 41.5 or less.

Assuming that the scores are evenly distributed in the intervals, how far into the interval must we go to find the 32nd case? Since there are 30 scores up to the top of the preceding interval and we want the 32nd score, the median will be the second score from the bottom of the interval from 35 to 41 ($32 - 30 = 2$). That is, the median will be the second of 8 scores in the interval. Thus, it is $\frac{2}{8}$ (or $\frac{1}{4}$) of the way into an interval containing 7 score units or $7 \times$ $\frac{2}{8}$ths of the way into the interval. Since $7 \times \frac{2}{8} = 1.75$ we conclude that the median is 1.75 score units into the interval with a lower real limit of 34.5. In conclusion, the median is $34.5 + 1.75$ or 36.25.

The procedure that has just been outlined is summarized in the following formula:

Md = lower real limit of interval containing ($N/2$)th case

$$+ \; i \left(\frac{N/2 - \text{Cum } f \text{ in interval below the one containing the } (N/2)\text{th case}}{f \text{ in interval containing } (N/2)\text{th case}} \right)$$

Although the formula appears to be very cumbersome, the rationale behind it and the use of it are really very simple. The steps involved in finding a median from a grouped distribution may be summarized as follows:

1. Determine the value of $N/2$. This is the same thing as finding 50% of N.
2. Consult the Cum f column to find the interval containing the ($N/2$)th case.
3. Add to the lower real limit of the interval i (the width of a class interval which may be determined by adding 1 to the difference between the limits of any interval) times $N/2$ minus the Cum f in the preceding interval divided by the frequency in the interval containing the ($N/2$)th case. The resulting value is the median.

Actually the formula presented may be used for finding the score value at any percentile, not just the 50th. In order to do this all we have to do is substitute any percentage of N for $N/2$. For example, to find the score at the 25th percentile, we would take 25% of N ($N \times .25$) or find the ($N/4$)th case.

Finally, to show the computations involved in finding the median using the formula introduced, let's use it to redetermine the median number of crackers consumed.

$$\text{Md} = 34.5 + 7\left(\frac{32 - 30}{8}\right) = 34.5 + 7\left(\frac{2}{8}\right) = 34.5 + \frac{14}{8}$$

$$= 34.5 + 1.75 = 36.25$$

In order to be certain that we have the procedure, let's consider another example. A test has been given to 83 students to determine their degree of apathy toward current events. The test consists of 60 items taken from a weekly news magazine and each student is asked to respond in terms of interest in the item. The score for each subject is the number of items marked "no interest." The grouped frequency distribution is shown below.

CI	f	Cum f
40–44	4	83
35–39	5	79
30–34	11	74
25–29	18	63
—20–24	⑦	45
15–19	11	38
10–14	13	27
5–9	14	14

The first step is to find the interval containing the median. Thus, the total N is divided by 2 giving us $N/2 = 83 \div 2 = 41.5$. The interval containing the 41.5th score or case is the one with limits from 20 to 24 (real limits: 19.5–24.5). The reason for this is that there are 38 scores of 19 or less and 45 scores of 24 or less which means that the 41.5th score must be in the interval from 20 to 24. Using the formula, we find:

$$\text{Md} = \text{lower real limit} + i \left(\frac{N/2 - \text{Cum } f \text{ in interval below}}{f} \right)$$

$$= 19.5 + 5 \left(\frac{41.5 - 38}{7} \right) = 19.5 + 5 \left(\frac{3.5}{7} \right) = 19.5 + 5(.5)$$

$$= 19.5 + 2.5 = 22$$

Checking Your Progress

Earlier in the chapter we found the median for a frequency distribution based on the high temperatures each day during the month of February in the town of Way Outback, Maine. A grouped frequency distribution based on that frequency distribution is shown below. Find the median.

CI	f	
44 – 52	1	28
35 – 43	4	27
26 – 34	4	23
17 – 25	5	19
8 – 16	5	14
(−1) – 7	1	9
(−10)– (−2)	4	8
(−19)–(−11)	1	4
(−28)–(−20)	2	3
(−37)–(−29)	1	1

(The correct answer is 16.5°.)

Uses of the Median

When should the median be reported? The median is a very useful statistic and should be used when: (1) you have a fairly small distribution and a few extreme scores or a badly skewed distribution and/or (2) there are some scores in the distribution that were not actually determined. An example of both situations was discussed in the section on the uses of the mean.

The distribution consisting of the scores 3, 5, 5, 7, and 17 was used to illustrate the case where the mean was not the best measure of central tendency to report because the distribution was small and badly skewed. The median of the distribution is 5 since the third or middle score has this value. The number 5 is much more representative of the distribution than the value computed for the mean or 7.4. Since the median is based on the number of scores and not on their values, it will not be influenced by the very deviant or extreme scores.

The second point, that the median is useful when there are scores in the distribution that were not actually determined, is illustrated by the learning experiment discussed in which some animals were unable to learn the task after brain damage. The actual distribution of scores was 15, 15, 15, 15, 12, 6, 5, 4, and 3 where a score of 15 indicated that an animal had been terminated from the study. The median in this case is the 5th score or 12 while the point was made that the mean should not be computed.

Although the median may be used in some further statistical operations (for example, the median test), it is not nearly as useful in this regard as the mean.

Mode

The mode is the easiest of the measures of central tendency to determine but, unfortunately, it is the least useful for further statistical manipulations. The *mode* is defined as the most frequently occurring score in a frequency distribution or the midpoint of the class interval with the largest frequency in a grouped frequency distribution. To determine its value we only have to look at the column of frequencies to see which is the largest and then look across to see which score or interval of scores has this frequency. Two examples based on frequency distributions of scores from a scrambled sentences test are given below.

mode

Scores of Males			Scores of Females	
X	f		X	f
13	1		12	2
12	1		11	1
11	2		10	1
10	1		9	2
9	3	Mo = 9, score with the highest frequency	8	3	Mo = 8, score with the highest frequency
6	1		7	1
4	1		6	1
			5	1
			4	1

To determine the value of the mode (Mo) for the distributions shown, a check of the frequency column was made to determine the highest value in it. Looking across from this value to the score column, we can determine that the Mo for the males was 9, while for the females it was 8. That is, more males correctly unscrambled 9 sentences than any other number, while more females correctly unscrambled 8 sentences.

To illustrate the location of the Mo in a grouped frequency distribution, let's reconsider one of the distributions introduced in chapter 3. The IQ test scores of 23 students in an honor's class were summarized in the following grouped frequency distribution.

CI	MP	f	CI	MP	f
170–174	172	1	140–144	142	5
165–169	167	0	135–139	137	1
160–164	162	2	130–134	132	0
155–159	157	3	125–129	127	2
150–154	152	6	120–124	122	1
145–149	147	2			

Looking at the frequency column we see that the largest number is 6 which is the frequency for the CI from 150 to 154. The midpoint of this interval is 152 and this value is reported as the mode.

Unfortunately, once we have determined the mode there is little we can do with it beyond reporting it, since we can't use it for any further statistical manipulations. The problem is that the mode is based on only one score in the data; a measure based on all of the scores would be much more useful since it would have more stability (would vary less) from sample to sample drawn from a population.

Our data can contain more than one score or class interval with a high frequency and the high frequencies can be exactly the same so that we can't decide on only one mode. A distribution with two **bimodal** modes is called *bimodal*, and we report both values.

Uses of the Mode

The mode is the measure of choice in two instances: (1) when we need the quickest possible estimate of the central tendency in the data or (2) when we want to report the score obtained by the largest number of subjects. Thus, the mode is a good descriptive measure, but it will not be used in inferential procedures. It is useful as a rough estimate of the mean and median, and it can be used to roughly check the accuracy of computation of the latter statistics.

The Position of the Measures of Central Tendency in a Frequency Polygon

In a symmetrical, unimodal distribution the mean, median, and mode are all the same. In a skewed distribution, however, the mean is pulled in the direction of the extreme scores (tail) and the median is between the mean and the mode. Examples of the relative locations of the three measures are shown in figure 4–3.

To further illustrate the position of the three measures and at

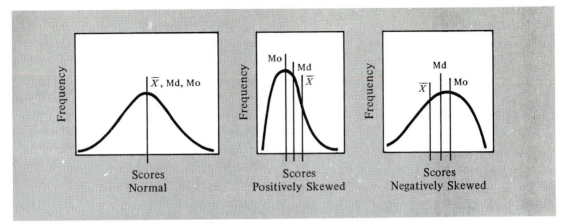

Figure 4–3: The relative positions of $\overline{X}$, Md, and Mo in a normal distribution, a positively skewed distribution, and a negatively skewed distribution.

the same time review computational procedures, suppose that we have the following highly simplified frequency distributions.

Distribution A—Positively Skewed

X	f	Cum f	fX
39	1	47	39
33	1	46	33
31	1	45	31
27	3	44	81
26	4	41	104
25	4	37	100
24	5	33	120
23	6	28	138
22	7	22	154
21	7	15	147
20	8	8	160
	47		1107

Mo = score with highest frequency or 20 since its frequency is 8

$$Md = \left(\frac{N+1}{2}\right) \text{th score} = \frac{47+1}{2} = \frac{48}{2} = 24\text{th score} = 23$$

$$\overline{X} = \frac{\Sigma fX}{N} = \frac{1107}{47} = 23.6$$

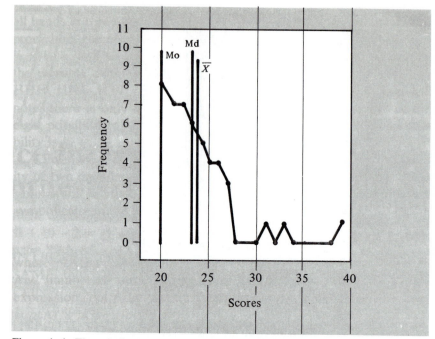

Figure 4–4: The relative locations of the three measures of central tendency in a positively skewed distribution.

The frequency polygon based on Distribution A is plotted in figure 4–4. On it are shown the relative locations of the measures of central tendency.

Distribution B—Negatively Skewed

X	f	Cum f	fX
9	5	34	45
8	5	29	40
7	7	24	49
6	6	17	36
5	5	11	25
4	3	6	12
3	1	3	3
2	1	2	2
1	1	1	1
	34		213

Mo = 7, since this is the score with the highest frequency, 7

Md = score halfway between the ($N/2$)th score and the ($N/2$)th
+ 1 score. $N/2 = 34/2 = 17$. The 17th score is 6. $N/2 + 1$
$= 17 + 1 = 18$th score, which is 7. Thus, Md $= (6 + 7)/2 = 13/2$
$= 6.5$

$\overline{X} = \Sigma fX/N = 213/34 = 6.3$

The frequency polygon based on Distribution B is shown in figure 4–5. Again, the measures of central tendency have been plotted to illustrate the relative locations.

Since the mean is pulled in the direction of the tail in a skewed distribution, if you are given any two of the measures you should be able to guess both the shape of the distribution and the location of the missing value. For example, if you knew that the mean of a distribution was 13 and the mode was 20, you would probably guess that the distribution was negatively skewed and that the median was somewhere between 13 and 20. If you were told that the mode was

Figure 4–5: The relative locations of the three measures of central tendency in a negatively skewed distribution.

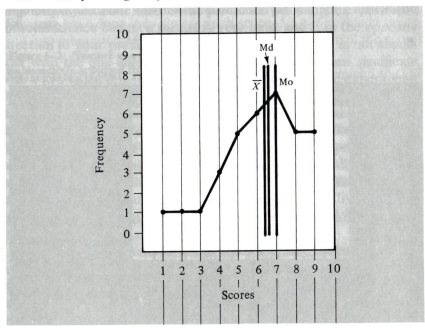

10 with a median of 15, the distribution would probably be positively skewed and the mean would be above 15.

Summary

In this chapter three measures of central tendency were discussed, the mean, the median, and the mode. The *mean* ($\overline{X}$) is the arithmetic average of the scores defined mathematically as the sum of the scores divided by the number of scores. The formula is $\overline{X} = \Sigma X/N$, or $\overline{X} = \Sigma fX/N$ for a frequency distribution. The midpoint of each class interval is used as a score in computing the mean from a grouped frequency distribution. The mean is the balancing point in the distribution, symbolized by the following: $\Sigma(X - \overline{X}) = 0$, or the sum of the deviation of each score about the mean is zero. The mean is the least variable of the three measures of central tendency and is used in many other statistical manipulations. It may not be the most representative measure in situations favoring the median; that is, badly skewed distributions and/or missing scores in the distribution. The mean of a sample is an unbiased estimator of the population mean or μ.

A brief discussion of *rounding* was presented and a set of conventions detailed. Thus, if the number to be rounded is less than 5, drop it. If it is greater than 5, round the preceding digit up. If the number to be rounded is exactly 5, round the preceding digit up if it is odd or leave it alone if it is even.

The *median* (Md) was defined as a point along the score scale separating the top 50% of the scores from the bottom 50%. In order to determine it from a frequency distribution, the median was redefined as the score in the middle of the distribution, the one above which half the scores lie and below which half lie.

A simple way to determine the location of the score that is the median in a frequency distribution is to consider the following:

1. If N is even, the median will be halfway between the $(N/2)$th score and the $(N/2)$th + 1 score. To determine the value of the median, first locate the two scores and then take their average.
2. If N is odd, the median will be the $[(N + 1)/2]$th score.

To find the median from a grouped frequency distribution, the class interval containing the $(N/2)$th score is found, and interpolation is then used to find the point where the score is located. The following formula was introduced to aid in the determination of the median from a grouped frequency distribution.

$$Md = \begin{array}{c} \text{lower real limit} \\ \text{of} \\ \text{interval} \\ \text{containing} \\ +i \; (N/2)\text{th case} \end{array} \left(\frac{N/2 - \text{Cum } f \text{ in interval below the one containing the } (N/2)\text{th case}}{f \text{ in interval containing } (N/2)\text{th case}} \right)$$

The median is the preferred measure when there are a few extreme scores in the distribution or when there are missing scores.

The *mode* (Mo) is defined as the most frequently occurring score in the distribution and is determined by locating the score(s) with the highest frequency. In a grouped frequency distribution, the mode is the midpoint of the class interval with the highest frequency. The mode is valuable in a descriptive sense but is not useful for further statistical procedures. Since it is so simply determined, it is useful as a first approximation of the central tendency in the data.

In a symmetrical distribution with only one mode, the mean, median, and the mode will all have the same value. In a skewed distribution, however, the mean will be pulled in the direction of the tail and the median will be between the mean and the mode.

Troubleshooting Your Computations

No matter how simple the statistic is, errors are possible. How will you know (or suspect) that an error has been made? Is there any advice that I can impart at this point that will ease your task?

The most basic piece of advice that I can give is that you should be aware of what constitutes a reasonable answer. You must try to get a feel for the type of answer that makes sense for the problem you are trying to solve. For example, if you are trying to determine a measure of central tendency for a sample distribution, the value you obtain should be not only in the distribution of scores you have but also in the *center* (more or less) of the distribution. Thus, before you start plugging numbers into some equation, sit back and look at the distribution of scores confronting you and try to guess a value for the statistic you want. In this way if you do make a mistake and obtain an impossible answer for the distribution at hand, at least you'll recognize it.

If you are dealing with a frequency distribution, be sure to take the frequencies into account. By this I mean that you should be sure that you are using the appropriate formula (e.g., $\Sigma fX/N$ rather than $\Sigma X/N$) and that you have multiplied each score by its frequency prior to summing.

The mode is so simple to determine that rarely does any mistake occur. The only advice I have here is to caution you to be sure that you have reported the *score* (or midpoint of a class interval) with the highest frequency rather than the highest frequency itself.

Finally, to help prevent computational errors I would advise that you perform all computations twice.

Exercises

1. In an experiment to determine the effect of a particular type of brain damage on the memory of rats, a group of rats was trained to make a visual discrimination, given a brain lesion, allowed to recover, and retrained on the original problem. Prior to retraining, the experimenter decides not to continue any animal that takes more than twice as long to relearn the task as had been taken originally; such an animal is assigned a savings score of -100%. The actual savings scores exhibited by the 9 animals in the group were: -100%, 10%, 43%, -100%, 65%, 75%, -80%, -100%, -35%. Determine each of the measures of central tendency, tell which you think is most appropriate, and say what you can about the shape of the distribution based on the three measures.

2. Determine the mean and the median for each of the following:
   (a) 27, 33, 10, 9, 6, 7, 11, 23, 27

   (b)

X	f
150	5
148	5
145	8
133	7
110	4
108	3
65	5
64	5
62	5
37	3

   (c)

X	f
5	2
4	3
3	4
2	1
-3	3
-10	2
-15	3
-30	2

3. Which measure of central tendency would be most appropriate when:
   (a) you have extreme scores or missing scores.
   (b) you need a quick estimate.
   (c) you need the value that will be most consistent from sample to sample.

4. (a) A unimodal distribution with Mo $= 30$, $\bar{X} = 17$ would be an example of a _____ distribution.
   (b) If the X were 67 with a Md $= 15$, this would be a _____ distribution.

5. An experimenter decides to test the effects of alcohol intake on the ability to learn a list of nonsense syllables. Half of the subjects are given a rum-flavored

drink while the other half are given the real thing. Because of time limitations, the experimenter decides to terminate any subject who has not achieved the criterion of learning within 100 trials. The data for each group are as follows:

Group Rum-Flavored Cola			Group Rum and Cola	
No. of Trials to Learn	f		No. of Trials to Learn	f
27	1	21	100+	3
25	2	20	52	2
21	3	18	46	4
20	3	15	33	2
18	5	12	24	3
16	2	7	21	2
15	3	5	19	3
14	1	2	18	2
12	1	1	13	1

Determine the three measures of central tendency. Which is the most appropriate? Suppose that we have discarded the 3 subjects in Group Rum and Cola who failed to meet the criterion. Recalculate the measures of central tendency and tell which is most appropriate.

6. In a statistics class, 14 males were given a reaction-time test involving the dropped ruler described in chapter 1. The frequency distribution was:

X	f
9	1
8	2
7	1
6	6
5	2
4	1
3	1

Determine each of the measures of central tendency.

7. The 14 females in the class had the following scores on the test mentioned in problem 6:

X	f
13	1
11	1
10	1
9	4
7	3
6	1
5	2
2	1

Determine the mean, median, and mode. Based upon the relative position of the measures of central tendency, what shape does the distribution have?

8. In this chapter it was stated that the mean is the balancing point in the distribution. Make up a simple example to illustrate this important property of the mean.

9. Preoperative weights were determined for 30 rats. Determine the mean, median, and modal preoperative weight from the grouped frequency distribution. The weights are given in grams.

CI	f
482–494	1
469–481	2
456–468	2
443–455	2
430–442	3
417–429	5
404–416	4
391–403	4
378–390	3
365–377	2
352–364	2

10. Using the rounding conventions described, solve the following:
    (a) Round 43.851 to tenths.
    (b) Round 2.879 to hundredths.
    (c) Round 3.333 to hundredths.
    (d) Round 13.865 to hundredths.

5

Measures of Dispersion

Introduction

In the first chapter we talked about the two major functions of statistics: to describe data and to make inferences from them. In chapters 2, 3, and 4 we discussed different ways to describe data: by organizing them into a frequency distribution for, perhaps, graphing purposes and by determining a number in the central part of the distribution to summarize the data. If we learn how to calculate one other measure we will be able to describe a frequency distribution fairly well. This number is related to the spread of the distribution or to the dispersion. Several terms (used interchangeably throughout this chapter) refer to the spread of the scores around the mean in a distribution. They are *dispersion, deviation,* and *variability*.

Perhaps examples might clarify the need for measuring the variability in the data in order to describe the data further. Suppose we look at the mean yearly amount of rainfall for two cities and find that each averages 150 inches. Just knowing the mean would tell us nothing about how the rainfall was distributed during the year. We might find that in one city the climate was extremely dry for ten months of the year with most of the 150 inches coming during a two-month period. By contrast, a small amount of rain might fall on the other city almost every day. If we just reported our measure of central tendency, however, there would be no way to distinguish the two cities in terms of rainfall.

Tennis is a very popular and rapidly growing sport. Consider the performance of two players, one a professional and the other a weekend player. We can certainly expect a tremendous difference in the variability exhibited by the two players, with the professional showing more consistency on a day-to-day basis.

These two examples illustrate the need for a measure of dispersion or variability. Four measures are discussed in this chapter: the range, the average deviation, the standard deviation, and the variance. Estimates of the population standard deviation and the variance from a sample are also discussed.

Each of the statistics discussed in this chapter will be computed from either simple arrays of scores or from frequency distributions.

They can easily be computed from grouped frequency distributions if the midpoints of the class intervals are used as the scores.

Range

The range is similar to the mode in that it is very easy to determine. Although it is useful in a descriptive sense, it will not be used in further statistical tests. The *range* is defined as the difference between the highest score in the distribution and the lowest score.

For example, suppose we have obtained the IQ scores of most of the population in the United States and have found a low score (LS) of 0 and a high score (HS) of 200. The range is from 0 to 200 or $200 - 0 = 200$. Again, in a problem at the end of chapter 4, a distribution was given where the high score was 5 and the low score was -30. What is the range?

$$R \text{ (Range)} = HS - LS = 5 - (-30) = 5 + 30 = 35$$

The range is a useful measure if you are only interested in a quick approximation of the variability in the data. But, since the range is based on only two scores in the distribution and these are the two extremes, it is obviously not a very sophisticated measure. It is entirely possible to have two distributions that do not differ in terms of the range but are nonetheless different in terms of the variability in them. This is illustrated by two hypothetical frequency polygons of IQ scores in figure 5–1.

Average Deviation

Although we will not use the average deviation (AD) for reporting differences in variability between distributions, it will be discussed briefly as a useful prelude to the most commonly used measure of dispersion, the standard deviation. Suppose we want to calculate the average deviation in a distribution, that is, the average amount that each score in the distribution differs from the mean. To do this, we would first calculate the deviation of each score from the mean ($X - \overline{X}$), add these deviations [$\Sigma(X - \overline{X})$], and divide by the number of scores. What would be wrong with this procedure?

In chapter 4 we found that one property of the mean was that the sum of the deviations around it is zero. Using this property and the procedure in the preceding paragraph, we would always find that the average deviation was zero. This would not be very useful so we must try another method—one that finds the sum of the deviations without getting zero every time.

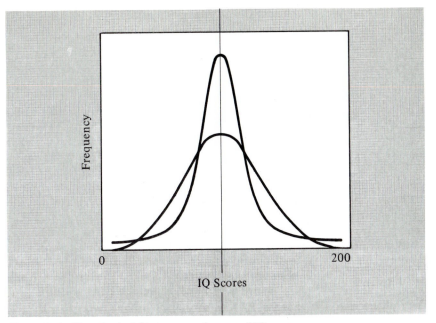

Figure 5–1: Hypothetical frequency polygons of IQ scores having the same measures of central tendency but differing in amount of dispersion.

Actually, there are several methods, one of which requires the summation of the absolute values of the deviations.

The *absolute value* of a number (symbolized by parallel vertical lines on either side of the number, e.g., |−3|) is the value of the number itself, without regard to sign. The absolute value of −5 is just 5 and the absolute value of +5 is likewise 5. Therefore, the formula for the average deviation is:

$$AD = \frac{\Sigma|X - \overline{X}|}{N}$$

Let's apply this formula to a couple of distributions to see if the resulting statistic provides us with any information that we could not discern from knowing the mean.

Distribution A	$X - \overline{X}$	$|X - \overline{X}|$
20	+5	5
19	+4	4
14	−1	1
12	−3	3
10	−5	5
75	0	18

absolute value

$$\overline{X} = \frac{\Sigma X}{N} = \frac{75}{5} = 15$$

$$AD = \frac{\Sigma |X - \overline{X}|}{N} = \frac{18}{5} = 3.6$$

Distribution B	$X - \overline{X}$	$|X - \overline{X}|$
29	+14	14
25	+10	10
15	0	0
5	−10	10
1	−14	14
75	0	48

$$\overline{X} = \frac{\Sigma X}{N} = \frac{75}{5} = 15$$

$$AD = \frac{\Sigma |X - \overline{X}|}{N} = \frac{48}{5} = 9.6$$

In each case the mean of the distribution is 15 and knowing the mean alone would not tell us about the very obvious difference in the distributions. The average deviations, however, are very different and tell us that Distribution B is much more variable than Distribution A (9.6 versus 3.6, respectively).

In the sample exercises at the end of chapter 4, problem 7 contained a frequency distribution of scores obtained by males on a simple reaction-time test. As another example to illustrate the computation of AD, let's reconsider the distribution.

X	f	fX	$X - \overline{X}$	$|X - \overline{X}|$	$f|X - \overline{X}|$
9	1	9	2.9	2.9	2.9
8	2	16	1.9	1.9	3.8
7	1	7	0.9	0.9	0.9
6	6	36	−0.1	0.1	0.6
5	2	10	−1.1	1.1	2.2
4	1	4	−2.1	2.1	2.1
3	1	3	−3.1	3.1	3.1
	14	85			15.6

$$\overline{X} = \frac{\Sigma fX}{N} = \frac{85}{14} = 6.1$$

$$AD = \frac{\Sigma f|X - \overline{X}|}{N} = \frac{15.6}{14} = 1.1$$

As you will note, the formula for AD wehn dealing with a frequency distribution is $\Sigma f|X - \overline{X}|/N$. Computationally the steps are as before with one addition: (1) subtract the mean from each score; (2) take the absolute value of the obtained differences; and (3) multiply the frequency of each score times the absolute value of the differences and sum the products. This final sum is divided by N to give AD. In this case the value of AD was 1.1.

Checking Your Progress

For comparison with the AD calculated above, determine the AD for the distribution of scores obtained by the females on the reaction-time test. The distribution is shown below.

X	f
13	1
11	1
10	1
9	4
7	3
6	1
5	2
2	1

(The correct answer is AD = 2.2.)

By this time you may have thought of another way to get around the problem of the negative signs when finding the deviation of each score from the mean—to square each value since a minus times a minus is a plus. But, of course, we must give a different name to the resulting statistic. We are going to call it the standard deviation.

Standard Deviation

The standard deviation (SD) is closely related to the AD discussed in the previous section. The *standard deviation* is defined as the square root of the sum of the squared deviation of the scores from

standard deviation

the mean divided by the number of scores; that is, it is the square root of the average squared deviation. To determine the average deviation, we summed the absolute values of the deviations and divided by their number. This time we square the deviations prior to summing and dividing by N. As a final step, the square root is taken. The procedure is expressed symbolically in the following:

$$SD = \sqrt{\frac{\Sigma(X - \overline{X})^2}{N}}$$

As you look at this formula, bear in mind that the formula assumes a frequency distribution in which each frequency is 1. If this is not true, then the formula is:

$$SD = \sqrt{\frac{\Sigma f(X - \overline{X})^2}{N}}$$

Using Distribution A from the previous section on the calculation of the AD, let's calculate the standard deviation.

X	$X - \overline{X}$	$(X - \overline{X})^2$
20	+5	25
19	+4	16
14	−1	1
12	−3	9
10	−5	25
75		76

$$\overline{X} = \frac{\Sigma X}{N} = \frac{75}{5} = 15$$

$$SD = \sqrt{\frac{\Sigma(X - \overline{X})^2}{N}} = \sqrt{\frac{76}{5}} = \sqrt{15.2} = 3.9$$

To begin, determine the mean (15) and subtract it from each score $(X - \overline{X})$. Then, square the resulting difference $[(X - \overline{X})^2]$, and find the sum of the squared differences (deviations). The average squared deviation is obtained by dividing the sum of the squared deviations by the number of them. The square root of the average squared deviation is the standard deviation.

For practice and for comparative purposes you might want to calculate the standard deviation from the data called Distribution B in the preceding section (answer: 10.9). You can see that the general results obtained by using the standard deviation are the same as those obtained by calculating the average deviation although the actual values are different. That is, there is more deviation about the mean in Distribution B than there is in Distribution A.

Rather than continue to use the defining formula for calculating the standard deviation, we can use a more efficient formula that doesn't require us to subtract the mean from each score. It is called either the *raw score formula* or the *computational formula* for the standard deviation and is derived from the defining formula. The raw score or computational formula is:

$$SD = \sqrt{\frac{\Sigma X^2}{N} - \left(\frac{\Sigma X}{N}\right)^2} \text{ or } \sqrt{\frac{\Sigma X^2}{N} - \overline{X}^2}, \text{ since } \frac{\Sigma X}{N} = \overline{X}$$

The formula when you have a frequency distribution is:

$$SD = \sqrt{\frac{\Sigma f X^2}{N} - \left(\frac{\Sigma f X}{N}\right)^2} \text{ or } \sqrt{\frac{\Sigma f X^2}{N} - \overline{X}^2}, \text{ where } \overline{X} = \frac{\Sigma f X}{N}$$

Let's use this formula to recalculate the standard deviation of Distribution A.

X	X^2
20	400
19	361
14	196
12	144
10	100
75	1201

$$SD = \sqrt{\frac{\Sigma X^2}{N} - \left(\frac{\Sigma X}{N}\right)^2}$$

$$= \sqrt{\frac{1201}{5} - \left(\frac{75}{5}\right)^2} = \sqrt{240.2 - 225} = \sqrt{15.2}$$

$$= 3.9$$

Thus, the answers are identical and we had fewer computations since we didn't have to find the deviation of each score from the mean.

Let's look at another example—one involving a frequency distribution. In a previous chapter I introduced some data based on the scores of 10 males performing a task of rearranging some scrambled sentences. The data are shown again below.

X	f	fX	fX^2
13	1	13	169
12	1	12	144
11	2	22	242
10	1	10	100
9	3	27	243
6	1	6	36
4	1	4	16
	10	94	950

$$\text{SD} = \sqrt{\frac{\Sigma fX^2}{N} - \left(\frac{\Sigma fX}{N}\right)^2}$$

$$= \sqrt{\frac{950}{10} - \left(\frac{94}{10}\right)^2} = \sqrt{95 - 88.4} = \sqrt{6.6}$$

$$= 2.6$$

I want to make an important point about this calculation. Many students make the mistake of thinking that all you have to do is square the values in the fX column in order to obtain the values under the heading fX^2. The problem with this is that if you square the numbers in the fX column you have really found f^2X^2, which is *not* what is required. The equation requires you to find fX^2, which is obtained by multiplying the scores in the X column by the scores in the fX column (fX times X equals fX^2). Equivalently you can square the values in the X column and then multiply by the frequencies. Remember the following:

$$(fX)^2 = f^2X^2 \neq fX^2 \text{ and } (fX) \cdot (X) = fX^2$$

Checking Your Progress and Visualization of SD

Now that we have gone through the computational steps of calculating the standard deviation, what do we actually have? Can we graphically depict the number we have derived? Fortunately, yes. To illustrate, let's take yet another example of a frequency distribution, calculate the standard deviation, and plot SD on the baseline of the frequency polygon derived from the frequency distribution. Suppose we have administered the scrambled sentences test to a class of 56 introductory psychology students and have obtained the following distribution of scores:

X	f		X	f
19	1		10	6
18	1		9	6
17	1		8	5
16	1		7	4
15	2		6	3
14	3		5	2
13	5		4	3
12	5		3	1
11	6		2	1

Find SD. (The correct answer is 3.7.)

Using the values from the frequency distribution, we can plot a frequency polygon (figure 5–2). Then, we can mark off the baseline

Figure 5–2: Visualization of the standard deviation.

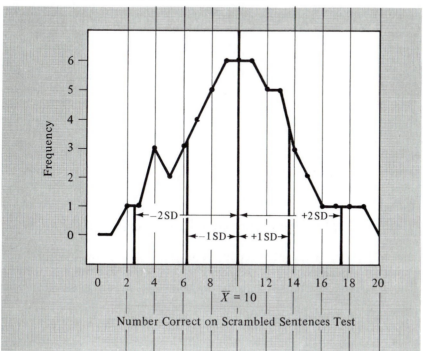

of the polygon on either side of the mean in standard deviation units, which, in this case, would have a width of 3.7—the value we calculated for the SD. Thus, the standard deviation can be visualized as a unit of measurement on the baseline of a frequency polygon. In the distribution shown in figure 5–2, a score of 13.7 falls one standard deviation unit above the mean, while someone scoring 6.3 lies one standard deviation unit below the mean, and so forth.

The procedure for visualizing the SD (i.e., viewing it as a width measure on the baseline of a frequency polygon) will assume added importance in the next chapter in the discussion of z-scores. For this reason, be sure you fully understand the visualization of SD.

Using the Pocket Calculator to Compute SD

Ten students recorded the number of hours they spent studying during the week prior to final exams. Let's use the determination of the SD of the resulting scores to illustrate the use of the pocket calculator. The scores were:

X	f
25	1
23	2
21	2
20	1
17	2
10	1
5	1
	10

The Σf or N is 10 and the computational formula for SD is:

$$\sqrt{\frac{\Sigma fX^2}{N} - \left(\frac{\Sigma fX}{N}\right)^2}$$

We will find $\Sigma fX^2/N$ first. The sequence of operations is:

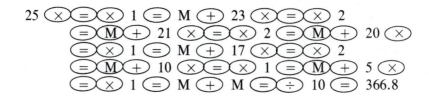

Although the operation appears tedious when written out this way, what we have done is to square each score (e.g., 25 ⊗ ⊜), multiply the squared score times its frequency (e.g. ⊗ ⊜), and add the result into memory (e.g., Ⓜ ⊕). When this has been done for each score, the total is recalled (Ⓜ ⊜) and divided by N (⊝10) giving $\Sigma fX^2/N$.

The value of $(\Sigma fX/N)^2$ is found by multiplying each score by its frequency and adding the product into memory. When all the scores have been treated in this fashion, the contents of memory are recalled, divided by N, and the result squared to give the desired answer. The sequence of operations is:

25 ⊗ 1 ⊜ Ⓜ ⊕ 23 ⊗ 2 ⊜ M ⊕ 21 ⊗ 2
⊜ Ⓜ ⊕ 20 ⊗ 1 ⊜ M ⊕ 17 ⊗ 2
⊜ Ⓜ ⊕ 10 ⊗ 1 ⊜ M ⊕ 5 ⊗ 1
⊜ Ⓜ ⊕ M ⊜ ⊝ 10 ⊜ ⊗ ⊜ 331.24

The final steps are to subtract $(\Sigma fX/N)^2$ from $\Sigma fX^2/N$ and to extract the square root:

366.8 ⊝ 331.24 ⊜ 35.56   √   5.96

As an exercise to convince yourself that this procedure really saves time, compute the SD of this distribution without using the memory function on your calculator.

Population SD and Its Estimate

Up to this point we have only considered the case of the standard deviation based on a sample distribution. In chapter 1 we stated that our interest often lies in making inferences from the sample to the population from which it was drawn. Therefore, how does the sample standard deviation relate to the corresponding population parameter?

Recall that in the previous chapter we said that the sample mean shows no systematic tendency to deviate from the population value, and thus $\bar{X}$ is an unbiased estimate of μ. Unfortunately this is not true in the case of the sample standard deviation. The sample value tends to be smaller than the corresponding population value, because the larger the sample the greater the likelihood of obtaining extreme scores which contribute disproportionately to the standard deviation. Since by definition the population is the largest possible "sample," it contains all the extreme scores and thus tends to have a larger standard deviation than samples taken from it. The symbol for the population standard deviation is σ (lowercase or little sigma).

Since we can't measure the entire population to determine the value for the standard deviation, and the sample value is a biased estimate, what do we do? Well, we must deal with the data we have collected, and therefore we need to do something to the sample standard deviation formula that will compensate for the tendency of SD to be smaller than σ. This is done in the following formula in which the value of the denominator is always slightly less than the same value in the formula for the sample standard deviation.

$$s = \sqrt{\frac{\Sigma(X - \overline{X})^2}{N - 1}}$$

With a frequency distribution the formula is:

$$s = \sqrt{\frac{\Sigma f(X - \overline{X})^2}{N - 1}}$$

Instead of dividing the sum of the squared deviations by N, we will divide by $N - 1$. Since $N - 1$ is less than N, the resulting fraction will always be larger. The new statistic s will be called the *estimate of the population standard deviation* based on the sample and is defined as the square root of the sum of the squared deviation of the scores from the mean divided by the number of scores minus one. The statistic s will be used when we want unbiased estimate of σ.

estimate of the
population standard
deviation

Since ordinarily we will not be dealing with the defining formula in the calculation of the SD of the sample, there is little point to an illustration of the use of the defining formula for the calculation of s. Instead I will introduce a computational or raw score formula for s and illustrate its use. The formula is:

$$s = \sqrt{\frac{\Sigma X^2 - \dfrac{(\Sigma X)^2}{N}}{N - 1}}$$

With a frequency distribution the formula is:

$$s = \sqrt{\frac{\Sigma f X^2 - \dfrac{(\Sigma f X)^2}{N}}{N - 1}}$$

To illustrate the similarity between the values of SD and s, let's compute s using a distribution of scores for which we have already determined SD. For example, we determined the SD for a distribution of scores of 10 males performing a task of rearranging scrambled sentences. In our previous computation we found $\Sigma fX^2 = 950$, $\Sigma fX = 94$, and $N = 10$. Using this information, what is s?

$$s = \sqrt{\frac{\Sigma fX^2 - \frac{(\Sigma fX)^2}{N}}{N-1}} = \sqrt{\frac{950 - \frac{(94)^2}{10}}{10-1}} = \sqrt{\frac{950 - \frac{8836}{10}}{9}}$$

$$= \sqrt{\frac{950 - 883.6}{9}} = \sqrt{\frac{66.4}{9}} = \sqrt{7.38} = 2.72$$

Since SD was 2.6, it is evident that ordinarily there is little difference between the two statistics. Only when we are dealing with an extremely small sample is there any substantial difference, as illustrated by the following small sample.

$$X = 20, 19, 14, 12, 10$$

$$\Sigma X = 75$$

$$\Sigma X^2 = 1201$$

$$N = 5$$

$$SD = 3.9 \text{ (computed earlier)}$$

$$s = \sqrt{\frac{\Sigma X^2 - \frac{(\Sigma X)^2}{N}}{N-1}}$$

$$= \sqrt{\frac{1201 - \frac{(75)^2}{5}}{5-1}}$$

$$= \sqrt{\frac{1201 - 1125}{4}} = \sqrt{19}$$

$$= 4.4$$

Checking Your Progress

Compute and compare SD and s for the distribution of scores made by 52 students on a philosophy test. The data are: $\Sigma fX = 1833$; $\Sigma fX^2 = 67{,}202.72$. (The correct answers are SD = 7.06 and s = 7.13.)

The Variance

Another statistic to be introduced at this time is the variance. Although it is not as useful in a descriptive sense as the standard deviation, it is very important in inferential statistics and will be dealt with extensively in a later chapter. Its calculation and definition is intimately related to the SD, and for this reason it is mentioned here.

To introduce the concept of SD, we first discussed the average deviation as a way to circumvent the property of the mean that $\Sigma(X - \overline{X}) = 0$. Next, I said that another way to bypass this property was to square the deviations before summing, thus eliminating all negative signs. This procedure led to the average squared deviation [$\Sigma(X - \overline{X})^2/N$] of which we took the square root and called the resulting statistic SD. Well, the average squared deviation is the *variance!*

variance

The variance is nothing more than the standard deviation squared or SD^2 for a sample, σ^2 for the population, and s^2 for the estimate of the population variance based upon the sample. In other words, it is merely the standard deviation without the square root sign. The following problem illustrates the calculation of the sample variance (SD^2) and the estimate of the population variance (s^2) from the sample.

As part of a study on hyperactivity in children, the number of physical abnormalities (e.g., malformed ears, curved fifth finger, third toe longer than second) has been determined for a sample of 23 children diagnosed as hyperactive. The data are:

X	f	fX	fX^2
14	1	14	196
13	2	26	338
12	3	36	432
11	3	33	363
10	5	50	500
9	3	27	243
8	2	16	128
7	1	7	49
6	2	12	72
5	1	5	25
	23	226	2346

$$SD^2 = \frac{\Sigma fX^2}{N} - \left(\frac{\Sigma fX}{N}\right)^2$$

$$= \frac{2346}{23} - \left(\frac{226}{23}\right)^2 = 102 - 9.83^2 = 102 - 96.63$$

$$= 5.37$$

$$s^2 = \frac{\Sigma fX^2 - \frac{(\Sigma fX)^2}{N}}{N - 1} = \frac{2346 - \frac{226^2}{23}}{22} = \frac{2346 - 2220.7}{22} = \frac{125.3}{22}$$

$$= 5.7$$

The computations are straightforward and exactly the same as when we computed SD and s, except that we didn't have to extract the square roots. The answers are 5.37 for the sample variance and 5.7 for the estimated population variance.

Another example of the computation of the variance may be worthwhile. As a preliminary to a study of the effects of marijuana on driving ability, the number of movements of the steering wheel in a one-minute simulated driving exercise was determined for 15 normal people. The data and computations are as follows:

Steering Adjustments	f	fX	fX²
25	2	50	1250
24	1	24	576
23	1	23	529
22	3	66	1452
20	1	20	400
18	1	18	324
17	2	34	578
16	1	16	256
14	1	14	196
10	1	10	100
8	1	8	64
	15	283	5725

$$SD^2 = \frac{\Sigma fX^2}{N} - \left(\frac{\Sigma fX}{N}\right)^2$$

$$= \frac{5725}{15} - \left(\frac{283}{15}\right)^2 = 381.7 - (18.9)^2 = 381.7 - 357.2$$

$$= 24.5$$

Checking Your Progress

A group of 10 college sophomores was trained on a barpressing task. The reward consisted of points needed to fulfill an experimental participation requirement. The schedule of reinforcement used was a fixed-interval (FI) schedule, meaning that the subject receives a reinforcement for the first barpress after the passage of a set period of time. The number of barpresses made by each student during a twenty-minute period is shown below. Find SD² and s^2.

Student No.	No. of Barpresses
1	55
2	74
3	83
4	43
5	25
6	38
7	44
8	49
9	54
10	137

(The correct answers are SD² = 908.96 and s^2 = 1009.96.)

Summary

Several measures of the spread or dispersion of the data were discussed. The simplest measure, but the least useful for further computations, is the *range:* R = HS − LS (where HS is the highest score and LS is the lowest score in the distribution).

   The second measure presented was the *average* or *mean deviation:* AD = $\Sigma|X - \overline{X}|/N$ (or $\Sigma f|X - \overline{X}|/N$ when dealing with a frequency distribution). The main purpose for presenting AD was a prelude to a more important measure, the standard deviation.

   The *standard deviation* is defined mathematically as the square root of the sum of the squared deviation of the scores from the mean divided by the number of scores, in other words, as the square root of the average squared deviation. The computational or raw score formula is:

$$\text{SD} = \sqrt{\frac{\Sigma X^2}{N} - \left(\frac{\Sigma X}{N}\right)^2}$$

When dealing with a frequency distribution, the formula is:

$$SD = \sqrt{\frac{\Sigma fX^2}{N} - \left(\frac{\Sigma fX}{N}\right)^2}$$

The standard deviation may be visualized as a unit of measurement that may be marked off on either side of the mean on the baseline of a frequency polygon.

Since SD is a biased estimate of σ (symbol for the population standard deviation, pronounced little sigma), another statistic, s, was introduced to estimate the *population standard deviation from sample data*. The computational formula for s is:

$$\sqrt{\frac{\Sigma X^2 - \frac{(\Sigma X)^2}{N}}{N - 1}}$$

When dealing with a frequency distribution, the formula is:

$$s = \sqrt{\frac{\Sigma fX^2 - \frac{(\Sigma fX)^2}{N}}{N - 1}}$$

The *variance* was defined as the average squared deviation or as the standard deviation squared, i.e., the standard deviation without the square root sign. The computational formulas for SD^2 are:

$$SD^2 = \frac{\Sigma X^2}{N} - \left(\frac{\Sigma X}{N}\right)^2 \text{ or } SD^2 = \frac{\Sigma fX^2}{N} - \left(\frac{\Sigma fX}{N}\right)^2$$

For s^2 the equations are:

$$s^2 = \frac{\Sigma X^2 - \frac{(\Sigma X)^2}{N}}{N - 1} \text{ or } s^2 = \frac{\Sigma fX^2 - \frac{(\Sigma fX)^2}{N}}{N - 1}$$

Troubleshooting Your Computations

This chapter dealt with statistics that are computationally more involved than anything encountered in chapter 4. For that reason we need to consider some possible clues to trouble and/or frequently made errors.

Having a "feel" for what is a reasonable answer is extremely important in computing SD (or any other statistic). For example, if you have a fairly large, symmetrical distribution, SD is going to be somewhere near one-sixth of the range. Further, if you have scores that are rather tightly bunched, then SD will be small relative to the case in which the scores are widely dispersed. If you obtain a value for SD that is greater than the range, you have made a gross computational error.

You must always get a positive value for SD, s, SD^2, and s^2. Often I have seen students obtain a negative number under the radical while computing SD and then "conveniently" lose it prior to reporting their final answer. In most cases the value of ΣfX^2 has been improperly computed with the result that $\Sigma fX^2/N$ is smaller than $\overline{X}^2$. At any rate, if you get a negative value for one of the measures of dispersion, it is incorrect.

You must remember to take the frequencies into account when dealing with a frequency distribution.

Finally, when computing SD or s, be sure to extract the square root.

Exercises

1. Given that the $\Sigma X = 1000$, $N = 100$, and $\Sigma X^2 = 10,400$, what are SD, s, and SD^2?

2. Find SD, SD^2, and s for the following distribution of scores: 10, 9, 8, 7, 6, 5, 4, 3, 2, 1.

3. Find SD for the following data: $\Sigma X^2 = 1308$, $\Sigma X = 120$, $N = 12$.

4. Find SD for the following data: $\Sigma X^2 = 1920$, $\Sigma X = 144$, $N = 12$.

5. Given the following frequency distribution, find R, $\overline{X}$, SD, s, and s^2.

X	f
9	1
8	2
7	4
6	5
5	8
4	3
3	3
2	2
1	1

In addition, plot the frequency polygon from these data and lay the SD off on the baseline.

6. On an examination in a statistics course, the scores were as follows: 71, 41, 62, 78, 94, 99, 100, 52, 68, 53, 85, 79, 31, 86, 40, 41, 85, 51, 76, 100, 22, 92, 95, 99, 92. Determine R, SD, and SD^2. From the data estimate the population standard deviation.

7. Over a three-year period, a clinical therapist in private practice recorded the number of sessions required by phobic patients to achieve symptomatic relief. The frequency distribution of the data is shown below. Determine SD^2 and s^2.

X	f
22	1
20	2
19	2
18	3
15	4
13	4
11	2
10	1
9	2
8	1

8. Under distracting conditions, 30 people learn a list of ten nonsense syllables. The experimenter records the number of repetitions of the list each person takes prior to achieving an errorless trial. The results are:

X	f	X	f
38	1	25	3
36	2	24	2
34	3	22	2
33	2	18	2
31	1	17	1
29	3	16	1
28	4	10	1
26	2		

Find SD and s^2 for the distribution.
9. On a test of aggressive behavior in mice, the latency of attack has been recorded for 25 animals. Find R, SD and s. The latencies are:

3.7	21.8	1.0	8.5	17.5
8.6	18.3	15.7	7.8	12.7
10.5	5.1	14.3	1.5	8.2
3.7	3.9	13.8	1.3	9.3
2.5	2.6	9.6	21.6	5.8

10. Why is SD considered to be a biased estimate of σ?
11. Match the following symbols with the correct statistic named below.

SD s^2
SD^2 σ
s σ^2

___ Population variance
___ Estimate of the population standard deviation
___ Population standard deviation
___ Sample standard deviation
___ Sample variance
___ Estimate of the population variance

Probability Distributions: The Binomial and the Normal Curve

Introduction

In the preceding chapters we have discussed a number of ways to describe data including the frequency distribution, graphing, computing a measure of central tendency, and determining measures of the spread or dispersion in the data. This chapter introduces material that leads to the heart of inferential statistics—the decision-making process. In order to discuss probability distributions, we must first explore briefly what is meant by the term probability.

Probability

Most of us intuitively use or encounter the idea of probability every day of our lives. For example, we may check the weather report and find that the probability of rain is 20%. On the basis of this information we may decide not to take an umbrella or a raincoat with us or, if we are more cautious, we may elect to be safe and not sorry.

If we decide to take a plane on a trip across the country rather than to drive, part of our decision may hinge on the knowledge that the probability of a fatal car wreck is much higher than that of a fatal plane crash. If we choose one steak restaurant over another, it may be because we have found that the probability of being served a choice cut of meat is higher at one than the other.

My point is that we are constantly assessing probabilities whether we do it explicitly or implicitly. Many of our decisions are based on these assessments, that is, whether we feel that an event is likely or unlikely to occur. Our feelings about the likelihood of an event's occurrence may be based on pure speculation or intuition, on previous experience with similar events (the wisdom of age), or on a knowledge of theoretical outcomes.

Incidentally, there are times when our intuitive ideas about probability are incorrect. One such idea, often called Gambler's Fallacy, is the mistaken belief that the probability of a particular event changes with a long string of the same event. For example, suppose that an unbiased coin is flipped nine times with a head appearing each time. What is the probability of a tail coming up on the tenth flip? The answer is that the probability of either a head or a tail is exactly the same as it was on the first flip; the string of heads has in no way increased the likelihood of a tail appearing even though we may subjectively feel that this has happened. Coins have no memory.

probability of an event   For our purposes the *probability of an event* is defined as the proportion of times an event would occur if the chances for occurrence were infinite. In other words, the probability of an event is the ratio of the number of times the event occurs to the total number of events. To illustrate the definition, what is the probability of obtaining a head from the toss of an unbiased coin? There are only two possibilities; either the coin will come up heads or tails, and either possibility is equally likely since the coin is unbiased. Thus, we say that the probability of either a head *or* a tail on any given toss is $\frac{1}{2}$.

In terms of the definition of probability we are saying that if the coin were flipped an infinite number of times, on half of the flips a head would appear. The ratio of the number of times the event (head) occurs to the total number of events is $\frac{1}{2}$ or .5 or 50%.

Similarly, suppose that we have one die (singular of dice). What is the probability of any particular number of spots from 1 to 6 appearing on any particular roll assuming that the die is unbiased? Since the die has six sides and each is equally likely to appear given an unbiased die, the probability of any particular number is $\frac{1}{6}$.

Addition Rule

On any particular flip of our unbiased coin, what is the probability of obtaining either a head *or* a tail? Since there are no other possibilities, the probability is 1 or 100%. That is, we will always obtain either a head or a tail when we flip the coin. As you can see, in order to obtain the probability of either a head *or* a tail on one flip of the coin, the probabilities of the two possibilities have been summed [$p(H) = .5$, $p(T) = .5$; $p(H \text{ or } T) = .5 + .5 = 1$]. For $p(H)$ read probability of a head; $p(T) =$ probability of a tail; $p(H \text{ or } T) =$ probability of a head or a tail.

Continuing, what is the probability of getting either 1 or 2 on one roll of our unbiased die? Since the probability of getting either number is $\frac{1}{6}$, the probability of obtaining either a 1 or a 2 is the sum of their individual probabilities or $\frac{1}{6} + \frac{1}{6} = \frac{2}{6}$ or .33. That is, $\frac{1}{3}$ of the time we would get either a 1 or a 2.

The preceding simple examples illustrate the *addition rule of probability* which states that for mutually exclusive random events the probability of either one event or another event is equal to the sum of the probabilities of the individual events.

addition rule of probability

Multiplication Rule

In the previous section we considered what might happen with only one flip of a coin or one roll of a die. What rule of probability can we apply when dealing with a series of events?

For example, suppose we have rolled a pair of dice (the outcome would be the same if we considered rolling one die twice). What is the probability of obtaining snake-eyes (a pair of ones)? All of the possible events that we might observe on one throw of the dice are shown in figure 6–1.

Note that, in the 36 possible events, there is only one way for snake-eyes to occur. Thus, the probability is $\frac{1}{36}$. The same result could also be obtained by multiplying the individual probabilities. In this case, the probability of obtaining a 1 on the first die is $\frac{1}{6}$ and the probability of a 1 on the second die is also $\frac{1}{6}$. The product of the individual probabilities is $\frac{1}{6} \times \frac{1}{6} = \frac{1}{36}$.

As another example, what would be the probability of getting

Figure 6–1: All possible events that might be observed following one throw of a pair of unbiased dice.

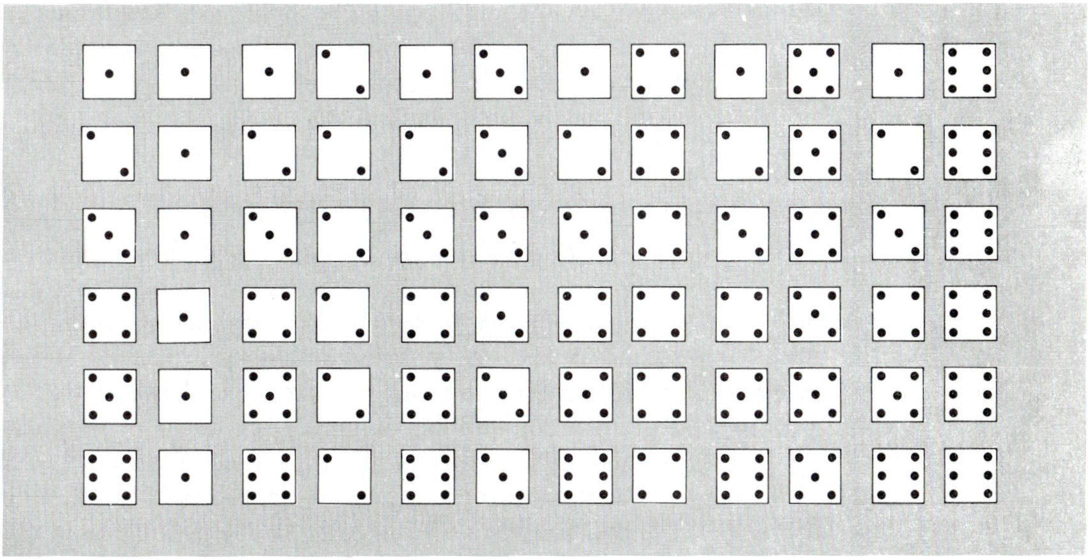

all heads in three flips of an unbiased coin? Using the multiplication procedure, the product of the individual probabilities would be $\frac{1}{2} \times \frac{1}{2} \times \frac{1}{2} = \frac{1}{8}$. This is the same answer that would be obtained if all of the possible events were described. Thus, the possible events are HHH, HHT, HTT, TTT, TTH, THH, THT, and HTH. As you will note, there is only one way that three heads can occur out of the eight possibilities for three flips of an unbiased coin and the probability is $\frac{1}{8}$.

multiplication rule   Formally stated, the *multiplication rule* says that the probability of two or more independent events occurring on separate occasions is the product of their individual probabilities. It is expressed symbolically in the following:

$$p(A,B) = p(A) \times p(B)$$

where $p(A,B)$ is the probability of the occurrence of both A and B. Any number of other independent events could be added to this expression. For example, for three events we would have $p(A,B,C) = p(A) \times p(B) \times p(C)$.

Events are independent if the occurrence of one event does not alter the probability of any other event. For example, whether or not a head appears on one toss of a coin does not alter the probability of a head appearing on a succeeding toss. On the other hand, if there are five colored balls in a box, three white and two red, the probability of selecting a red ball is $\frac{2}{5}$ initially. If a red ball is selected on the first draw and not replaced, the probability of selecting a red ball on the next draw is $\frac{1}{4}$. In the second case, we could not say that the events were independent since the probability has been altered by the occurrence of the first event.

The Binomial Probability Distribution

In the previous section, you were exposed to a very simple and abbreviated introduction to probability theory. It is now time to consider a simple theoretical probability distribution, the binomial.

The binomial distribution is based on events in which there are only two possible outcomes on each occurrence and its construction is often illustrated by coin flipping examples. To begin, suppose that we have flipped an unbiased coin three times. As before, the possible outcomes we might observe are HHH, HHT, HTT, TTT, TTH, THH, THT, and HTH. One way to look at the possible outcomes involves calling the heads "hits" and the tails "misses" (alternatively, "successes" and "failures"). Using this approach, the following table can be constructed.

Possible Outcomes of an
Unbiased Coin Flipped Three
Times

Outcome	No. of Hits
HHH	3
HHT	2
THH	2
HTH	2
HTT	1
THT	1
TTH	1
TTT	0

A frequency distribution can be constructed from the table, and from this a bar graph can be made. This has been done in figure 6–2.

Finally, we can convert the frequencies into probabilities and plot these rather than the frequencies. This procedure is shown in figure 6–3.

Figure 6–2: Number of ways that "hits" may occur when an unbiased coin is flipped three times.

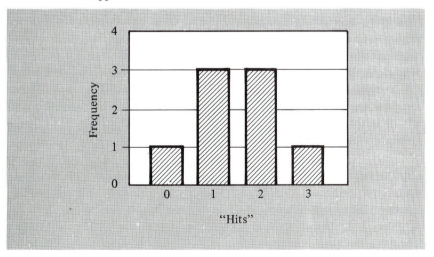

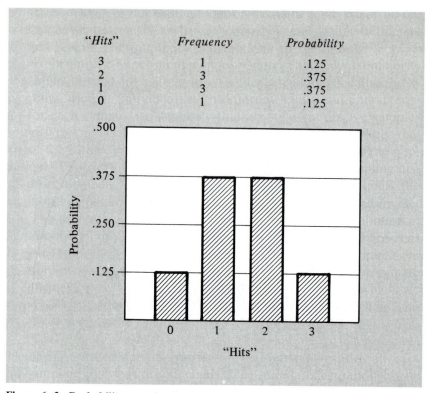

"Hits"	Frequency	Probability
3	1	.125
2	3	.375
1	3	.375
0	1	.125

Figure 6–3: Probability associated with each number of "hits."

One thing that we can note from both figures 6–2 and 6–3 is that the bar graph in each case is symmetrical. This will always be true for the binomial distribution when $p = \frac{1}{2}$.

Let's take our example a step further. What are the possible outcomes if we flip our unbiased coin yet a fourth time? The possible outcomes are:

HHHH	HHHT	HHTT	HTTT	TTTT
	HHTH	HTHT	THTT	
	HTHH	HTTH	TTHT	
	THHH	THHT	TTTH	
		THTH		
		TTHH		

The frequency distribution of hits and the probabilities of the hits are:

Hits	f	p
4	1	.0625
3	4	.2500
2	6	.3750
1	4	.2500
0	1	.0625
	16	1.0000

A bar graph depicting the probability of hits is shown in figure 6–4.

The construction of polygons (similar to the ones illustrated in figures 6–3 and 6–4) using successively larger values of N would reveal two very important features of the binomial distribution: (1) when $p = \frac{1}{2}$, the distribution is symmetrical, and, (2) as N increases in value, the distribution more closely approximates the *normal probability distribution*. Because of this approximation of the normal by the binomial distribution, the normal distribution is often substituted for the binomial distribution in evaluating binomial data. For this reason, the rest of the chapter will be devoted to the discussion of the normal distribution.

Figure 6–4: Bar graph showing the probability of a given number of hits in four flips of an unbiased coin.

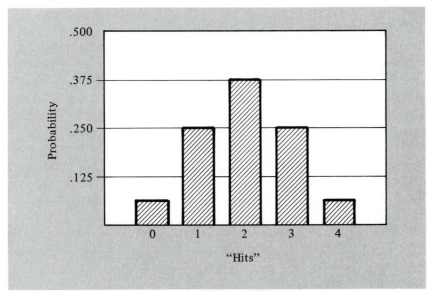

The Normal Probability Distribution

In chapter 3 we mentioned the normal or bell-shaped curve and said that its properties were very important because many measurements produce frequency polygons that are very similar to the normal curve. Examples of physical and behavioral characteristics that are approximately normally distributed are such things as height, weight, blood pressure, IQ scores, and reaction-time scores. The point is that many empirical distributions (distributions based on actual measurement and observation) are similar enough to the normal curve distribution for us to make statements about them using the known properties of the normal curve.

Perhaps more important in inferential statistics, the normal distribution is the limiting case for a number of other distributions we will discuss. The discussion of the binomial distribution noted that as the size of N increases, the binomial distribution more closely approximates the normal curve. In the next chapter, a distribution called the sampling distribution of means will be introduced. One of its properties is that, as the samples comprising it increase in size, the distribution becomes more nearly normal. Additionally, in a later chapter we will discuss the distribution of chi square which approaches a normal distribution as N increases. Thus, even if we are working with distributions other than the normal curve, we can often assume a normal distribution with large samples.

Characteristics of the Normal Curve

I've alluded frequently to the properties of the normal curve without actually specifying them. To begin, in the standard normal curve, which is generated from an equation and not from any actual data, the mean is zero and the standard deviation is one. Drawing the curve and laying off the value of the standard deviation on the baseline, we have the curve shown in figure 6–5.

Notice that some percentages have been entered above the curve. For example, between the mean and one standard deviation unit above the mean the number 34.13% appears. What does this mean? If we consider that the total area under the curve is 100% (the area between the curve and the baseline), then 34.13% of the total area under the curve lies between the mean and one standard deviation unit above the mean. Since the curve is symmetrical, the same thing is true to the left (or below) the mean, also. Continuing, we find that 13.59% of the area lies between one and two standard deviation units on either side of the mean. Summing the two areas

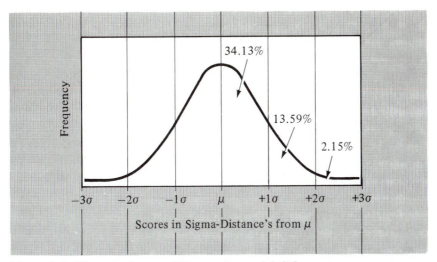

Figure 6–5: The normal curve with several areas labeled.

that we have considered on each side of the mean, we find that 47.72% (34.13% + 13.59%) of the area lies between the mean and two standard deviation units on either side of it. Finally, we see that only 2.15% of the total area under the normal curve lies between two and three standard deviation units above or below the mean. Summing all the areas we have considered, we can see that almost the entire normal curve is contained between ±3 standard deviation units of the mean (99.74%).

Since the normal curve is symmetrical, we really need only to consider one side of the distribution since the values on the other side will be the same. Fortunately for us, the areas under the normal curve have been determined for many different standard deviation units from the mean and are given in table A in the appendix. However, the distances from the mean in the table are given based on a mean of 0 and a standard deviation of 1 (that is, in terms of the standard normal curve). It is extremely unlikely that we will ever encounter a sample from a population in which the mean is exactly 0 and the standard deviation is 1. How will we enter the table? We will do it by converting our score values into *standard scores* or, as they are often called, *z*-scores.

z-scores

A *z-score* is defined as the deviation of a raw score from the mean in standard deviation units. In other words, a *z*-score tells us how far from the mean a raw score is in standard deviation units.

z-score

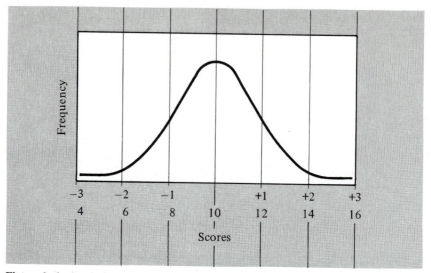

Figure 6–6: A relatively normal distribution with $\overline{X} = 10$ and SD = 2.

An example may help to illustrate the definition. Suppose we have a relatively normal distribution with mean of 10 and standard deviation of 2. How many standard deviation units away from the mean is a score of 14? The problem is shown graphically in figure 6–6.

Marking off the baseline of our frequency polygon in standard deviation units, it is apparent that 14 is two standard deviation units above the mean. Thus, the z-score for 14 (that is, how far it is from the mean in standard deviation units) is 2. Similarly, the z-score for 8 is -1, for 6 is -2, and so forth.

From the definition of a z-score, the deviation of a score from the mean in standard deviation units, comes a very simple formula for finding the z-score corresponding to any raw score:

$$z = \frac{X - \overline{X}}{SD}$$

Using this formula and the above distribution, we can determine the z-score for any raw score in which we are interested. For example, what is the z-score for a score of 4.5?

$$z = \frac{X - \overline{X}}{SD} = \frac{4.5 - 10}{2} = \frac{-5.5}{2} = -2.75$$

The negative value for z tells us that our raw score is below the mean. How many standard deviation units away from the mean is a score of 15?

$$z = \frac{15 - 10}{2} = \frac{5}{2} = 2.5$$

We can also use the z-score formula for finding the raw score that lies at a particular distance from the mean. Suppose that you were asked, what score lies 2.5 standard deviation units above the mean? In this case you are told that $z = 2.5$ since the definition of z is how far a raw score lies from the mean in standard deviation units. Looking at figure 6–6, we can see that the raw score 2.5 standard deviation units above the mean is halfway between the scores of 14 and 16; i.e., 15. However, we can also determine the value of the score by using the formula for converting a raw score into a z-score. In this case, since we are looking for X rather than z we will solve the equation for X.

Thus, $z = (X - \overline{X})/\text{SD}$ and $2.5 = (X - 10)/2$. Solving for X we find $(2)(2.5) = X - 10$ or $5 = X - 10$. Adding 10 to both sides of the equation gives us $10 + 5 = X$ or $15 = X$, and reversing terms we see that $X = 15$.

Another way to approach a problem of this type is to solve our original formula for the z-score for X initially. Thus, we find that $X = z\text{SD} + \overline{X}$. Now that we have this formula, let's use it again to find a score when we know how far it is from the mean in standard deviation units. For example, what is the score that lies 2.4 standard deviation units below the mean? In this case $z = -2.4$ (negative z-score indicating that it is below the mean), $\overline{X} = 10$ and $\text{SD} = 2$. Solving for X we have $X = (-2.4)(2) + 10 = -4.8 + 10 = 5.2$. Therefore, 5.2 lies 2.4 standard deviation units below the mean.

It is worth emphasizing here that you only need to know two formulas in order to solve any problem involving areas under the normal curve: (1) the formula for the z-score or $z = (X - \overline{X})/\text{SD}$ and (2) the same formula solved for X which is used for converting a z-score into a raw score ($X = z\text{SD} + \overline{X}$).

Checking Your Progress

Suppose we have measured the heights of all the basketball players in the National Basketball Association and have found that the average height is 77 inches with a standard deviation of 2.2. What is the

z-score for a player who is 73 inches tall? 83 inches? What is the height of a player who is 2.6 standard deviation units below the mean? (The correct answers are -1.82, 2.73, and 71.28 inches, respectively.)

Using the Normal Curve Table

Now that we know how to convert a raw score into a z-score and vice versa, what do we do with this knowledge? We can use it to provide us with an entry in the normal curve table which can provide information about the population from which our sample was drawn. Consider the following questions:

1. If a person takes an IQ test and is told that his score is at the 75th percentile, what is his score?
2. If someone tells you that his IQ is 130 and asks you to give him his percentile rank (how he scores in relation to the rest of the population), what would you tell him?
3. If someone asks you which IQ scores are so deviant that they are achieved by less than 5% of the population, how do you answer?

A knowledge of the properties of the normal curve and an appreciation of how to use the table in this book can help you answer these questions and more. But, before we try to answer the questions, let's examine the portion of the normal curve table shown in table 6–1.

The normal curve table indicates that we can find the percentage of the total area under the normal curve between the mean and any particular z-score we have. This statement is very important and must be fully understood to avoid misunderstanding what the table tells us. If we have converted some raw score to a z-score, we can find it in the margins of the table and then look in the body of the table to determine what percentage of the normal curve lies between the z-score and the mean.

In the left margin of the table you will see that the z-scores are given in the outer row of numbers. For example, to determine the percentage area under the curve between the mean and a z-score of 0.52, go down the left margin until you locate 0.5 and across from 0.5 until you come to the column labeled .02. The number at this point (19.85) is the area you are looking for. In other words, between the mean of a normal distribution and a z-score of 0.52 lies approx-

Table 6–1: Reproduction of a portion of the normal curve table. The complete version is found in the Appendix.

z	.00	.01	.02	.03	.04	.05	.06	.07	.08	.09
0.0	00.00	00.40	00.80	01.20	01.60	01.99	02.39	02.79	03.19	03.59
0.1	03.98	04.38	04.78	05.17	05.57	05.96	06.36	06.75	07.14	07.53
0.2	07.93	08.32	08.71	09.10	09.48	09.87	10.26	10.64	11.03	11.41
0.3	11.79	12.17	12.55	12.93	13.31	13.68	14.06	14.43	14.80	15.17
0.4	15.54	15.91	16.28	16.64	17.00	17.36	17.72	18.08	18.44	18.79
0.5	19.15	19.50	19.85	20.19	20.54	20.88	21.23	21.57	21.90	22.24
0.6	22.57	22.91	23.24	23.57	23.89	24.22	24.54	24.86	25.17	25.49
0.7	25.80	26.11	26.42	26.73	27.04	27.34	27.64	27.94	28.23	28.52
0.8	28.81	29.10	29.39	29.67	29.95	30.23	30.51	30.78	31.06	31.33
0.9	31.59	31.86	32.12	32.38	32.64	32.90	33.15	33.40	33.65	33.89

Source: The original data for this table came from Karl Pearson (ed.), *Tables for Statisticians and Biometricians*, Vol. 1, 3rd ed., Table II, pp. 2–8, and are used with permission of Cambridge University Press. The adaptation of these data was taken from Lindquist, E. L., *A First Course in Statistics* (rev. ed.), Houghton Mifflin Co., copyright ©1942, and is shown here with permission of the publisher.

imately 20% of the normal curve. The procedure that has just been described is shown in table 6–2.

What about negative z-scores? Since the normal curve is symmetrical, there is no need to reproduce both halves of it. For this reason only the right half is reproduced in the table. If you were asked to find the area under the curve between the mean and a z-

Table 6–2. A portion of the normal curve table is shown and the procedure for finding an area corresponding to a z-score is outlined.

0.52
↓

z	.00	.01	.02
0.0	00.00	00.40	00.80
0.1	03.98	04.38	04.78
0.2	07.93	08.32	08.71
0.3	11.79	12.17	12.55
0.4	15.54	15.91	16.28
0.52 ⟶ 0.5	19.15	19.50	19.85

Source: Derived from appendix table A.

score of -1.36, you would look up 1.36 and report that the area was 41.31% of the normal curve. Remember that a negative z-score indicates that we are dealing with the portion of the distribution below the mean. The areas are always positive.

We can also use the normal curve table to determine a score if we know that it has a particular area of the curve associated with it. In this case we will first look in the body of the table until we come to the area in which we are interested, look out to the margins of the table until we find the z-score that cuts it off, and convert this z-score into a raw score.

For example, suppose we want to know the z-score at the 70th percentile. The problem is shown graphically in figure 6–7. From figure 6–7 we can see that we need to find the z-score below which lies 70% of the distribution. Since half the curve lies to the left of the mean, the area above the mean up to the score we want to find is 20% (50% + 20% = 70%). Again, the areas in the body of the table represent the percentage of the curve between the mean and any z-score. Thus, to find the z-score at the top of 20% above the mean, we first look in the body of the table until we find 20% (or whatever is closest to it) and then look at the left margin to get the whole number and first decimal place for z. The second decimal place is determined by finding the marginal value at the top of the column in which our percentage is located. The procedures described are shown in table 6–3.

Figure 6–7: A normal curve illustrating the problem in which we want to find the z-score at the 70th percentile.

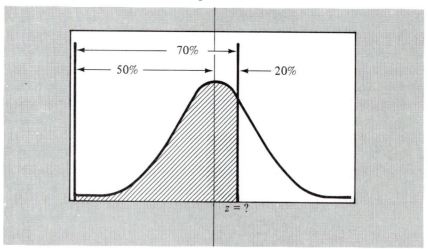

Table 6–3: A portion of the normal curve table and the procedure used to find the z-score at the 70th percentile.

0.52

$\downarrow$

z	.00	.01	.02	.03
0.0	00.00	00.40	00.80	01.20
0.1	03.98	04.38	04.78	05.17
0.2	07.93	08.32	08.71	09.10
0.3	11.79	12.17	12.55	12.93
0.4	15.54	15.91	16.28	16.64
0.52 $\longrightarrow$ 0.5	19.15	19.50	19.85	20.19

Source: Derived from appendix table A.

Finding the Percentile Rank of a Score

If a person has an IQ score of 132, what is the percentile rank associated with this score? To begin, *percentile rank* is defined as the percentage of cases up to and including the one in which we are interested. Thus, our problem becomes one of finding the percentage of the population that scores 132 or less.

percentile rank

The following steps should always be taken prior to working any problem involving the normal curve: draw the normal curve, label it according to the information given in the problem, and then determine the area(s) or score(s) needed. Let's assume for this problem and for any others like it that the mean for the distribution of IQ scores is 100 and the standard deviation is 16. An appropriately labeled curve is shown in figure 6–8.

Given a raw score (132), we must first convert it to a z-score. The z-score for an IQ of 132 is $z = (X - \overline{X})/SD = (132 - 100)/16 = 32/16 = 2$. Looking in appendix table A it is evident that 47.72% of the curve falls between a z-score of 2.00 and the mean. The new information has been added to the graph shown in figure 6–8, and this is shown in figure 6–9.

Since we are interested in the percentile rank of someone scoring 132, we need to find the total area below 132. In the preceding step, we found that the area between 100 and 132 is 47.72%. We know that the area to the left of the mean is exactly 50% of the total curve since the total area is 100% and half of the curve lies on either side of the mean. Therefore, the area below a score of 132 is 50 + 47.72 = 97.72% of the curve. We conclude that a person scoring 132

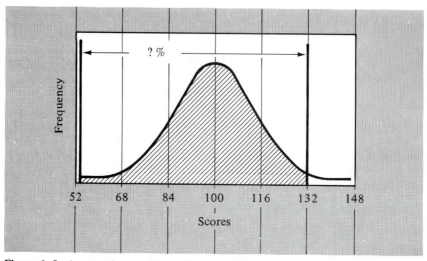

Figure 6–8: A normal curve illustrating a problem in which we
want to find the percentile rank of a score of 132.

Figure 6–9: Normal curve showing area of 47.72% between the
mean and the score of 132 obtained from appendix table A.

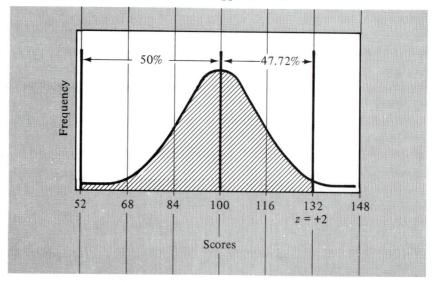

has an IQ score equal to or higher than approximately 98% of the population.

Let's try another problem. What is the percentile rank of some-one with an IQ score of 91? Again the first steps are to draw the normal curve and label the appropriate information. This has been done in figure 6–10.

From the figure it is apparent that we need to find the area under the curve below the score of 91. In order to use the normal curve table we must first convert the raw score to a z-score. Thus, $z = (91 - 100)/16 = -9/16 = -0.56$. (The negative z-score simply tells us that we are dealing with a score to the left of the mean.) We find from the table that 21.23% of the curve lies between $z = 0.56$ (or -0.56) and the mean. In figure 6–11 this new information has been added to the previous graph, and it is evident that 21.23% is not the area we want. Rather we need to find the area *below* this.

Since the total area to the left of the mean is 50% and the whole is equal to the sum of its parts, the area below $z = -0.56$ is $50 - 21.23 = 28.77\%$. We conclude, then, that the percentile rank of someone with an IQ of 91 is 28.77, or that the person scores as well as or better than about 29% of the population. The final step in the solution of the problem is shown in figure 6–12.

Figure 6–10: Normal curve illustrating a problem in which we want to find the percentile rank of a score of 91.

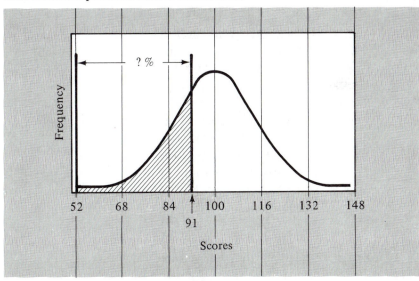

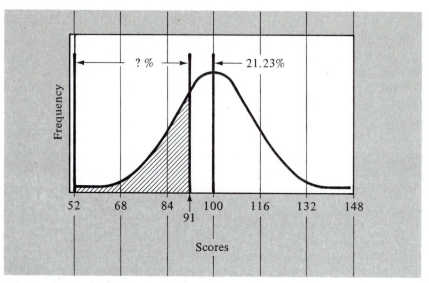

Figure 6–11: Normal curve on which has been entered the information from appendix table A that 21.23% of the curve lies between the mean and the score of 91.

Figure 6–12: Normal curve showing the solution to the problem of finding the percentile rank of a score of 91.

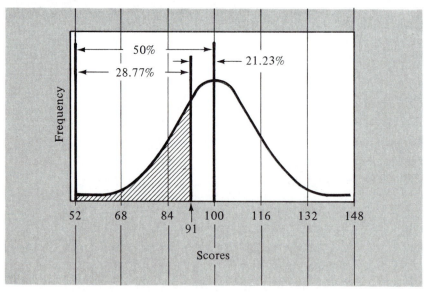

Checking Your Progress

As a final exercise in the determination of percentile rank, suppose you have trained 1000 rats to run from one end of a six-foot straight alley runway to the other. On the final run for each animal you have recorded the speed of the run in feet per second. The mean running speed for the 1000 rats was 2.4 feet/second with a standard deviation of 0.8 feet/second. What is the percentile rank of a rat that traverses the runway at a speed of 3.7 feet/second? 1.8 feet/second? (The correct answers are 94.74 and 22.66%, respectively.)

Finding the Percentage of the Normal Curve above a Given Score

To find the percentile rank of a score we had to find the percentage of the normal curve below the score. A related problem is to find the percentage of the curve above a particular point. For example, we might want to know what percentage of the population has an IQ score of 120 or above? As in the previous section, we will first draw the normal curve distribution and locate the area we want to find. The problem is pictured in figure 6–13.

As before we have been given a raw score (120) and must first convert this score into a z-score so that we can use the normal curve

Figure 6–13: Normal curve illustrating the problem of finding the percentage area above an IQ score of 120.

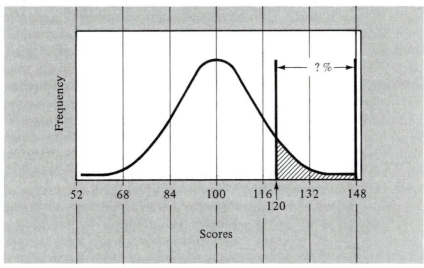

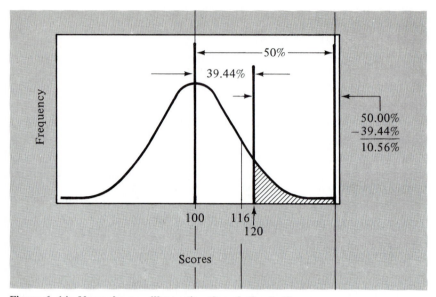

Figure 6–14: Normal curve illustrating the solution to the problem of finding the percentage area above the IQ score of 120.

table. Thus, $z = (120 - 100)/16 = 20/16 = 1.25$. Looking in appendix table A we see that 39.44% of the curve lies between the mean and a z-score of 1.25. The new information has been entered into the original diagram of the normal curve, and the solution to the problem appears in figure 6–14.

Since the total area under the curve to the right of the mean is 50%, the area above 120 must be 50% − 39.44% = 10.56%. We conclude that approximately 11% of the population has IQ scores above 120.

Another piece of useful information about the normal curve is that the percentage area under the curve is the same thing as percentage frequency. For example, if we administer an IQ test to 100 randomly selected individuals we could expect that 11% or 11 of them would score 120 or above. Let's try another example to be sure that we grasp both this last point and the idea of how to locate areas above a particular score.

Suppose that we have given an IQ test to 250 randomly selected individuals. How many would we expect to score above 80? As before, we will draw a diagram of the normal curve and put in the information we have. Then we will examine it to see if we can determine the area we want to find. The problem is shown in figure 6–15.

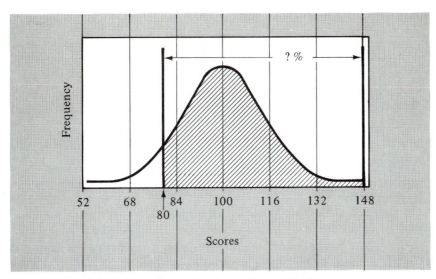

**Figure 6–15: Normal curve illustrating the problem of finding
the area above an IQ score of 80.**

In order to use the normal curve table, we must first convert
the IQ score of 80 into a z-score. This is easily done as follows: z
$= (80 - 100)/16 = -20/16 = -1.25$. Consulting appendix table A we
find that 39.44% of the normal curve lies between the mean and a z
of -1.25. Entering this information into our graph gives us figure 6–
16.

**Figure 6–16: Normal curve showing that the area from the
mean to the IQ score of 80 is 39.44%.**

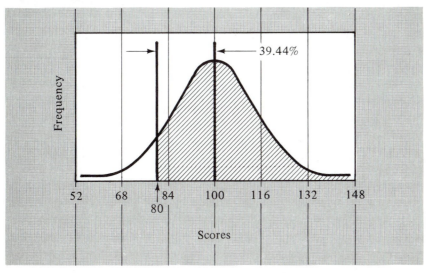

Since 50% of the normal curve lies to the right of the mean, the total area above an IQ score of 80 is 50% + 39.44% = 89.44%. But this is not all the question asks us to find. We also want to know how many people from the group of 250 are likely to score 80 or above. Thus, we need to take 89.44% of 250 which is the same as (.8944) (250) = 223.6 or, realistically, 224 people.

Checking Your Progress

In the previous section, the data from 1000 rats trained on a straight alley runway were introduced. Thus, you found a mean running speed of 2.4 feet/second with a standard deviation of 0.8 feet/second. On the basis of the normal curve distribution, if you trained 300 more rats, how many of them would you expect to have running speeds of 3.28 feet/second or more? The answer is 41 rats. When dealing with the number of living organisms (like rats and people), it makes sense to round your answer to the nearest whole number.

Locating the Score That Cuts Off a Particular Area

So far we have only considered cases in which we have been given a particular score and are asked to find some area under the curve. What if we reverse the procedure and locate a score that corresponds to some particular area of the curve? For example, a student in an introductory psychology class came to me after a lecture on the IQ test and told me that he had taken an IQ test on campus but that the examiner had not told him his score. The examiner had told him, however, that in terms of the rest of the population his percentile rank was 75%. What was his IQ score?

As usual we need to diagram the information we have in order to try to determine what we need to find. This has been done in figure 6–17.

The problem is to locate the score which has a percentile rank of 75; i.e., 75% of the normal curve lies below it. We know immediately that the score is above the mean since it has a rank higher than 50%. We must look in the normal curve table until we find a z-score such that between the mean and the z-score lies 25% of the curve (75% − 50% = 25%).

Thus, we look for 25% in the body of the table and when we find it we will go out to the margins to determine the closest z-score. Doing this we find that between the mean and a z-score of 0.67 lies 24.86% of the curve and that between the mean and a z-score of 0.68

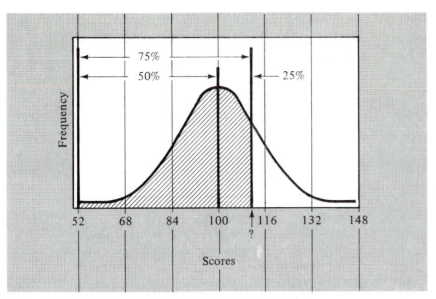

Figure 6–17: Normal curve illustrating the problem of finding the score at the 75th percentile.

lies 25.17%. Since 25% is closer to 24.86 than it is to 25.17, we will use 0.67 as the appropriate z-score.

Now that we have the z-score at the 75th percentile all that remains is to convert the z-score into a raw score using the formula $X = z\text{SD} + \overline{X}$. The computations are as follows: $X = (0.67)(16) + 100 = 10.72 + 100 = 110.72$ or about 111. Finally, a person at the 75th percentile on an IQ test has an IQ score of approximately 111. To be sure that we have the technique, let's try another problem of the same general type.

What is the IQ score at the 20th percentile? Put another way, what IQ score cuts off the lowest 20% of the population? The problem is shown in figure 6–18.

When working problems involving the normal curve table, we must always keep in mind what information the table contains. The table tells us the percentage area between the mean and a particular z-score. Thus, to find the z-score that cuts off the lowest 20% of the distribution we have to look up 30%, rather than 20%. This is because of the way the table is arranged; that is, from the mean out rather than from the extremes into the mean.

At any rate, when we look for 30% in the body of the table, we find that it lies between -0.84 (29.95%) and -0.85 (30.23%). Since

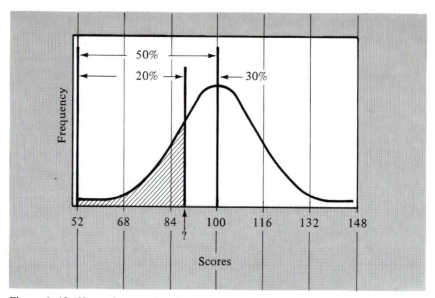

Figure 6–18: Normal curve showing the problem of finding the score at the 20th percentile.

it is obviously much closer to -0.84, we will convert this z-score into a raw score.

$$X = z\text{SD} + \overline{X} = (-0.84)(16) + 100 = -13.44 + 100 = 86.56$$

In conclusion, anyone scoring below 87 on an IQ test would be in the bottom 20% of the population.

Checking Your Progress

Over a ten-year period, 2000 students have taken standardized tests in introductory psychology. The average grade was 73.5 and the standard deviation was 9.8. Assuming a normal distribution of scores, what score would a student have to make in order to be in the upper 15% of the distribution? Lower 30%? Don't forget the way the table is compiled, from the mean out to the tail, rather than from the tail into the mean. (The answers are 83.7 and 68.4, respectively.)

Determining a Percentage between Two Scores
We have considered how to find a percentage area below a score and how to determine an area above a score. What about determining a percentage area between two scores (or the number

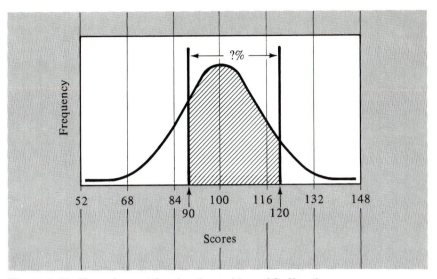

Figure 6–19: Normal curve showing the problem of finding the area between the scores of 90 and 120.

of cases between two scores)? For example, suppose that you are asked to determine the number of people in a random sample of 1000 that have IQ scores between 90 and 120. The problem is shown graphically in figure 6–19.

From the figure you can see that the problem is to determine the area between the scores of 90 and 120, and to convert this area to a frequency based on an N of 1000. To use the normal curve table, the two raw scores (90 and 120) must first be converted to z-scores. The z-score for 90 (symbolically: z_{90}) is $(X - \overline{X})/\text{SD} = (90 - 100)/16 = -10/16 = -0.625$ or -0.62 applying the rule of rounding introduced earlier (when the last digit is more than 5, round up; less than 5, drop it; equal to 5, drop it if the preceding digit is even, round up if the preceding digit is odd). Also, $z_{120} = (120 - 100)/16 = 20/16 = 1.25$.

From the normal curve table we find that 23.24% of the curve lies between the mean and a z-score of -0.62, and that 39.44% of the curve lies between the mean and a z-score of 1.25. Adding this new information to figure 6–19 gives us the curve shown in figure 6–20.

Figure 6–20 tells us that the total area from 90 to 120 is 23.24% + 39.44% = 62.68%. The last step is to find 62.88% of 1000 which is the same as (.6268)(1000) = 626.8 or 627 people would have IQ scores between 90 and 120.

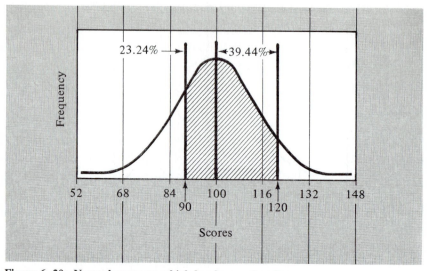

Figure 6–20: Normal curve on which has been entered areas obtained from appendix table A between 90 and the mean (23.24%) and between 120 and the mean (39.44%).

A slightly more difficult variation of this problem involves finding an area between two scores both of which are on the same side of the mean. To illustrate, suppose you want to know the number of people out of a sample of 1000 that would have IQ scores between 52 and 68. The problem is shown in figure 6–21.

Figure 6–21: Normal curve illustrating the problem of finding the area between IQ scores of 52 and 68.

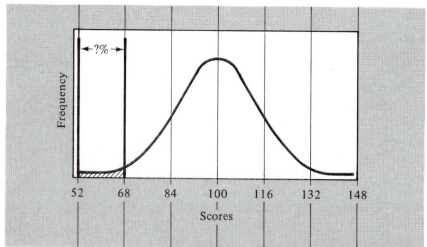

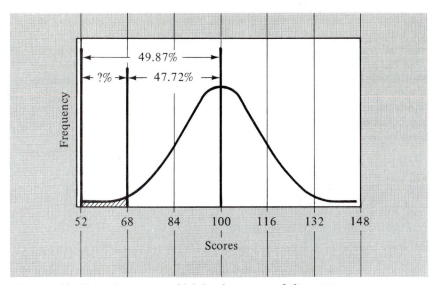

**Figure 6–22: Normal curve on which has been entered the areas
from 52 to the mean (49.87%) and from 68 to the mean
(47.72%).**

As before, our task is to determine the area between the two scores (between the scores of 52 and 68) and then to convert this area into a frequency. The z-scores are $z_{52} = (52 - 100)/16 = -48/16 = -3.00$ and $z_{68} = (68 - 100)/16 = -32/16 = -2.00$. Between the mean and a z-score of -3.00 lies 49.87% of the curve and between the mean and a z-score of -2.00 lies 47.72% of the curve. The new information is shown on figure 6–22.

From figure 6–22 it is clear that the area we are seeking is 49.87 $-$ 47.72 = 2.15% of the area under the normal curve. Finally, 2.15% of 1000 is the same as $(.0215)(1000) = 21.5$ or 22 people would have IQ scores between 52 and 68.

Checking Your Progress

For a second time, let's consider the example based on 2000 students who have taken a test in introductory psychology ($\overline{X} = 73.5$, SD $= 9.8$). What percentage of them made scores between 70 and 90? How many scored between 80 and 95? Between 50 and 60? If a D was given for scores 60–69, how many students earned a D? (The answers are 59.41%, 481 students, 151 students, and 478 students, respectively.)

Problems Involving Probability and the Normal Curve

The normal curve distribution is often called a probability distribution, and while we have discussed percentage areas under the curve, we could just as easily have talked about probabilities. At any rate, we can easily convert the percentage area we determine from the normal curve table to a probability value by using the following formula:

$$probability = \% \ area \div 100$$

For example, if we say that the percentage area under the curve is 2.15 between 2 and 3 standard deviation units of the mean, then the probability of someone having a score in this area is $2.15 \div 100 = 0.0215$. Conversely, if you are given a problem in which the likelihood of an event is expressed in terms of probability rather than percentage area, you can convert the probability into percentage area by multiplying by 100. Let's look at a problem of each type to be sure that you have the idea.

For example, you might be asked to determine the probability that someone picked at random would have an IQ score of 136 or above when tested? When the diagram shown in figure 6–23 is constructed, we see that our immediate problem is to determine the percentage area above 136.

Figure 6–23: Normal curve illustrating the problem of finding the probability of an IQ score of 136 or above.

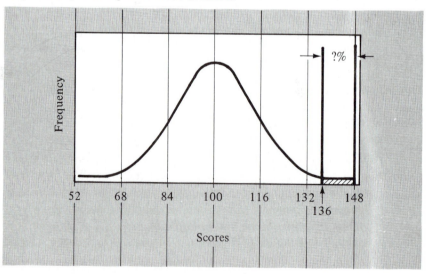

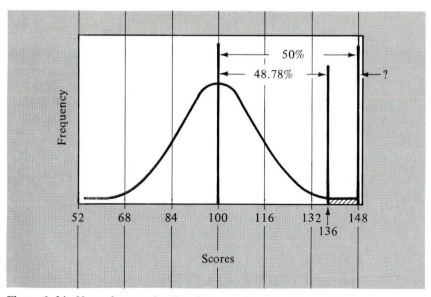

Figure 6–24: Normal curve showing the percentage area between the mean and an IQ score of 136.

As before, the first step is to convert the raw score into a z-score and the z-score for 136 is $z_{136} = (136 - 100)/16 = 36/16 = 2.25$. According to the normal curve table, 48.78% of the normal curve lies between the mean and $z = 2.25$. With this new information, figure 6–24 is constructed.

Since the total area above the mean is 50%, the area we want is $50\% - 48.78\% = 1.22\%$. Converting this area to a probability value, we have $p = 1.22 \div 100 = 0.0122$. Since the range of probability values is from 0 to 1, a value of 0.0122 expresses a low probability event. Thus, it is unlikely that we would encounter someone with an IQ score of 136 or higher.

A related problem asks us to determine what IQ scores are so unlikely that they would occur with a probability of 0.10 or less? In a way, this is a trick question since the direction of the deviance from the mean is not stated. Thus, we are actually dealing with both ends of the normal curve and not just the top or bottom half.

The first step this time is to convert the probability value to a percentage area, since that is what we are used to working with. Thus, percentage area $= p \times 100 = 0.10 \times 100 = 10\%$. Having obtained a percentage area, we can reword the problem to ask which IQ scores are so unlikely that they occur 10% or less of the time. In addition, an appropriately labeled diagram of the normal curve is shown in figure 6–25.

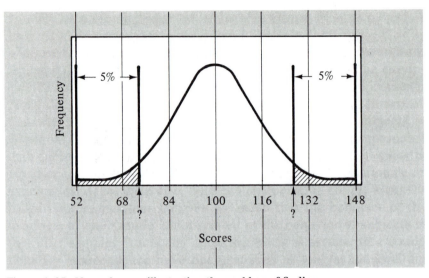

Figure 6–25: Normal curve illustrating the problem of finding the scores cutting off the deviant 10% of the distribution (scores occurring with a probability of .10 or less).

Notice in figure 6–25 that the deviant 10% of the curve has been split into two equal parts with 5% above the mean and 5% below it. The reason for this is, as I mentioned earlier, that the direction of the deviation from the mean was not stated in the problem. Thus, extremely high IQ scores are just as unlikely as extremely low ones. If I had asked you to find scores that occurred less than 1% of the time, then you would have divided the 1% into ½ of 1% on either side of the mean. Similarly, 5% would be divided into 2.5% on either side of the mean, and so forth.

The problem now becomes one of finding a z-score when we know a percentage area under the curve and converting this z-score into a raw score. Because of the table's arrangement, we can't look up 5% directly. Instead we look up the z-score that has 45% of the normal curve between it and the mean. Since $z = 1.64$ is associated with an area of 44.95 and $z = 1.65$ is associated with an area of 45.05, the z-score that cuts off 45% must be approximately halfway between 1.64 and 1.65 (approximately 1.645). How do you decide which score to use? I suggest that you apply the rule of rounding stated earlier and round to 1.64, since 4 is an even number.

We have determined that the z-scores that cut off the deviant 10% of the population are ± 1.64. The final step in the problem is to convert these two z-scores into raw scores. $X = z\text{SD} + \overline{X} =$

(± 1.64)(16) + 100 = ± 26.24 + 100 = 73.76 and 126.24. In conclusion, the IQ scores that are so unlikely that they occur with a probability of 0.10 or less are those less than 74 and greater than 126.

Checking Your Progress

In the example previously considered based on 2000 introductory students, the mean score on a test was 73.5 with SD = 9.8. What was the probability that someone would score 95 or better? Below what score would a student be in the lower 10% of the class? What scores are so deviant that the probability of their occurrence is 0.05 or less? (The answers are p = 0.0143, 60.96, 54.3 and 92.7, respectively.)

Summary

Probability is defined as the proportion of times an event would occur if the chances for occurrence were infinite or as the ratio of the number of times the event occurs to the total number of events. Two simple rules from probability theory are the addition and multiplication rules. The *addition rule* states that the probability of either one event or another event is equal to the sum of the probabilities of the individual events. The *multiplication rule* states that the probability of two or more independent events occurring on separate occasions is the product of their individual probabilities.

A simple probability distribution called the binomial distribution was described. The *binomial distribution* is based on events in which there are only two possible outcomes on each occurrence. As N increases the binomial distribution becomes more and more similar to the normal curve distribution and the normal distribution is often used to evaluate binomial data.

The *normal curve distribution* was described and a number of techniques were introduced for deriving information from it. Even though the actual distribution of scores in a sample taken from some population may not be normally distributed, we can still apply the characteristics of the normal curve as long as we can assume normality in the population from which the sample was taken. For much of the data in the social sciences, this is a valid assumption.

The actual techniques involved in obtaining information from the normal curve table are relatively simple. For example, there are only two basic formulas that you need to know and one is derived from the other: the formula for converting a raw score to a standard score or z-score is $z = (X - \overline{X})/\text{SD}$ and the equation for converting a z-score to a raw score is $X = z\text{SD} + \overline{X}$. As long as you remember that (1) the normal curve table gives the area under the normal curve from the mean to the z-score you are looking up; and that (2) half of the area under the curve lies on one side of the mean and the other half on the other side of the mean (i.e., that the normal curve is symmetrical), you should have no difficulty.

The steps you should follow in attacking any problem of the type discussed in this chapter are as follows:

1. Draw a small diagram of the normal curve and enter any information you have.
2. Use this diagram to try to decide what area(s) or score(s) you want to find.
3. Given raw scores, you should first convert these into z-scores so you can use the normal curve table. The conversion formula is: $z = (X - \overline{X})/\text{SD}$.
4. Given some area under the curve, you must look up the appropriate area (not necessarily the one you have been given) in the body of the table and find the z-score associated with it. Usually, you will want to convert this z-score into a raw score using the formula: $X = z\text{SD} + \overline{X}$.
5. Given a probability of occurrence rather than a percentage area, you should first convert this probability into a percentage area so that you can use the normal curve table. The conversion formula is: % area $= p \times 100$. If asked to find a probability associated with some particular score, you first determine the percentage area and then convert this to probability: $p = \%\text{ area}/100$.
6. If asked to find scores that are so deviant that they occur less than a certain percent of the time (or with a certain probability), you are looking at both ends of the distribution. So, you want to divide the percentage area (or the probability) in half and label your diagram accordingly.

Troubleshooting Your Computations

Most of the errors made in solving normal curve problems come from not really understanding what the problem asks you to find. To aid your understanding, I have suggested that you first draw a small curve, fill in any information you are given, and try to label it in terms of what you are seeking. Assuming that you do this correctly, you might ask yourself if your answer is reasonable in terms of your drawing? For example, if the area you are seeking is very small, your final answer should be correspondingly small.

A frequently made error involves not completing the problem, that is, the final answer is not in the appropriate form. For example, if the problem requires a frequency (e.g., number of persons with a certain range of scores), then any percentage area you find should be converted to a frequency. Similarly, percentage area should be converted to probability, if this is required.

Exercises

1. Briefly discuss the binomial distribution and how it is related to the normal distribution.
2. Is the normal distribution based on the generation of data or is it theoretical?
3. Define z-score as many different ways as you can.
4. Using the formula for a z-score, derive the equation for converting a z-score into a raw score.
5. Over a period of several months, a shoe salesman recorded shoe size in adult males entering his store. The data he gathered are: $N = 587$, $\Sigma X = 4989.5$, $\Sigma X^2 = 43731.5$. Assuming that shoe sizes are normally distributed in the population, answer these questions:
   (a) What is the percentile rank of a man who wears a size 5 shoe? Size 11.5?
   (b) How many of the men the saleman observed had shoe sizes between 7 and 10?
   (c) What shoe sizes are so unlikely that the probability of their being observed is .05 or less?
   (d) Assuming sales of 1000 pairs of men's shoes in a year, how many pairs of size 11.5 or larger should the salesman stock for sale in a year?
6. Define Gambler's Fallacy. Do you think that knowing what it is will affect your behavior?
7. Over a five-year period 175 undergraduate students have taken statistics in our department. On the final examination the average score was 76% with a standard deviation of 7. Assuming a normally distributed population from which the sample was drawn, answer the following questions:
   (a) What is the percentile rank of someone scoring 95? 60?
   (b) How many students scored between 80 and 90?
   (c) How many students scored 92 or better?
   (d) If a score of 90 or better is necessary for successful performance in our graduate course in statistics, how many undergraduates should not bother to apply to our graduate program?
   (e) What scores are so unlikely that their probability of occurrence is .05 or less? Occur less than 20% of the time?
   (f) The percentile rank of a student on this test was 83%. What was his score?
   (g) What is the probability of a score of 58 or less on the test?

8. In an introductory psychology class, 83 male students have taken a masculinity-feminity rating scale. The possible ratings are from 1 to 7 with a low score indicating low masculinity while a high score indicates high masculinity. The average rating was 4.23 with a SD = 1.02. Assuming a normal distribution, answer the following questions:

   (a) What is the percentile rank of a student with an average rating of 3.11?

   (b) How many of the 83 students had scores between 4.88 and 5.62?

   (c) What scores are so deviant that their probability of occurrence is 0.01 or less?

   (d) What is the probability associated with a score of 2.55 or less? 6.11 or more?

   (e) What is the score at the 83rd percentile?

9. The police department of a major city has found that the average height of their 1250 officers is 71 inches with a standard deviation of 2.3 inches. Assuming a normal distribution of heights, determine the following:

   (a) The number of officers who are at least 75 inches tall.

   (b) The number of officers who are between 65 and 72 inches in height.

   (c) The probability of being arrested by an officer who is 66 inches tall or less.

   (d) If an officer is at the 35th percentile in terms of height, how tall is he or she?

   (e) Assuming an equal amount of service, the top 10% of the policemen in terms of height also make higher salaries than their less-favored fellow officers. How tall does an officer have to be to get a better salary?

10. In an introductory psychology class, 100 students were given 20 words to define. The data from this test were as follows: $\Sigma X = 1000$, $\Sigma X^2 = 10,400$. Answer the questions below.

    (a) What is the percentile rank of a person scoring 8.8?

    (b) How many people score above 13?

    (c) What percentage of the class scored between 7 and 10.5?

    (d) What scores are so deviant that less than 7% of the class make them?

    (e) What is the probability that someone will score 12 or above?

7

Confidence Intervals and Hypothesis Testing

Introduction

This chapter marks the beginning of an introduction to inferential statistics. That is, the techniques introduced here and in the next several chapters will enable you to apply decisions made from sample data to the real world which is presumably reflected in the sample. Many concepts in inferential statistics are less easily grasped than material previously encountered and may require several readings for you to achieve some measure of insight.

In chapter 6 we discussed the properties of the normal curve and learned how to use the normal curve table to find areas under the curve. In this chapter we will discuss a distribution, similar to the normal curve, that is used to construct confidence intervals (an interval of scores around the sample mean) and to test hypotheses about our sample and the population from which it was drawn. The first step is to define the new distribution, the sampling distribution of means.

Sampling Distribution of Means

Consider the population of female undergraduate college students. Suppose a researcher was interested in determining the average amount of marijuana smoked per week by the members of this population. To approach this problem he might select a random sample of a given size (say 20) from the population and ask each of his subjects to estimate the amount in grams of marijuana smoked per week. (A random sample is one in which every individual in the population has an equal chance of being included.) After obtaining the answers our researcher computes a mean.

Being blessed with unlimited resources, the researcher continues to take random samples all with the same N from the population until it has been completely sampled. For each sample a mean is computed just as it was for the first.

To describe the mountain of data with which he is faced, our enterprising researcher decides to arrange the sample means into a frequency distribution and then to plot a frequency polygon from the resulting distribution. What are the properties of this frequency polygon?

To begin, the experimenter quickly notes that the vast majority of sample means differ from each other. That is, because he is selecting different individuals with different habits and characteristics for each sample, it is unlikely that any two successive samples would have precisely equivalent means. In fact, it is unlikely that any of the sample means would exactly equal the mean of the population. However, and this is the *first property* of the sampling distribution of means, the mean of all the sample means equals the mean of the population or μ.

The second and third properties of the sampling distribution of means concern the shape of the distribution. The *second property* is that the larger the size of each sample selected from the population, the more nearly the sampling distribution of means will approximate the normal curve. Additionally, if the population from which we have drawn the sample is normally distributed, the sampling distribution of means will be normal for any size sample.

The *third property* is that the larger the size of each sample selected from the population, the smaller the standard deviation of the sampling distribution of means. The standard deviation of the sampling distribution of means is called the *standard error of the mean* and is symbolized by $\sigma_{\bar{X}}$ (pronounced sigma sub X-bar). Statisticians have found that mathematically $\sigma_{\bar{X}}$ is equal to the population standard deviation divided by the square root of the sample size; i.e., $\sigma_{\bar{X}} = \sigma/\sqrt{N}$.

To help you understand the third property of the sampling distribution of means, think of it this way. The larger the size of each sample we extract from the population, the closer the sample mean will be to the mean of the population. That is, we are more likely with large samples to obtain a distribution of scores that accurately reflects the population situation. With large samples there is less deviation of the sample means from the population mean; that is, less variability about the population mean. The smaller variability with larger samples is reflected by a smaller standard error.

To summarize, we have imagined the construction of a frequency polygon from the distribution of sample means which were calculated from successive random samples of a given size which were drawn from a population. The family of frequency polygons based on different size samples taken from a population defines the *sampling distribution of means*. The shape of the frequency polygon is symmetrical and is approximately normal with large samples. The

standard error of the mean

sampling distribution of means

mean of the sampling distribution of means is equal to the population mean, and the standard deviation (called the standard error) becomes smaller as the sample size increases. A pictorial summary of the sampling distribution of means is shown in figure 7–1.

Before leaving the discussion of the sampling distribution of means, it will be useful to define a z-score for the new distribution. In chapter 6 a z-score was defined as the deviation of a raw score from the mean in standard deviation units, and the formula was $(X - \overline{X})/\text{SD}$ for a sample. Continuing with the same definition of a z-score, we see that each score in the distribution is a sample mean ($\overline{X}$), and the mean of the distribution is the population mean (μ).

Figure 7–1: A sequence of drawings illustrating the derivation and properties of the sampling distribution of means.

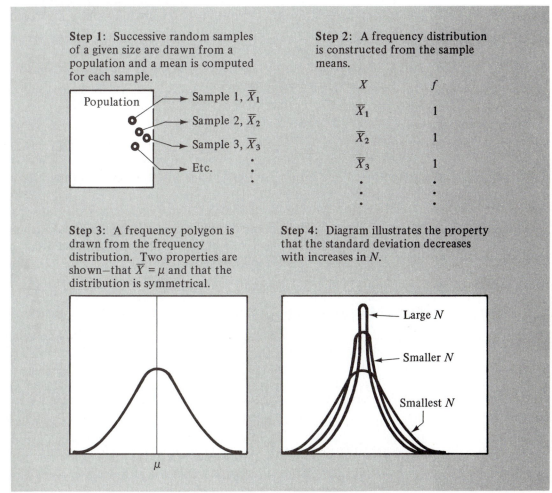

Step 1: Successive random samples of a given size are drawn from a population and a mean is computed for each sample.

Population → Sample 1, $\overline{X}_1$
→ Sample 2, $\overline{X}_2$
→ Sample 3, $\overline{X}_3$
→ Etc.

Step 2: A frequency distribution is constructed from the sample means.

X	f
$\overline{X}_1$	1
$\overline{X}_2$	1
$\overline{X}_3$	1
.	.
.	.
.	.

Step 3: A frequency polygon is drawn from the frequency distribution. Two properties are shown—that $\overline{X} = \mu$ and that the distribution is symmetrical.

μ

Step 4: Diagram illustrates the property that the standard deviation decreases with increases in N.

← Large N
← Smaller N
Smallest N

The standard deviation is the standard error of the mean ($\sigma_{\bar{X}}$). Thus, the z-score for our sampling distribution of means is found by:

$$z = \frac{\bar{X} - \mu}{\sigma_{\bar{X}}}$$

There are two terms in our formula for z that we cannot determine, μ and $\sigma_{\bar{X}}$. We can either use $\bar{X}$ to estimate μ or we can make guesses about it, but what are we going to do about $\sigma_{\bar{X}}$? We are going to estimate its value with $s_{\bar{X}}$, which we will call the estimated standard error of the mean. The equation for $s_{\bar{X}}$ is:

$$s_{\bar{X}} = \frac{SD}{\sqrt{N - 1}}$$

where N is the number of subjects in the sample and SD is the sample standard deviation. Substituting the estimated standard error of the mean, $s_{\bar{X}}$, for $\sigma_{\bar{X}}$ in the formula for z, we have $t = (\bar{X} - \mu)/s_{\bar{X}}$. This formula is called t because we have estimated $\sigma_{\bar{X}}$, and the family of curves based on this statistic is known as the distribution of t.

An equivalent equation for $s_{\bar{X}}$ is:

$$s_{\bar{X}} = \frac{s}{\sqrt{N}}$$

However, since SD is slightly easier to compute than s, $s_{\bar{X}}$ will be computed by the originally introduced equation in the remainder of the chapter.

Now that the sampling distribution of means has been defined and some of its properties discussed, what can be done with it and the related distribution of t? The first use that will be discussed is in the construction of confidence intervals.

Confidence Intervals

Suppose that an experimental psychologist wanted to do a learning experiment with newborn children in order to establish the average rate at which a neonate could form an avoidance response to a mildly noxious stimulus (for example, a puff of air to the eyelid). Since it is impossible to measure the population of neonates, the experimenter randomly selects a sample of 23 children and assesses their learning skills. From the data collected a mean number of trials to criterion of 46.33 is computed. But what does this figure mean in terms of the population of neonates? If the study were done time and again with random samples of 23 children, would the results always be similar to this? What is the mean of means or μ?

Unfortunately, we can't answer the last question. However, one of the things that we learned in chapter 4 was that the mean of a sample, $\overline{X}$, shows no systematic tendencies in relation to the mean of the population, μ, and for this reason is said to be an unbiased estimate of μ. Thus, we can use the sample mean as an estimate of μ. When we do this we must realize that it is very unlikely for $\overline{X}$ to exactly equal μ. Is there any way to increase our chances of having captured the population value? Yes, and it has to do with designating a *range* of values rather than only one in guessing about the location of μ. The range of values is called a confidence interval. A *confidence interval* will be formally defined as a range of score values within which we are reasonably certain lies the population mean.

confidence interval

How confident do we want to be in our guess about the value of μ? Do we want to be 80% sure, or 90%, or 63%, or what? Well, I suspect that 90% probably sounds pretty good, but most of you would balk at anything less than this. Statisticians, being very conservative people, have traditionally tended to favor either 95% or 99% certainty, and, for this reason, we will discuss the derivation of 95% and 99% confidence intervals. Think of it this way, if we establish a range of values around our sample mean within which we are 95% (or 99%) sure that μ is contained, it is exceedingly unlikely that μ will be outside the range. It is not impossible, but highly unlikely.

Now that we have decided how confident we want to be, let's derive a formula for 95% and 99% confidence intervals. In the last chapter we talked about the normal curve and learned how to find scores cutting off deviant portions of the curve. One problem we considered involved finding the scores that were so deviant that they occurred less than 5% (or 1%) of the time. This could also be expressed as finding the scores that occurred with a probability of 0.05 (or 0.01) or less. To find these scores we first drew a normal curve, divided the 5% (or 1%) in half and labeled each end of the curve appropriately. We then looked in the normal curve table to find the z-scores cutting off the deviant percentage of the curve and converted these scores to raw scores using the equation for this purpose, $X = z\text{SD} + \overline{X}$. The problem is shown graphically in figure 7–2.

Note from the graph that while we were seeking the scores cutting off the deviant 5% (or 1%) of the normal curve distribution we simultaneously found the scores between which lies 95% or 99% of

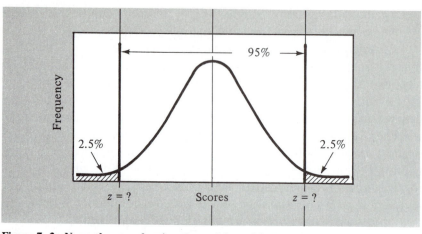

Figure 7–2: Normal curve showing the problem of finding the scores cutting off the deviant 5% of the distribution or the scores between which lies 95% of the curve.

the distribution. Thus, we already have a technique for finding the 99% and 95% confidence intervals. All we need to do is to modify the equations slightly to take into account the new distribution introduced in this chapter, the sampling distribution of means.

Consider the situations where our samples are infinite in size or where we have drawn our samples from a normally distributed population. In these limiting cases the sampling distribution of means is normally distributed and the formulas for finding the 99% and 95% confidence intervals would be $X = z_{\bar{X}} + \mu$ or $X = \pm 2.58 \, \sigma_{\bar{X}} + \mu$ for the 99% interval and $X = \pm 1.96 \sigma_{\bar{X}} + \mu$ for the 95% interval. The z-scores of ± 2.58 and ± 1.96 are the scores cutting off the deviant 1% and 5% of the normal curve, respectively.

Since we still don't know either μ or $\sigma_{\bar{X}}$, we will estimate their value with $\bar{X}$ and $s_{\bar{X}}$, respectively. The equations introduced in the previous paragraph now become $X = \pm t_{.01} \, s_{\bar{X}} + \bar{X}$ for the 99% confidence interval and $X = \pm t_{.05} \, s_{\bar{X}} + \bar{X}$ for the 95% confidence interval. As you will note, instead of using the z-scores of ± 2.58 and ± 1.96, we will need to determine the corresponding values of t.

The values for t are both positive and negative since we are looking for scores on either side of $\bar{X}$. In addition, we can add the appropriate subscripts depending on whether we are finding the 95% or the 99% confidence interval. The appropriate subscripts are $t_{.05}$ (which means the t-scores that cut off the deviant 5% of the distribution or occur with a probability of 0.05 or less) and $t_{.01}$. Putting all of this together, the formula for the 95% confidence interval

(CI) $= \pm t_{.05} \, s_{\overline{x}} + \overline{X}$ and the formula for the 99% confidence interval $= \pm t_{.01} \, s_{\overline{x}} + \overline{X}$. Looking at these equations we see that we have already encountered two of the three terms needed and shouldn't have any difficulty determining them. Thus, $s_X = SD/\sqrt{N-1}$ and $\overline{X} = \Sigma X/N$. But, where do we get the t-scores?

To determine the relevant values of t, we will refer to a table (table B) which lists the t-scores that cut off either the deviant 5% or 1% of the distribution depending on the size of the sample. Ordinarily, when we talk about the deviant 5% or 1% of the distribution we will be considering both ends of the distribution. Another way to express this idea is to say that we are considering *both tails* of the distribution of t-scores. For this reason, when we are using the table pertaining to the distribution of t, we will generally use the values under the heading ending with the designation "two-tailed test." A portion of the table of t-scores has been reproduced in table 7–1.

According to the title of table 7–1, it contains critical values of t, that is, values of t cutting off deviant portions of the distribution. Continuing down in the table, we encounter the words "Level of

*Table 7–1: A portion of table **B** showing values of t cutting off deviant portions of the sampling distribution of means depending on the degrees of freedom. The complete table may be found in the appendix.*

	Level of Significance for One-Tailed Test			
	5%	2.5%	1%	.5%
	Level of Significance for Two-Tailed Test			
df	10%	5%	2%	1%
1	6.3138	12.7062	31.8207	63.6574
2	2.9200	4.3027	6.9646	9.9248
3	2.3534	3.1824	4.5407	5.8409
4	2.1318	2.7764	3.7469	4.6041
5	2.0150	2.5706	3.3649	4.0322
6	1.9432	2.4469	3.1427	3.7074
7	1.8946	2.3646	2.9980	3.4995
8	1.8595	2.3060	2.8965	3.3554
9	1.8331	2.2622	2.8214	3.2498
10	1.8125	2.2281	2.7638	3.1693

Source: This table is adapted from Owen, D.B., *Handbook of Statistical Tables,* Addison-Wesley, 1962, pp. 28–30, with permission of the author and publisher.

significance for one-tailed test'' with four different percentages below them. Since we are not considering one-tailed tests at the moment, let's ignore these words and continue on in the table. A discussion of one-tailed tests will be provided in chapter 8.

Now we come to the heading ''Level of significance for two-tailed test'' with each of the previous percentages doubled. The numbers in each column below the percentages are the values of t cutting off the deviant percentage of the distribution indicated by the percentage that heads the column in which you are looking. As with the normal curve table, only the positive half of the curve is given in the table so that for a two-tailed test each of the values of t in the table is assumed to be both positive and negative.

At the far left of the table there is a column of numbers with the heading *df*, which is the abbreviation for degrees of freedom. The

degrees of freedom

term *degrees of freedom* is defined as the number of values that are free to vary after certain restrictions have been placed on the data. Thus, if one restriction is placed on a group of numbers (e.g., the sum must be a certain value), then all of the numbers are free to vary except the last one which is determined by the restriction that has been placed. To illustrate, suppose we want to pick five numbers with the restriction that the sum must be equal to 50. We could let the first number be 5, the second 13, the third 21, the fourth 6, and the fifth, well, the fifth would be determined by whatever we had chosen for the first four numbers. In this case, the fifth number must be 5 since the sum of the first four was 45 and the sum of all five must be 50. The point is that we could have chosen any values for the first four numbers but the last number would be determined by what we had chosen for the first four and by the restriction placed on the data. In summary, the *df* is equal to $N - 1$ when one restriction has been placed on the data, or to the number of values minus the one restriction.

The concept of degrees of freedom is very complex, and I have only scratched the surface with this discussion. For our purposes, it is sufficient to point out that the *df* for t when we are dealing with one sample is $N - 1$. For example, if we have a sample of size N = 46, the $df = N - 1 = 46 - 1 = 45$, and the t-scores cutting off the deviant 5% of the distribution are ± 2.0141.

But, enough of all the abstractions, definitions, and talking about formulas. Let's do some problem solving; that is, determine some confidence intervals. At the beginning of this section, I described a learning experiment with newborn children in which the average number of trials to criterion was 46.33 for a sample of size

$N = 23$. Suppose that the SD was 6.51. What is the 95% confidence interval for μ?

The formula is 95% confidence interval $= \pm t_{.05}\, s_{\bar{x}} + \bar{X}$. We know that $\bar{X} = 46.33$ and $s_{\bar{x}} = \text{SD}/\sqrt{N-1} = 6.51/\sqrt{23-1} = 6.51/\sqrt{22} = 6.51/4.69 = 1.39$. The t-scores cutting off the deviant 5% of the distribution with $df = N - 1 = 23 - 1 = 22$ are ± 2.0739. Entering the information into the equation, we find that the 95% confidence interval $= \pm 2.0739(1.39) + 46.33 = \pm 2.88 + 46.33 = 43.45$ to 49.21. Thus, the range of values within which we are 95% sure μ is contained is from 43.45 to 49.21. The 99% confidence interval could be obtained in the same fashion with the only difference being in the values of t which are ± 2.8188. The 99% confidence interval is from 42.41 to 50.25.

Let's try another example. In a study to determine the bar-pressing rate of mongoloid children, 55 have been tested on a continuous reinforcement schedule. (A continuous reinforcement schedule, CRF, is one in which the child is rewarded, in this case with candy, for each press of a lever extending from a panel.) The average response rate in a thirty-minute period for the sample was 573 responses with a standard deviation of 34.7. What is the 95% confidence interval?

95% confidence internal $= \pm t_{.05}\, s_{\bar{x}} + \bar{X}$

$$s_{\bar{x}} = \frac{\text{SD}}{\sqrt{N-1}} = \frac{34.7}{\sqrt{55-1}} = \frac{34.7}{\sqrt{54}} = \frac{34.7}{7.35}$$
$$= 4.72$$

$$t_{.05}(df = N - 1 = 55 - 1 = 54) = \pm 2.0086$$

$$\text{95\% confidence interval} = \pm 2.0086(4.72) + 573 = \pm 9.48 + 573$$
$$= 563.52 \text{ to } 582.48$$

You will note that the critical values of t for 54 degrees of freedom were not actually shown in table 7–1 and that the value used was that for $df = 50$. If the sample size is larger than 30, the table is incomplete and the actual value of t may not be given. In this case we will use the value for the most nearly correct df.

Because the distribution of t more and more closely approximates the normal curve as N increases, many textbook authors use z-scores rather than t-scores to construct confidence intervals when N is greater than some arbitrary number, e.g., 50. I feel that this results in unnecessary confusion and will continue to use t-scores, regardless of the size of N.

Checking Your Progress

Suppose that the digit span of 31 adults has been measured with the result that $\Sigma X = 207.7$ and $\Sigma X^2 = 1399.34$. What are the 95% and 99% confidence intervals for μ? (The answers are 6.52 to 6.88 and 6.45 to 6.95, respectively.)

Hypothesis Testing (One Sample t-Test)

In the section on confidence intervals we used a distribution that is approximately normal with large samples to establish a range of values within which we have a certain degree of confidence that μ is contained. Another, and perhaps even more important use to which we can put the distribution of t is to test guesses about the value of μ.

Let's consider a specific example and develop a testing procedure from it. A professor in an introductory psychology class has been rated on his teaching performance by 56 students. His average rating on a 5-point scale is 4.21 with SD = 0.55. On the basis of university performance as a whole, we might guess that average teaching performance would be reflected by a rating of 4.0. If we guess (hypothesize) the population mean to be 4.0, what is the probability of a rating as deviant as 4.21?

Using the procedures developed in chapter 6 for finding the probability of a deviant score or scores, the first step is to calculate a z-score for the raw score of 4.21. However, in this chapter we are considering the distribution of t rather than z, so our first step is to compute a t-score:

$$t = \frac{\bar{X} - \mu}{s_{\bar{X}}} = \frac{4.21 - 4.00}{s_{\bar{X}}}$$

$$s_{\bar{X}} = \frac{SD}{\sqrt{N-1}} = \frac{.55}{\sqrt{56-1}} = \frac{.55}{\sqrt{55}} = \frac{.55}{7.42} = 0.074$$

$$t = \frac{4.21 - 4.00}{0.074} = \frac{.21}{0.074} = 2.84$$

What does this t-score of 2.84 mean? Verbally it means that a rating of 4.21 is 2.84 $s_{\bar{X}}$ units above a mean of 4.0 on the sampling distribution of means with $N = 56$. This is shown graphically in figure 7–3.

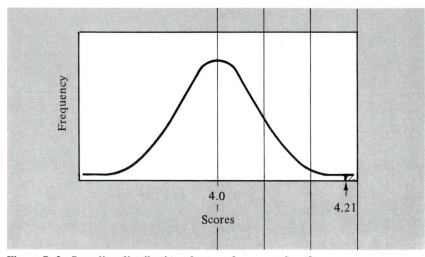

Figure 7–3: Sampling distribution of means from samples of size $N = 56$. Score of 4.21 is 2.84 $s_{\bar{x}}$ units above the mean of 4.0.

Originally we wanted to know what the probability is of obtaining a rating as deviant as 4.21, assuming that $\mu = 4.0$. Since 4.21 is 2.84 estimated standard error units above the mean, the score 2.84 units below the mean $[4.0 - (2.84)(0.074) = 4.0 - 0.21 = 3.79]$ is equally deviant, and the original problem really asked us to find the area of the curve above 4.21 and below 3.79. We could add the areas together, convert to probability, and we would have determined the probability of obtaining a score as deviant as 4.21, given that $\mu = 4.0$.

However, since we are not dealing with the normal curve but rather with a family of curves none of which is well described in appendix table B, we cannot actually determine the probability. We can do something that is almost equally valuable and much easier. We can compare our obtained *t*-score with table values known to cut off the deviant 5% or 1% of the distribution for a given sample size.

For the example we have been considering, we found t to be 2.84 and the $df = N - 1 = 56 - 1 = 55$. Looking in table 7–1 we see that the *t*-scores cutting off the deviant 5% and 1% of the sampling distribution of means when the size of each sample is 56 ($df = 55$) are approximately 2.01 and 2.68, respectively. Since our obtained t is more deviant (i.e., farther from μ than either of the critical values), the logical thing to do is to reject the guess that $\mu = 4.0$.

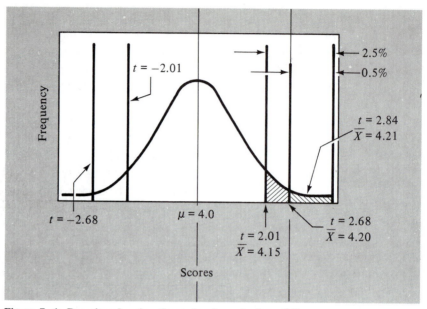

Figure 7–4: Drawing showing the region for rejection of the hypothesis that $\mu = 4.0$. $t = \pm2.01$ cuts off the deviant 5% (2.5% on either side of μ) of the sampling distribution of means with $N = 56$. $t = \pm2.68$ cuts off the deviant 1%. The raw scores corresponding to the t-scores are 3.85, 4.15 and 3.80, 4.20, respectively. $t = 2.84$ ($X = 4.21$) is in the region for rejection of μ.

In other words, our observed rating of 4.21 is very unlikely if the population mean is 4.0. We can conclude that our rated professor was drawn from a different population with a different mean. We still don't know what the population mean is; we just know that it is very unlikely that it is 4.0. Figure 7–4 illustrates what has been done with this problem.

Here is what we have done to this point. A sample has been selected from a population with a hypothetical mean of 4.0. The sample mean of 4.21 has been found to be very unlikely given the assumption that $\mu = 4.0$. We concluded, therefore, that our sample was quite probably taken from a population in which μ was not equal to 4.0. The hypothesis testing procedure we have outlined is called "testing the null hypothesis."

The null hypothesis, symbolized by H_0, in this particular case is that the sample mean and the guessed value of μ do not differ. The null hypothesis is stated symbolically by $\overline{X} - \mu = 0$ or H_0: $\overline{X} - \mu = 0$. Equivalently, H_0: $\overline{X} = \mu$.

An alternative to the null hypothesis is that $\overline{X} - \mu \neq$ 0 or that $\overline{X} \neq \mu$ (symbolically, H_1: $\overline{X} - \mu \neq 0$ or H_1: $\overline{X} \neq \mu$). This alternative hypothesis is called bidirectional (i.e., taking into account both tails of the distribution), since the direction of the difference between $\overline{X}$ and μ is not specified. A unidirectional hypothesis exists if H_1: $\overline{X} - \mu > 0$ or H_1: $\overline{X} - \mu < 0$.

In the example we have considered the sample mean was found to be unlikely given the hypothesized value of μ. Thus, we rejected the null hypothesis.

In summary, the steps for testing the null hypothesis are:

1. Make a guess (usually on the basis of previous research) about the value of μ. For example, based on several studies involving a large number of rats, the rats took an average of 22.5 trials to learn a problem. Thus, it is reasonable to guess that the population mean is 22.5.
2. From the guess about the population mean, establish the null hypothesis (H_0: $\overline{X} = \mu$).
3. Determine how far the sample mean deviates from the guessed value of μ in estimated standard error units. In other words, compute a t-score with the formula $t = (\overline{X} - \mu)/s_{\overline{x}}$.
4. Compare the obtained t-score with table values of t known to cut off the deviant 5% and 1% of the distribution of t for samples of a given size. Sample size is converted to df by determining $N - 1$. If the obtained value of t is larger in absolute value than either critical value in the table, reject H_0 and conclude that it is very unlikely that the sample came from a population in which μ is what it was guessed to be.

Let's look at another example. Suppose that over a several year period a professor has found that the average grade on the final examination for all students taking a course in statistics is 75%. One semester the final exam is given and the grades are found to be slightly lower, with an average of 73.8 for a sample of size $N = 61$. The standard deviation is 8.3. Assuming that $\mu = 75$, what is the probability of obtaining a sample with a mean as deviant as 73.8? Is the probability low enough for the professor to reject the null hypothesis and conclude that perhaps a review of teaching and/or testing procedures is in order?

Another term that is often used to describe the hypothesis testing procedure is "testing for significance." When H_0 is rejected, statisticians often say that a significant difference has been found between $\overline{X}$ and μ, and that it corresponds to either the 5% or the 1% level of significance depending upon how far away from μ the sample $\overline{X}$ lies in $s_{\overline{x}}$ units.

As before, the first step is to calculate a t-score.

$$t = \frac{\overline{X} - \mu}{s_{\overline{x}}}$$

$$s_X = \frac{SD}{\sqrt{N-1}} = \frac{8.3}{\sqrt{61-1}} = \frac{8.3}{\sqrt{60}} = \frac{8.3}{7.75} = 1.07$$

$$t = \frac{73.8 - 75}{1.07} = \frac{-1.2}{1.07} = -1.12, \, df = N - 1 = 61 - 1 = 60$$

Looking at the table of t-scores, we find that the critical values for $df = 60$ are 2.0003 at the 5% level and 2.6603 at the 1% level. That is, t-scores of ± 2.0003 cut off the deviant 5% of the distribution of t for samples of size $N = 61$. Since our computed t-score is -1.12 (1.12 in absolute value), it is less than either of the critical values and we cannot reject H_0. In other words, the probability is quite high of obtaining a sample of size $N = 61$ with a mean of 73.8 when the population mean is 75.

Continuing to look at the table of t-scores, we see that if we have $df = \infty$ the values required for significance are 1.96 at the 5% level and 2.58 at the 1% level. One of the properties of the distribution of t is that it approaches the normal curve as sample size increases. It should not be surprising, therefore, that 1.96 and 2.58 are the z-scores that cut off the deviant 5% and 1% of the normal curve, respectively. Finally, it should be noted that 1.96 is the smallest value of t that is required for rejection of the null hypothesis for a two-tailed test at the 5% level. For this reason, if any obtained t is less than 1.96 in absolute value, there is no need to look in the table since it cannot be significant.

Checking Your Progress

A new college president has been hired at a large state university. He has just given his first speech to the general faculty. As the faculty members are leaving, 35 are randomly selected and asked to rate the speech on a scale from 1 to 7 with 1 being terrible, 4 average, and 7 fantastic. The average rating is 4.4 with SD = .93. Test the hypothesis that $\mu = 4$; that is, that the faculty as a whole was neutral towards the speech. (The answer is $t = 2.52$, $df = 34$, $p < 0.05$.)

Type-I and Type-II Errors

Hypothesis testing as it has been discussed in this chapter involves making a guess about a population parameter (μ) and then determining whether or not a sample mean differs enough from the guessed value of μ so that we can reject the hypothetical μ. The actual test is performed by computing how far the sample mean deviates from the guessed μ in $s_{\bar{X}}$ units (in other words, by computing t). The computed t-score is then compared with t-scores known to cut off either the deviant 5% or 1% of the distribution for a given value of df. If the computed t is larger than the table value at the 5% (or 1%) level of significance, the null hypothesis (that there is no difference between the sample mean and the mean of the population) is rejected. Thus, we can conclude that the probability is .05 (.01) or less of obtaining a sample $\bar{X}$ as deviant as we obtained from a population with the μ that we guessed. If the obtained value of t is smaller than the table values, we do not reject the null hypothesis.

This process of rejecting or failing to reject the null hypothesis is sometimes called "making a decision." In statistics, as in life, sometimes we make the wrong decision. Thus, one type of incorrect decision involves rejecting the null hypothesis when in fact it is true. That is, we may conclude on the basis of our sample value that there is a difference between the hypothetical μ and $\bar{X}$ when this is not true.

This type of judgmental error is known as a *Type-I or α error* and is defined as rejecting H_0 when it is true. The levels of significance (5% and 1%) are often called α levels, and the probability of making a Type-I error depends directly on α. Thus, if $\alpha = .05$, then the probability of rejecting a true H_0 is .05 or 5 times in 100. That is, if we drew 100 samples from a population in which μ is what we have guessed it to be, 5 of those samples would have means deviant enough from μ for us to reject H_0. However, 5 times out of 100 is not very often and that is why we rejected H_0 initially.

If we want to be more conservative and come closer to ensuring that we don't mistakenly reject a true H_0, we can lower the α level to .01 (1% level of significance) or to .001 and so on. However, while decreasing the probability of a Type-I error we are simultaneously increasing the probability of a *Type-II or β error* which is defined as failing to reject H_0 when it is false. Further, while the probability of a Type-I error is determined by the α level, the probability of a Type-II error will not be known.

In practice, the $\alpha = .05$ level or the 5% level of significance is widely used and most scientists are willing to accept rejection of H_0

Type-I (or) α error

Type-II (or) β error

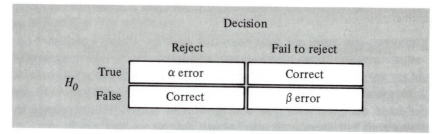

Figure 7–5: Chart illustrating the possible consequences of decision making as discussed in this chapter.

at the 5% level as reflecting a true difference. If, however, there is great concern about only reporting true differences, then a more conservative value of α may be chosen, for example, .01 or .001 or less. The problem with the ultraconservative approach is that a true difference may be discarded because it does not quite reach the required values of the small α. In other words, the ultraconservative approach means an increase in the likelihood of a Type-II error.

The possible consequences of hypothesis testing as outlined in this chapter are summarized in figure 7–5. The figure reflects the two possible decisions that can be made, either to reject or to fail to reject the null hypothesis which may be either true or false. Rejection of a true H_0 results in an α error while rejection of a false H_0 is correct. Failure to reject a true H_0 is correct while failing to reject a false H_0 leads to a β error.

Power of a Statistical Test

In the previous section a Type-I or α error was defined as rejecting a true null hypothesis while a Type-II or β error was defined as failing to reject a false hypothesis. Further it was stated that decreasing the likelihood of an α error by lowering α results in an increase in the probability of a β error. That is, by making it less likely that we will mistakenly reject a true null, we are making it increasingly more difficult to reject *any* null hypothesis, even one that is false.

power   A related concern is the *power* of a test which is defined as the probability that our test will detect a false hypothesis. Power may be determined by solving the equation:

$$\text{Power} = 1 - \beta$$

Unfortunately, determining the power of a test requires information that we do not have concerning the actual state of affairs in the pop-

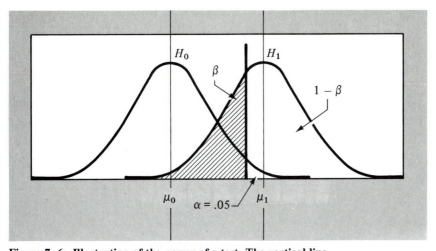

Figure 7–6: Illustration of the power of a test. The vertical line represents the lower boundary for rejection of the null hypothesis under H_0. The shaded area under H_1 to the left of the line is β while the unshaded area to the right is $1 - \beta$ or the power of the test.

ulation. That is, we would need to know exact parameters which are what we have been estimating with our sample values. Although we cannot determine β (and from it $1 - \beta$), we can discuss some factors contributing to the power of a test. To better understand the factors, let's consider the distributions shown in figure 7–6.

In figure 7–6 there are two partially overlapping distributions designated H_0 and H_1. The distribution called H_0 is what we would expect to observe if H_0 were true while H_1 represents the true state of affairs. Assuming that $\alpha = .05$ and that we are using a one-tailed test (one which considers only one tail of the distribution rather than both tails), a vertical line has been drawn on the graph illustrating the region of rejection of H_0. That is, any sample mean from H_1 that happened to fall in the unshaded region to the right of the rejection line would enable us to reject H_0. This unshaded portion of the graph is labeled $1 - \beta$ or the power of the test.

However, you can see that a substantial portion of distribution H_1 lies to the left of the rejection line. This portion of H_1 has been shaded and is labeled β. That is, any sample drawn from H_1 with a mean in the shaded portion will not result in the rejection of H_0 which is really false. Thus, observation of a sample in this area will result in a β error. Now let's look at the factors affecting power.

As already mentioned, the value of α affects β which in turn

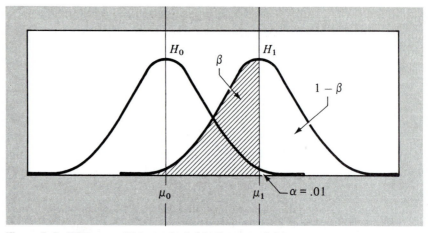

Figure 7–7: With $\alpha = .01$ instead of .05, the area of β is increased with a corresponding decrease in the power of the test $(1 - \beta)$.

determines $1 - \beta$. Thus, the smaller we set the α level, the larger β will be, which in turn means that our statistical test will have less power. In constructing the line of rejection shown in figure 7–6, α was set at .05. Suppose we make $\alpha = .01$ instead. In the new situation, shown in figure 7–7 we can see that the shaded area β is now larger than it was with $\alpha = .05$, while the power of the test $(1 - \beta)$ has decreased.

A second factor affecting the power of a test is the size of the sample that we have drawn from the population. Specifically, the larger the size of N, the greater the power of the test will be. The reason for this concerns one of the properties of the sampling distribution of means—as the size of the samples increases, $\sigma_{\bar{x}}$ decreases. In other words, with larger and larger N's, the sampling distribution becomes more and more compact. The effect of sample size on the power of a test is shown in figure 7–8 in which the distributions have been drawn to reflect a larger N than that shown in figure 7–6. As you can see, although the mean of each distribution is the same as before, the greater compactness results in less overlap, a smaller β, and a larger power.

A third factor affecting power concerns the distance between the mean under H_0 and the true mean under H_1. That is, the greater the discrepancy between the hypothesized value and the true value, the greater the power of the test will be. Figure 7–9 illustrates that power increases when the mean under H_1 is farther away from the mean under H_0 than it was in figure 7–6.

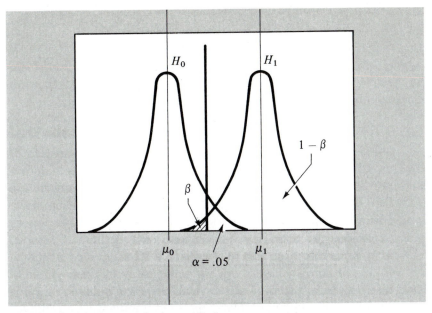

Figure 7–8: A larger sample size results in more compact distributions, a smaller region of overlap between H_0 and H_1, and a more powerful test.

Figure 7–9: When the means under H_0 and H_1 are farther apart, β is decreased and $1 - \beta$ or the power is increased.

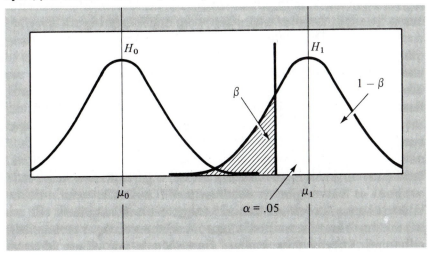

Summary

A new distribution was introduced, the *sampling distribution of means*. The sampling distribution of means was constructed from the means of successive random samples of a given size taken from some population. Its properties are:

1. It is symmetrical in shape and approaches normality with large samples even if the population from which the samples are drawn is not normal.
2. It has a normal distribution for any sample size if the samples are drawn from a normally distributed population.
3. Its mean is equal to the mean of the population (μ).
4. Its standard deviation ($\sigma_{\bar{x}}$, called the standard error of the mean) will become smaller, as the size of the sample becomes larger.

The sampling distribution of means and a related family of curves were used to construct *confidence intervals* (defined as a range of scores within which we have a certain degree of confidence that μ is contained) and to test hypotheses about the exact value of μ.

The two confidence intervals discussed were the 95% confidence interval and the 99% confidence interval. The formula for the 95% confidence interval is $\pm t_{.05} s_{\bar{x}} + \bar{X}$ where $t_{.05}$ is a value obtained from a table of t-scores that cut off the deviant 5% and 1% of the distribution of t. The particular value of t used depends on the *degrees of freedom* or *df* which is defined as the number of values free to vary after certain restrictions have been placed on the data. In the case of t with one sample, $df = N - 1$. The value s_x is an estimate of $\sigma_{\bar{x}}$ and is computed from the formula $s_{\bar{x}} = \text{SD}/\sqrt{N - 1}$. The formula for the 99% confidence interval is $\pm t_{.01} s_{\bar{x}} + \bar{X}$.

Hypothesis testing involves making an assumption about the value of μ and testing this assumption in relation to an observed sample mean. That is, if the $\bar{X}$ (or any as deviant or more deviant from μ) observed is very unlikely given a value for μ, the hypothesized value for μ is rejected. The actual steps are:

1. Make a guess about μ. From this guess the null hypothesis (H_0) is made. The null hypothesis is that the sample mean and the guessed value of μ do not differ ($H_0: \bar{X} - \mu = 0$).
2. Determine how far $\bar{X}$ deviates from the guessed value of μ in $s_{\bar{x}}$ units. In other words, calculate a t-score using the formula $t = (\bar{X} - \mu)/s_{\bar{x}}$.

3. Compare the computed t-score with the values of t in table B with the appropriate df $(N - 1)$. If the observed t-score is equal to or greater than the table values in absolute value, reject H_0. If it is less than the table values, do not reject H_0.

Hypothesis testing is also known as testing for significance and the values of t cutting off the deviant 5% and 1% of the distribution of t define the 5% and 1% levels of significance, respectively.

Two types of error may be made when testing H_0. The *Type-I or α error* is defined as rejection of a true null and has a probability equal to the α level. The *Type-II or β error* is defined as failing to reject a false H_0. The probability of this type of error increases with decreases in α.

The *power of a test* is defined as the probability of detecting or rejecting a false H_0. Power is determined by the formula:

$$\text{Power} = 1 - \beta$$

Three factors affecting power are the α level used, the size of N, and the distance between H_0 and H_1, a true alternate hypothesis.

Troubleshooting Your Computations

The computations covered in this chapter have for the most part been quite simple and require an understanding of what you are trying to find more than mathematical ability. However, there are some questions that you should ask yourself after you have worked the problems in this chapter.

First of all, have you obtained a confidence interval that seems reasonable in light of the sample information you have? For example, to be reasonable, the confidence interval should contain the mean of the sample. When you found the t-score to plug into the formula for the confidence interval, did you use df or N? You should have used df $(N - 1)$ rather than N.

When computing and reporting the t-score, did you retain the appropriate sign throughout the computations? That is, if the mean of your sample is less than the value hypothesized for μ, the t-score should be negative.

After making a decision to reject or not to reject the null hypothesis, go back and review the decision-making process. Consider whether or not your obtained t-score was larger in absolute value than the table value of t cutting off the deviant 5% of the distribution of t-scores for samples with the df you observed. If so, you should have rejected H_0; if not, you should not have rejected H_0.

Exercises

1. (a) Given $X = 10$, SD = 4, $N = 18$, find the 99% confidence interval for μ.
   (b) If $N = 147$, what is the 95% confidence interval for μ? Note that 146 is closer to 120 than it is to ∞.
2. Find the 99% and 95% confidence intervals for μ for each of the following samples.
   (a) $X = 15$, $N = 17$, SD = 5.
   (b) $\Sigma X = 240$, $N = 40$, $s_{\bar{x}} = 1.6$.
   (c) $N = 170$, $\Sigma X = 14{,}450$, $\Sigma X^2 = 1{,}235{,}432.5$.
3. Some data have been collected with the following results:

X	f	X	f
37	1	29	3
36	1	27	2
34	3	26	1
32	1	25	1
31	5	20	1
30	4		

   Find the 95% and 99% confidence intervals for μ.
4. 137 rats are food deprived for 24 hours and their running time in a six-foot runway is recorded. The data are $\Sigma X = 1781$ seconds, $\Sigma X^2 = 25{,}345$. Test the hypothesis that $\mu = 11.5$ seconds.
5. A sample consisting of 30 pairs of identical twins is extracted from the population and one member of each pair is given an IQ test. The average score for the sample is 95.3 with a SD of 10.1. Assuming that the average IQ score for the population is 100, can you reject the null hypothesis? What is the 95% confidence interval for this sample?
6. Over a several year period, hundreds of rats have been subjected to damage to an area of the brain known as the septal region. One behavioral effect of this damage is that there is a tremendous increase in barpressing rate for positive reinforcement, with rats averaging around 500 responses in a twenty-minute period. An experimenter subjects a random sample of 22 rats to septal damage and tests them on a barpressing task. The results in terms of the number of presses in a twenty-minute period are $X = 487$ and SD = 75. Test the hypothesis that $\mu = 500$. In addition, find the 99% confidence interval for μ.
7. Briefly define the following terms:
   (a) power of a test
   (b) α error
   (c) β error
   (d) one-tailed test
8. How was the sampling distribution of means derived and what are its properties?

9. The brainstem auditory response latency for normal human males has been found to be 5.68 milliseconds. A random sample of 10 males is selected and each subject drinks an ounce of alcohol thirty minutes prior to a test for brainstem auditory response latency. The average latency is found to be 5.85 milliseconds with SD = .14. Test the hypothesis that the alcohol has no effect on average latency.

10. In the chapter, we discussed the derivation of the sampling distribution of means. Suppose we have a finite population consisting of the scores 1, 3, 5, and 7. All possible samples of size $N = 2$ have been extracted from it and are listed below.

1, 1	5, 1	3, 5	5, 5
1, 3	1, 7	5, 3	5, 7
3, 1	7, 1	3, 7	7, 5
1, 5	3, 3	7, 3	7, 7

From these samples construct the sampling distribution of means and show that the mean of the distribution is equal to μ. Also demonstrate that $\sigma_{\bar{x}} = \sigma/\sqrt{N}$.

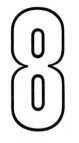

Significance of the Difference between Two Sample Means

Introduction

Chapter 7 presented the *t*-test as a means of evaluating the validity of a guess about the population mean on the basis of a sample value. The material to be discussed in this chapter is but an extension of what we reviewed in chapter 7. Rather than considering one sample extracted from a population at a time, we will consider two samples taken simultaneously. A simple experiment will help illustrate the task before us.

Sampling Distribution of the Differences between Sample Means

An experimenter wants to know whether or not alcohol ingestion affects digit span (number of digits that can be retained in memory for a brief period of time). A call for volunteers is made and 20 volunteers are randomly and equally assigned to either an alcohol group (Group AL) or to a nonalcohol, placebo group (Group PL). Each subject is given a drink consisting of cola plus either rum flavoring (Group PL) or an ounce of rum (Group AL). After thirty minutes each subject is given a simple digit-span test to determine their maximum digit span. The results are shown below.

Group AL	Group PL
5	7
6	7
7	8
4	6
4	7
3	7
5	8
7	5
7	6
6	7

The average digit span of subjects in Group PL was 6.8 (68 ÷ 10 = 6.8) while the people in Group AL didn't do as well ($\bar{X}$ = 54 ÷ 10 = 5.4). What would the results be if this experiment were repeated time after time with different subjects? Would the experimenter always (or almost always) find a larger digit span in Group PL or does the result obtained reflect merely a chance occurrence? Can we say, on the basis of this one experiment, that subjects in Group AL come from a different population (with a different mean) than subjects in Group PL?

independent samples

Let's leave our example for a while and look at the rationale on which a test of the difference between independent sample means is based. By *independent samples* we mean that the behavior of the members of one sample is not related to the behavior of subjects in the other sample. Practically speaking, we will assume that conditions for independence have been satisfied as long as subjects are selected at random from a large group and are assigned randomly to the different treatment conditions.

In chapter 7 to introduce the sampling distribution of means we first considered some population. From this population we drew single random samples all with the same size N, and from the means of these samples we constructed the sampling distribution of means. Suppose that instead of drawing single samples from the population, we draw *pairs* of random samples. As before, we calculate the mean for some behavioral measure for each sample, but this time we take the difference between the pair of sample means. For any pair of samples drawn at random from the same population, it is unlikely that each would have the same mean because of sampling error.

Now what do we have? We have a population from which we have drawn pairs of samples, we have the means that we have calculated for each sample of a pair, and we have the difference between the means for each pair of samples. We can now make a frequency distribution based on the differences between sample means and from this distribution plot a frequency polygon. The shape of the resulting polygon will be symmetrical, and, if the samples are large enough, will be approximately normal. The procedure up to this point is shown in figure 8–1.

Since the scores plotted along the baseline of the frequency polygon are differences between pairs of sample means, the distribution is called the sampling distribution of the differences. In chapter 7 we talked about three important properties of the sampling distribution of means. The sampling distribution of differences also has three important properties, two of which are the same as corre-

Step 1: Pairs of random samples are drawn from a population.

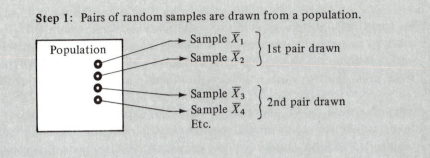

Step 2: The mean for some behavioral measure is found for each sample and the difference is found for each pair of samples.

$\overline{X}$ of 1st sample		$\overline{X}$ of 2nd sample		Difference
$\overline{X}_1$	$-$	$\overline{X}_2$	$=$	d_1
$\overline{X}_3$	$-$	$\overline{X}_4$	$=$	d_2
$\cdot$		$\cdot$		$\cdot$
$\cdot$		$\cdot$		$\cdot$
$\cdot$		$\cdot$		$\cdot$

Step 3: The frequency polygon of the difference scores has been plotted.

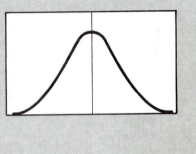

Figure 8–1: Illustration of the development of the sampling distribution of differences.

sponding properties of the sampling distribution of means. But to begin, let's discuss the one that is different.

In the previous chapter, we saw that the mean of the sampling distribution of means was equal to the population mean or μ. The mean of the sampling distribution of differences, on the other hand, is *zero*. Why is this?

Remember that all samples are assumed to be drawn from the same population. Because of sampling error we would expect that in some cases the mean of the first sample of a pair chosen would be larger than the second mean and the difference between them would be positive, while in other cases the mean of the second sample would be the larger so that the difference would be negative. Then, when the mean of all the differences was calculated, the result would be zero. If this is not convincing to you, let me try another approach.

Suppose we look only at the frequency distribution of the means of the first sample from each pair of samples taken from the population, that is, all the ones labeled X_1, X_3, X_5, etc., from figure 8–1. If we plotted the frequency polygon based on these sample means, it would be the sampling distribution of means and its mean would be equal to the population mean or μ. Continuing, suppose that we next look only at the means of the second sample of each pair; that is, X_2, X_4, X_6, and so forth. Again the mean of the frequency distribution made of these sample means would be equal to the population mean, which would also be μ since the samples were taken from the same population as before. However, we have been considering differences between sample means and the sampling distribution of the differences the mean of which is $\mu - \mu = 0$.

The remaining properties of the sampling distribution of differences are concerned with the shape of the distribution and are the same as corresponding properties of the sampling distribution of means. Thus, the larger the size of the samples chosen from the population, the closer the sampling distribution of differences approximates the normal curve. Additionally, the larger the size of the samples drawn from the population, the smaller the standard deviation of the sampling distribution of differences will be. The standard deviation of the new distribution is called *the standard error of the differences* and is symbolized by $\sigma_{\overline{X}_1 - \overline{X}_2}$ (pronounced sigma sub X-bar sub 1 minus X-bar sub 2).

This last property (that is, that the standard error of the differences decreases with increases in sample size) may be appreciated if you consider that the larger the size of each sample, the closer the mean of the sample will be to the population mean. In turn, the closer the mean of each sample of a pair of samples is to the population value, the closer the sample means will be to each other. If the means of a pair of samples are close to each other, then the difference between their means will be small (i.e., close to zero) and their variability around the mean of the sampling distribution of means will be diminished.

Although we can talk about it in theory, in reality we will not be able to determine the standard error of the differences. Fortunately, however, we can estimate it with $s_{\overline{X}_1 - \overline{X}_2}$ which we will call the *estimated standard error of the differences*. The defining formula is:

$$s_{\overline{X}_1 - \overline{X}_2} = \sqrt{s^2_{\overline{X}_1} + s^2_{\overline{X}_2} - 2rs_{\overline{X}_1}s_{\overline{X}_2}}$$

As in chapter 7, $s_{\overline{X}}$ is the estimated standard error of the means for which the formula is $SD/\sqrt{N - 1}$. The only unfamiliar term in the equation is r which is the symbol for something called a correlation coefficient. The correlation coefficient, r, is a measure of the degree of relationship between scores in a pair of samples. Since we assumed that the pairs of samples are independent, there is no relationship between them and r becomes zero. With this the final term in the equation $(-2rs_{\bar{x}_1}s_{\bar{x}_2})$ drops out leaving:

$$s_{\bar{x}_1-\bar{x}_2} = \sqrt{s^2_{\bar{x}_1}+s^2_{\bar{x}_2}}$$

This last equation is the defining equation for $s_{\bar{x}_1} - \bar{x}_2$ for independent samples. Unfortunately, the equation can only be used if the samples have equal N's. For this reason I will introduce a computational formula that can be used with equal or unequal N's. The computational or raw score formula is:

$$s_{\bar{x}_1} - \bar{x}_2 = \sqrt{\left(\frac{N_1SD_1^2 + N_2SD_2^2}{N_1 + N_2 - 2}\right)\left(\frac{1}{N_1} + \frac{1}{N_2}\right)}$$

where N_1 and N_2 are the number of subjects in the first and second samples, respectively. The variances of each sample are symbolized by SD_1^2 and SD_2^2.

We are now in a position to determine whether or not two sample means differ significantly, that is, come from different populations with different means. We can do this in the same way that we tested hypotheses about μ in chapter 7. As you will recall, we first determined how far away from the guessed μ the sample mean was in $s_{\bar{x}}$ units. In other words, we computed a t-score and then looked in table B to see if the computed t was larger in absolute value than the values of t known to cut off the deviant 5% and 1% of the distribution of t-scores for samples of a given size which was converted to df. If so, we rejected the hypothesis that our sample was drawn from a population in which μ had the value we had guessed.

The hypothesis testing procedure is the same when we are considering pairs of samples rather than only one at a time. Again, the first step will be to determine how far our observed difference in sample means deviates from the mean of the sampling distribution of differences in $s_{\bar{x}_1-\bar{x}_2}$ units. In other words, we will compute a t-score just as we did in the previous chapter. The equation for t is just another variation on the basic formula for a standard score or a z-score.

A z-score in chapter 6 was defined as the deviation of a raw score from the mean in standard deviation units. Applying this definition to the sampling distribution of differences, the formula for z would be:

$$z = \frac{(\bar{X}_1 - \bar{X}_2) - (\mu_1 - \mu_2)}{\sigma_{\bar{X}_1-\bar{X}_2}}$$

Thus, $(\bar{X}_1 - \bar{X}_2)$ is the designation of a score in the sampling distribution of differences. Similarly, the mean of the distribution could be symbolized by $(\mu_1 - \mu_2)$, and we have said that one of the properties of the distribution is that the mean is zero so that $\mu_1 - \mu_2 = 0$. Finally, the standard deviation of the sampling distribution of differences is the standard error of the differences or $\sigma_{\bar{X}_1 - \bar{X}_2}$.

Since we cannot determine $\sigma_{\bar{X}_1 - \bar{X}_2}$, we use $s_{\bar{X}_1 - \bar{X}_2}$ to estimate it. Substituting this value into the equation for z gives us

$$t = \frac{(\bar{X}_1 - \bar{X}_2) - (\mu_1 - \mu_2)}{s_{\bar{X}_1 - \bar{X}_2}}$$

Since $\mu_1 - \mu_2 = 0$, the equation for t is normally written:

$$t = \frac{\bar{X}_1 - \bar{X}_2}{s_{\bar{X}_1 - \bar{X}_2}}$$

After a t-score is computed, it is compared with the table values known to cut off the deviant 5% and 1% of the distribution of t-scores for samples of given sizes (converted to df). Now that we have discussed how the t-test is going to be performed, let's go back to the original problem, calculate t, and determine whether or not the samples were drawn from the same population.

Computation of t

For our first problem let's reconsider the example used to begin the discussion of the sampling distribution of the differences. The data from our placebo and alcohol groups are:

Group AL	Group PL
5	7
6	7
7	8
4	6
4	7
3	7
5	8
7	5
7	6
6	7

The formula for *t* is:

$$t = \frac{\overline{X}_1 - \overline{X}_2}{s_{\overline{X}_1} - \overline{X}_2} = \frac{\overline{X}_1 - \overline{X}_2}{\sqrt{\left(\dfrac{N_1 SD_1^2 + N_2 SD_2^2}{N_1 + N_2 - 2}\right)\left(\dfrac{1}{N_1} + \dfrac{1}{N_2}\right)}}$$

Analyzing the formula, we see that we need the following values: $\overline{X}_1$, $\overline{X}_2$, N_1, SD_1^2, and SD_2^2. Earlier in the chapter I said that $\overline{X}_1$ was 5.4 and that $\overline{X}_2 = 6.8$. Additionally, N_1 and N_2 are both equal to 10. Thus, all we need to find is the variance of each sample. The computational formula for the variance is:

$$SD^2 = \frac{\Sigma X^2}{N} - \overline{X}^2$$

The variance of Group AL is 1.84 while that of Group PL is 0.76. Computation of these two values is shown below.

Group AL:

$$\Sigma X_1^2 = 5^2 + 6^2 + \ldots + 6^2 = 310$$

$$SD^2 = \frac{\Sigma X^2}{N} - \overline{X}^2 = \frac{310}{10} - 5.4^2 = 31 - 29.16 = 1.84$$

Group PL:

$$\Sigma X_2^2 = 7^2 + 7^2 + \ldots + 7^2 = 470$$

$$SD^2 = \frac{470}{10} - 6.8^2 = 47 - 46.24 = 0.76$$

We now have everything we need to calculate *t* and filling in the equation we have:

$$t = \frac{\overline{X}_1 - \overline{X}_2}{\sqrt{\left(\dfrac{N_1 SD_1^2 + N_2 SD_2^2}{N_1 + N_2 - 2}\right)\left(\dfrac{1}{N_1} + \dfrac{1}{N_2}\right)}}$$

$$= \frac{5.4 - 6.8}{\sqrt{\left(\dfrac{10 \cdot 1.84 + 10 \cdot 0.76}{10 + 10 - 2}\right)\left(\dfrac{1}{10} + \dfrac{1}{10}\right)}}$$

$$t = \frac{-1.4}{\sqrt{\left(\dfrac{18.4 + 7.6}{18}\right)(0.1 + 0.1)}} = \frac{-1.4}{\sqrt{\left(\dfrac{26}{18}\right)(0.2)}}$$

$$t = \frac{-1.4}{\sqrt{(1.44)(0.2)}} = \frac{-1.4}{\sqrt{0.288}} = \frac{-1.4}{0.54} = -2.59$$

What we have found is that a difference in sample means as large as we observed is 2.59 standard error units away from a mean of zero. Can we reject the null hypothesis or not? What is the null hypothesis? The null hypothesis in this case is that both samples were drawn from the same population and that the mean of the sampling distribution of differences is zero. This is often symbolized by H_0: $\mu_1 - \mu_2 = 0$.

In order to use appendix table B containing critical values of t, we need to know what df is. For single samples such as we considered in the last chapter, we said that $df = N - 1$. For pairs of independent samples, the degrees of freedom are $N - 1$ for each sample giving us $(N_1 - 1) + (N_2 - 1) = N_1 + N_2 - 2$ which is part of the denominator of the t-ratio. For our particular example, $df = 10 + 10 - 2 = 18$ and the critical values of t from table B are 2.1009 at the 5% level and 2.8784 at the 1% level. Thus, for $df = 18$ t-scores of ± 2.1009 cut off the deviant 5% of the distribution of t-scores, while scores of ± 2.8784 cut off the deviant 1% for a two-tailed test.

The t-ratio we observed was -2.59 which in absolute value is larger than the table value required for significance (for rejection of H_0) at the 5% level but is less than the value required for rejection at the 1% level. We conclude, therefore, that the probability is less than 0.05 of obtaining a difference in sample means as large as we observed if the samples were both drawn from the same population. In other words, there is a significant difference between the groups, and digit span is lowered by alcohol consumption.

One-tailed versus Two-tailed Tests

Although I mentioned one-tailed and two-tailed tests in chapter 7 when I introduced appendix table B, I didn't really go into much detail at that time and, in fact, suggested or implied that most tests of significance were two-tailed tests. This section should clarify the issue.

two-tailed test   A *two-tailed test* is one that considers both ends of the distribution, whether it is the normal curve distribution, the distribution of t, or whatever. With a two-tailed test we have made no predictions concerning the direction of the difference in means. That is, a negative t-score was considered just as unlikely as the corresponding positive value since we were considering both ends of the distribution. In summary, then, a two-tailed test is one where we look at both tails of the distribution, and where we are not required to make any guesses about possible outcomes prior to beginning the experiment.

There are some situations, however, in which we can make a prediction about the possible outcome of an experiment prior to conducting it. For example, suppose a researcher wants to do a study to determine the effects of marijuana on time estimation. On the basis of anecdotal evidence and previous research, the experimenter decides that he can predict the direction of the experiment's outcome and he states at the outset that he expects to find that users overestimate the passage of time. In this case he would be able to employ a one-tailed test.

The *one-tailed test* only considers one end of the distribution—   one-tailed test
the end predicted by the experimenter on the basis of previous research, anecdotal evidence, intuition, logic, or whatever. Since only one end or tail of the distribution is considered, the one-tailed test is a more powerful test if the prediction comes true and if the experimental result is in the appropriate direction. By more powerful, I mean that it will be easier for the experimenter to reject the null hypothesis, i.e., the value required for significance in the table will be lower for the one-tailed test than it will be for the two-tailed test at the same level of significance. For example, with infinite *df* the critical value of *t* at the 5% level for a one-tailed test is 1.64, while the corresponding value for a two-tailed test is 1.96.

There is a danger associated with using the one-tailed test, however. Since you must make some prediction prior to the experiment, if the difference between means is very large and is in the *opposite* direction to your prediction, you will conclude that it is not significant with the one-tailed test where it might have been significant with a two-tailed test. For this reason and also because experimenters tend to acknowledge a rationale for the one-tailed test *after* the data are all in, many people caution against the use of the one-tailed test for any reason. My position is that often an experimenter is able that the use of the more sensitive test is warranted. If you can legitimately apply a one-tailed test to your data, use the probability values for the one-tailed test shown in the table of significant values of *t*.

Another Example of the Use of the *t*-Test for Independent Samples

Suppose we want to determine whether or not females do better than males on a test that involves mainly verbal skills. To do this let's say that we have given 37 students (17 males and 20 females) a test in which they are asked to unscramble 20 sentences within a ten-minute time period. Each student receives a score based on the number of sentences she or he can correctly unscramble within the allotted period. The frequency distributions are as follows:

Males		Females	
X	f	X	f
11	3	15	2
10	1	14	2
9	3	13	3
8	4	11	4
6	2	10	2
5	1	9	3
4	2	8	2
2	1	6	1
		3	1

As before the first thing we should do is to write the formula and study it to see what we have to calculate. We have:

$$t = \frac{\bar{X}_1 - \bar{X}_2}{\sqrt{\left(\dfrac{N_1 \text{SD}_1^2 + N_2 \text{SD}_2^2}{N_1 + N_2 - 2}\right)\left(\dfrac{1}{N_1} + \dfrac{1}{N_2}\right)}}$$

Again we need to know six things: N_1, N_2, $\bar{X}_1$, $\bar{X}_2$, SD_1^2, and SD_2^2. The N's are found by summing the numbers in the frequency column, and the N for males is 17 while for females it is 20. The formula for the mean is $\Sigma fX/N$ and for the sample variance is $\Sigma fX^2/N - \bar{X}^2$. In order to compute the means and variances we need to know ΣfX and ΣfX^2.

Males				Females			
X_1	f	fX_1	fX_1^2	X_2	f	fX_2	fX_2^2
11	3	33	363	15	2	30	450
10	1	10	100	14	2	28	392
9	3	27	243	13	3	39	507
8	4	32	256	11	4	44	484
6	2	12	72	10	2	20	200
5	1	5	25	9	3	27	243
4	2	8	32	8	2	16	128
2	1	2	4	6	1	6	36
	17	129	1095	3	1	3	9
					20	213	2449

The means and variances are computed below.

Male:

$$\bar{X}_1 = \frac{\Sigma f X_1}{N} = \frac{129}{17} = 7.59$$

$$SD_1^2 = \frac{\Sigma f X_1^2}{N} - \bar{X}_1^2 = \frac{1095}{17} - 7.59^2 = 64.41 - 57.61 = 6.8$$

Female:

$$\bar{X}_2 = \frac{\Sigma f X_2}{N} = \frac{213}{20} = 10.65$$

$$SD_2^2 = \frac{\Sigma f X_2^2}{N} - \bar{X}_2^2 = \frac{2449}{20} - 10.65^2 = 122.45 - 113.42 = 9.03$$

We now have all the values needed to compute the t-score and we find that:

$$t = \frac{7.59 - 10.65}{\sqrt{\left(\dfrac{17 \cdot 6.8 + 20 \cdot 9.03}{17 + 20 - 2}\right)\left(\dfrac{1}{17} + \dfrac{1}{20}\right)}}$$

$$= \frac{-3.06}{\sqrt{\left(\dfrac{115.6 + 180.6}{35}\right)(.06 + .05)}}$$

$$= \frac{-3.06}{\sqrt{\left(\dfrac{296.2}{35}\right)(.11)}} = \frac{-3.06}{\sqrt{(8.46)(.11)}} = \frac{-3.06}{\sqrt{.93}} = \frac{-3.06}{.96} = -3.19$$

with $df = N_1 + N_2 - 2 = 17 + 20 - 2 = 35$

The minus value obtained for t tells us that the mean of the first group (males) was smaller than that for the second group (females). Since we will be using a two-tailed test, we are interested in the absolute value of the t-score in our comparison with table values. Thus, for the two-tailed test it really doesn't matter whether the t-score is positive or not; the sign simply tells us the direction of the difference in sample means.

If we had predicted at the outset of the experiment that females would perform better than males and we had listed the males as group number 1, then for a one-tailed test the t-score would have to be negative. Under these conditions a positive t could never be significant no matter how large it was.

Looking in appendix table B for the critical values of *t* when *df* = 35, we see that 2.0301 is required for significance at the 5% level while 2.7238 is required at the 1% level. Since the *t*-score we computed of −3.19 is larger in absolute value than either of the table values, we can reject the null hypothesis that the two samples were drawn from the same population and say that the outcome we observed has a probability less than 0.01. We conclude from these results that females in fact are superior when it comes to rearranging scrambled sentences.

Checking Your Progress

Suppose you are given 20 rats. You subject half of them to damage to the VMH and give the other half control operations. (The VMH or ventromedial hypothalamus is a tiny area of the brain called by some physiological psychologists the satiety center because damage to the structure usually results in dramatic weight gain.) After two weeks you weigh all subjects and obtain the following weights in grams:

Group VMH	Group CO
437	383
455	355
483	313
392	410
455	289
469	344
513	418
452	400
444	344
410	310

Determine whether or not the brain damage had an effect on weight. The correct answer for *t* is 5.28, which for *df* = 18 is significant ($p < .01$).

Assumptions of the Two Sample *t*-Test

Although I have not previously mentioned it, in order to use the *t* distribution for tests of significance between means, two assumptions must be made. First, we must assume that the populations from which we drew our samples are normal. Second, we must assume that the population variances are homogeneous, that is, that $\sigma_1^2 = \sigma_2^2$, where σ_1^2 and σ_2^2 are the variances of the two populations from which we are sampling.

Fortunately, both assumptions can apparently be violated with little effect upon the conclusions made from the *t*-test. Of the two assumptions, the first is considered less important than the second. As long as sample sizes are fairly large, even large deviations from normality seem to make little difference in the conclusions. For this reason, if you have reason to suspect that the population distributions are badly skewed, you should use large samples in your experiment.

The assumption of homogeneity of variance is considered more important, however. In fact, in some texts a test for homogeneity of variance is presented and is performed prior to computation of *t*. However, most modern authorities agree that such a test is not worth the effort involved. As long as samples of equal size are used, relatively great departure from homogeneity will have little effect upon conclusions drawn from the *t*-test. The moral is: if in doubt about homogeneity, use samples of equal size.

Dependent Samples and the *t*-Test

At the beginning of this chapter the sampling distribution of the differences was constructed by extracting pairs of random samples from a population. Further, the assumption was made that the pairs were independent (unrelated) to each other. Let's consider how the sampling distribution of differences might differ if, instead of having independent samples, our samples were dependent or related to each other. For example, we might be selecting wife-husband pairs or pairs of siblings from the population and then assigning the members of each pair randomly to one or the other of our pair of samples.

Earlier we found that the sampling distribution of differences was composed of difference scores between pairs of sample means. People who are related to each other (husband-wife pairs, siblings, for example) are likely to be more similar to each other on a variety of behavioral characteristics than are two individuals selected from the population at random. The result of this greater relatedness between related samples is that the difference in means will tend to be smaller than differences between means of independent samples. Since the scores that make up the sampling distribution of differences for related samples are relatively small, they will be closer to the mean of the distribution which we said earlier was zero. Thus, the scores deviate less from the mean with related samples. The major difference with the sampling distribution of differences between related samples is that the standard deviation of the distribution ($\sigma_{\overline{X}_1-\overline{X}_2}$, which is estimated by $s_{\overline{X}_1-\overline{X}_2}$) is smaller.

Since the t-ratio consists of the difference between sample means divided by $s_{\overline{X}_1-\overline{X}_2}$, the relatively small value of the denominator results in a relatively large value for t and makes rejection of the null hypothesis more likely. This, then, is one of the main reasons for using matched or related samples in an experiment; it decreases the standard error of the differences and results in a larger t-score.

The equation for the t-test with related samples is the same as it was for independent samples:

$$t = \frac{\overline{X}_1 - \overline{X}_2}{s_{\overline{X}_1-\overline{X}_2}}, \text{ where } s_{\overline{X}_1-\overline{X}_2} = \sqrt{s_{\overline{X}_1} + s_{\overline{X}_2} - 2rs_{\overline{X}_1}s_{\overline{X}_2}}$$

This formula for the estimated standard error of the differences was introduced at the beginning of the chapter with the discussion of the t-test for independent samples. At that time we found that the last portion of the equation ($-2rs_{\overline{X}_1}s_{\overline{X}_2}$) drops out, since r is assumed to be zero with independent samples. With dependent samples, however, r is not zero and the estimated standard error is reduced by the amount of $-2rs_{\overline{X}_1}s_{\overline{X}_2}$. Actually, computation of the t-ratio for dependent samples is quite tedious using the formula introduced so far, and, for this reason, a technique known as the direct difference method will be introduced.

Direct Difference Method

In order to discuss the *direct difference method,* let's consider a specific example of a type of problem for which the t-test for dependent samples would be relevant. In the example, another case is presented in which the use of the t-test for dependent samples would be appropriate. This is the situation where we have the same individuals subjected to each of two treatments.

A pharmaceutical company hires a psychologist to test the effectiveness of Kilpain, a new pain killer they have manufactured. The experimenter decides to test the analgesic or pain-reducing effect of Kilpain on a pain other than headache. The pain is produced by instructing subjects to keep their hands immersed in a pail of icewater. The response measure or dependent variable is the length of time that each subject can tolerate the immersion.

A group of 12 persons is selected at random—half receive a

dose of Kilpain; the other half, a placebo. After a delay of ten minutes to allow the drug to take effect, each person is asked to place the preferred hand in the water and to keep it there until the pain becomes unbearable. The next day, the subjects return to be tested again, but this time they receive the drug other than the one they were given for the first test. Thus, each subject receives both drugs but the order of presentation has been varied in order to rule out the possibility that the order of presenting the drugs affects the results. A double-blind technique of drug presentation is employed; that is, neither the administrator nor the subject know which drug is being given prior to a particular test.

The results of the experiment are as follows:

Subject No.	Kilpain (time in sec.)	Placebo (time in sec.)
1	60	45
2	20	15
3	47	49
4	63	50
5	53	56
6	90	70
7	76	55
8	28	14
9	90	65
10	16	10
11	32	16
12	86	57

We have 12 pairs of scores. To use the direct difference method we first subtract the second of the pair of scores from the first and call this the difference (D). All further calculations are based on the differences between each pair of scores rather than on the scores themselves.

The formula for the *t*-ratio for the direct difference method is $t = \bar{X}_D/s_{\bar{X}_D}$ which you should read as the mean of the differences divided by the estimated standard error of the differences. The mean of the differences or $\bar{X}_D$ is defined as the *algebraic* sum of the differences divided by the number of pairs of scores or N. By algebraic sum of the differences I simply mean that you must remember to take the sign of the difference into account when summing. The estimated standard error of the differences is found by computing

$s_{\bar{X}_D} = SD_D/\sqrt{N-1}$, where SD_D is the standard deviation of the differences. Actually, $\bar{X}_D$ is equivalent to $\bar{X}_1 - \bar{X}_2$ and

$$s_{\bar{X}_D} = s_{\bar{X}_1-\bar{X}_2} = \sqrt{s_{\bar{X}_1}^2 + s_{\bar{X}_2}^2 - 2rs_{\bar{X}_1}s_{\bar{X}_2}}$$

Substituting

$$\frac{SD_D}{\sqrt{N-1}} \text{ for } s_{\bar{X}_D}$$

in the formula for t and simplifying leads us to the following equation for the t-score:

$$t = \frac{\bar{X}_D \sqrt{N-1}}{SD_D}$$

Now that the equation for t has been described, we can go back to our original problem, find the difference scores, and from them determine the mean and standard deviation of the differences. This has been done below.

Subject No.	Kilpain (time in sec.)	Placebo (time in sec.)	Difference (D)	D²
1	60	45	15	225
2	20	15	5	25
3	47	49	−2	4
4	63	50	13	169
5	53	56	−3	9
6	90	70	20	400
7	76	55	21	441
8	28	14	14	196
9	90	65	25	625
10	16	10	6	36
11	32	16	16	256
12	86	57	29	841
			159	3227

$$\bar{X}_D = \frac{\Sigma D}{N} = \frac{159}{12} = 13.25$$

$$SD_D = \sqrt{\frac{\Sigma D^2}{N} - \bar{X}_D^2} = \sqrt{\frac{3227}{12} - 13.25^2} = \sqrt{268.92 - 175.56}$$

$$= \sqrt{93.36} = 9.66$$

Inserting the values of $\overline{X}_D$ and SD_D into the equation for t gives us:

$$t = \frac{\overline{X}_D \sqrt{N-1}}{SD_D} = \frac{13.25 \sqrt{12-1}}{9.66} = \frac{13.25 \sqrt{11}}{9.66} = \frac{13.25(3.32)}{9.66}$$

$$= \frac{43.99}{9.66} = 4.55, \text{ with } df = N - 1 = 12 - 1 = 11$$

With $df = 11$, the values of t that cut off the deviant 5% and 1% are 2.2010 and 3.1058, respectively. Our computed t-score is 4.55 which is much larger than either of the critical table values. Therefore, we reject the null hypothesis that both groups come from the same population and conclude that Kilpain is significantly more effective than a placebo in the treatment of a pain other than headache.

Another example may be instructive. To fulfill the requirements for a class in experimental psychology, 10 students are given a one-minute test on a mirror-tracing task in which the knowledge they receive concerning their efforts comes from their mirror reflection. A comparison is made of the average time spent in accurately tracing a star with the preferred and nonpreferred hands. The results of the experiment are shown below. The experimental question is whether or not the hand used affects the accuracy of mirror tracing.

Student	Preferred Hand (ave. time in sec.)	Nonpreferred Hand (ave. time in sec.)	D	D²
John	35	37	−2	4
Mary	22	18	4	16
Doug	43	32	11	121
Bill	15	17	−2	4
Ann	31	25	6	36
Nancy	25	29	−4	16
Karen	38	31	7	49
Mike	26	29	−3	9
Jack	33	33	0	0
Harold	10	5	5	25
			22	280

$$\overline{X}_D = \frac{\Sigma D}{N} = \frac{22}{10} = 2.2$$

$$SD_D = \sqrt{\frac{\Sigma D^2}{N} - \overline{X}_D^2} = \sqrt{\frac{280}{10} - 2.2^2} = \sqrt{28 - 4.84}$$

$$= \sqrt{23.16} = 4.81$$

$$t = \frac{\overline{X}_D \sqrt{N - 1}}{SD_D} = \frac{2.2 \sqrt{10 - 1}}{4.81} = \frac{2.2 \sqrt{9}}{4.81} = \frac{2.2(3)}{4.81} = \frac{6.6}{4.81}$$

$$= 1.37.$$

with $df = N - 1 = 10 - 1 = 9$

  With $df = 9$ the values of t required for significance are 2.2622 and 3.2498 at the 5% and 1% levels, respectively. Since the obtained value ($t = 1.37$) is less than 2.2622 we cannot reject the null hypothesis. Thus, from this study at least there is no evidence that the hand that is used in mirror tracing has an effect on accuracy.

Checking Your Progress

Ten pairs of individuals, matched as carefully as possible in terms of age, sex, smoking habits, drug usage, education, IQ, etc., have been given exposure to either marijuana or a placebo in the form of cookies and then tested after thirty minutes on a simple task. The task consists of crossing out all of the letters "a" on a sheet of paper containing a random assortment of letters. The number of errors, letters not crossed out, made by each subject in a two-minute test is shown below. Compute a t-score by the direct difference method and test it for significance.

Pair	Marijuana	Placebo
1	15	12
2	13	14
3	16	13
4	22	16
5	8	7
6	13	10
7	12	14
8	9	7
9	5	4
10	6	3

The correct answer is $t = 2.64$ which for $df = 9$ is significant ($p < .05$).

Summary

This chapter has discussed a technique that allows us to make a comparison of the results from two independent samples and from two dependent samples. The technique is called the *t-test,* and the null hypothesis tested is that the two samples come from the same population. If the value of *t* that we calculate is very unlikely (assuming the two samples come from the same population), then we reject this assumption and conclude that the samples probably come from different populations with different means.

The computational formula for the *t*-test based on independent (unrelated) samples is:

$$t = \frac{\overline{X}_1 - \overline{X}_2}{s_{\overline{X}_1 - \overline{X}_2}}, \text{ where}$$

$$s_{\overline{X}_1 - \overline{X}_2} = \sqrt{\left(\frac{N_1 SD_1^2 + N_2 SD_2^2}{N_1 + N_2 - 2}\right)\left(\frac{1}{N_1} + \frac{1}{N_2}\right)}$$

The means of the first and second samples are denoted by $\overline{X}_1$ and $\overline{X}_2$, respectively. N_1 and N_2 are the numbers of subjects in the first and second samples and SD_1^2 and SD_2^2 are the variances of the first and second samples, respectively. For the test of significance the obtained value of *t* is compared with the table values using the appropriate degrees of freedom $(N_1 + N_2 - 2)$ and if found to be larger in absolute value, the null hypothesis is rejected.

For matched or dependent samples, the *t*-ratio may be computed from the following formula: $t = \overline{X}_D \sqrt{N - 1}/SD_D$ where $\overline{X}_D$ is the mean of the differences between each pair of scores. The mean is determined by summing algebraically the differences and dividing by the number of pairs of scores or *N*. In addition, $SD_D = \sqrt{\Sigma D^2/N - \overline{X}_D^2}$. The *t*-score obtained by the direct difference method is compared with table values with $df = N - 1$.

A brief discussion was presented in the chapter of the difference between *one-tailed* and *two-tailed tests of significance*. If the direction of the difference in means can be predicted before the data have been collected for an experiment, then the one-tailed test is appropriate and is a more powerful test than the two-tailed test since only one tail of the sampling distribution of means or differences is considered. With the two-tailed test, however, both ends of the distribution are considered.

Two assumptions for the two sample *t*-test are that the populations from which the samples are taken are normally distributed and that the variances of the population are homogeneous. Both assumptions may be violated with little effect on the conclusions drawn with the t-test.

Troubleshooting Your Computations

In this chapter we have considered two methods for comparing sample means. One method was used when the samples were considered to be independent (unrelated) of each other, while the other was used with related samples. When choosing the form of the t-test to apply, you must be careful to select the one appropriate to your data. If you have collected data on matched pairs or on husband-wife pairs or you are comparing two behaviors from the same individuals, the t-test for dependent samples will be appropriate. On the other hand, if your subjects have been selected at random from a population and randomly assigned to the two groups, you will want to analyze their data with the t-test for independent samples.

    Because of the complexity of the computational formula for the t-test for independent samples, a number of errors can be made. For example, occasionally students compute $s_{\bar{X}_1 - \bar{X}_2}$ and report its value for t. Additionally, be sure that the value under the square root sign for $s_{\bar{X}_1 - \bar{X}_2}$ is positive. A negative value under the radical indicates a gross computational error.

    Don't forget about the term $1/N_1 + 1/N_2$ in the formula for $s_{\bar{X}_1 - \bar{X}_2}$. Some students omit it entirely. My suggestion for computing it is to first change the fractions to decimals and then add.

    Be sure that the final t-score you derive has the correct sign. It's easy to lose the negative sign in the last few steps, so be careful. Remember that, if the mean of the first group is smaller than the mean of the second group, t will be negative.

    In computing the t-score for dependent samples, remember that all computations are performed on the difference scores rather than on the raw scores themselves. Adding the difference scores algebraically causes difficulties for students weak in algebra. One check on the accuracy of your computation of $\bar{X}_D$ is to compute $\bar{X}_1$ and $\bar{X}_2$ and find the difference between them. It should be $\bar{X}_D$.

Exercises

1. An experiment was performed to measure the effect of radiation upon running speed in rats. Twenty rats were randomly selected from an animal colony and arbitrarily assigned to a radiation group or to a control group. The time taken to run from one end of a six-foot runway to the other was measured for each animal following manipulation of the independent variable. The results were as follows:

Group Radiation (time in sec.)	Group Nonradiation (time in sec.)
10	13
15	8
13	14
5	11
27	8
7	7
16	2
20	2
21	17
13	5

Determine whether or not the groups differ significantly. Give the table values required for significance.

2. The members of 13 wife-husband pairs were randomly assigned to one of two treatment conditions. One group learned a list of nonsense syllables while a tape of a speech by former President A was playing. The second group learned the same list of syllables while a tape of a speech by President B was playing. The results in terms of the number of presentations of the list prior to an error-less recital were as follows:

Wife-Husband Pair No.	Group A	Group B
1	26	23
2	13	16
3	10	6
4	24	19
5	24	25
6	25	21
7	23	25
8	20	17
9	16	17
10	13	5
11	15	10
12	19	15
13	22	20

Determine which president's speech was more distracting and whether or not the difference is significant. Give table values required for significance.

3. Forty students are randomly selected from a large introductory psychology class. Half of the students view a five-minute segment of film taken from the movie *Jaws* which shows a man being eaten by a shark (Group A) while the other half watch a five-minute scene from the same movie in which three men get boisterously drunk (Group B). After seeing the film strips, each student is given a foam bat and placed into a room with a humanoid dummy. They are told to hit the dummy as much as they want as part of a study on the effectiveness of aggressive therapy. The number of blows administered in a five-minute period are recorded.

Group A		Group B	
X	f	X	f
37	1	25	1
35	2	23	3
34	3	22	2
30	2	21	5
27	4	19	4
22	3	18	2
19	2	17	2
18	3	10	1

Compare the two groups in terms of the aggressiveness displayed.

4. A group of 10 rats is first trained on a brightness discrimination task to a criterion of 9 correct responses in 10 trials. Following this the same animals are trained on a pattern discrimination task to the same criterion. Compare the groups to see if one task was easier to learn than the other. Scores shown are the number of errors made prior to achieving the criterion.

Rat No.	Brightness Discrimination	Pattern Discrimination
1	22	14
2	16	8
3	10	5
4	15	7
5	25	13
6	33	15
7	8	10
8	26	15
9	18	11
10	13	14

Why do you think that the pattern discrimination would be easier to learn than the brightness discrimination in this experiment?

5. Ten people learned two lists of nonsense syllables. Both lists were of equal difficulty. Test to see whether the order of learning had an effect on the number of trials to learn.

Person No.	List A	List B
1	13	8
2	11	12
3	15	10
4	7	4
5	10	7
6	16	14
7	4	5
8	9	5
9	9	6
10	8	9

6. An experimenter wants to see if marijuana will be of benefit to phobic patients. With the cooperation of a clinical psychologist, 12 females with extreme snake phobia are located and randomly assigned either to a group receiving the active ingredient of the marijuana plant or to a group receiving a portion of the plant that does not contain the active ingredient. The subjects are fully aware of the nature of the experiment but are ignorant of the group to which they have been assigned.

   The marijuana is administered in the form of a brownie and a double-blind control procedure is employed; that is, neither the subject nor the administrator of the cookie knows whether or not it contains the active ingredient. After a thirty-minute delay to allow the drug to have an effect, a Behavioral Avoidance Test is administered in which each subject approaches as closely as possible an aquarium containing a live snake. The floor in front of the aquarium is marked off in feet from the aquarium to the door of the room. Failure to enter the room results in a score of 10 feet. Each subject receives a score in feet indicating the closeness of her approach to the aquarium. Determine whether or not marijuana had an effect on snake phobia.

Group Inactive	Group Active
10	6
8	5
9	4
7	2
5	1
3	0

7. What are the assumptions for the two sample t-test? Why is so little space devoted to their discussion?
8. Using the definition of a z-score, demonstrate that the defining formula for a two sample t-test is just another variation on the basic formula for z.
9. A study is performed to determine brainstem auditory response latency as a function of alcohol ingestion. Using appropriate control procedures, 6 persons have had their auditory response latency measured both before and after alcohol intake. The results are:

Person No.	Before	After
1	5.80	5.90
2	5.88	6.05
3	5.38	5.64
4	5.40	5.58
5	5.90	6.05
6	5.71	5.87

   Determine whether or not alcohol ingestion affects auditory response latency.
10. Forty students are randomly assigned to two different groups. One group learns a list of nonsense syllables with high association value (each syllable elicits many associations) while the other group learns syllables with low association

value. The number of repetitions prior to an errorless criterion is recorded for each student. The results are:

High Association Value		Low Association Value	
No. of Repetitions	f	No. of Repetitions	f
23	1	35	1
21	3	33	2
20	2	31	1
19	3	28	3
18	5	25	4
16	1	22	1
15	2	21	1
14	1	20	3
10	1	18	2
8	1	17	2

Compare the groups.

9

One-Way Analysis of Variance

Introduction

In chapter 8, we used the *t*-test to compare the results from two samples in order to see if they differed significantly; that is, were drawn from different populations. As you probably realize, there are often occasions when we will want to compare more than two groups at a time. The most widely used test for this purpose in psychology is called the *analysis of variance* or sometimes just ANOVA (ANalysis Of VAriance). In this case, the name of the test is highly descriptive of what we are actually going to do. We are going to develop a way to analyze the variance in our experimental groups.

analysis of variance

Before introducing the actual ANOVA techniques, let's consider some possible experiments where the techniques would be appropriate. Physiological psychologists are often interested in the effects of different types of brain damage on the learning ability of rats. In a recent study, for example, I compared the abilities of rats with damage to the septal area of the brain with control animals and with animals that had had their olfactory bulbs removed. Thus, there were three groups: septals, olfactory bulb damaged, and controls. The *t*-test as discussed in the previous chapters is now inadequate to enable us to determine whether or not significant differences exist between the groups. While the *t*-test might be used, there are some good reasons not to apply it in cases such as this.

One reason not to apply the *t*-test is that computation of multiple *t*-tests would be very tedious. More importantly, the more tests you do on the same data, the more likely it becomes that you will get a spurious significant difference; that is, you will reject the null hypothesis when it is really true (Type-I error).

Many other illustrations exist of the need for a test to compare the results from more than two groups. For example, we might be interested in comparing different methods of teaching to determine which is most effective. Three methods we might want to compare are the traditional lecture approach, the totally self-paced method (the student is given a textbook, told what to read, and tested on the material read), and a self-paced method with weekly discussion sessions.

Another possibility is the clinical psychologist who wants to compare three or more different treatment techniques with phobic patients to see which is most effective in terms of the number of sessions to effect symptom removal. A psychopharmacologist might be interested in comparing the effectiveness of several different drugs in modifying behavior or perhaps in comparing the effectiveness of different dosages of the same drug. Without belaboring the point, the list of possible studies that might involve more than two groups is really endless.

Variability and the Sum of Squares

To begin the discussion of variability and the sum of squares, it should be helpful to introduce an actual example of the type of problem in which the techniques to be discussed in this chapter would be appropriate. Suppose that a clinical psychologist has reason to believe that certain psychoactive drugs (drugs known to have an effect on behavior) may be beneficial in the treatment of specific fears or phobias. To test this belief, the psychologist designs an experiment in which female patients are given one of three different substances baked into a cookie. The substances to be tested are: (1) an extract from the stems of the marijuana plant, (2) an extract from the flowers of the plant, and (3) LSD. The extract from the stems of the plant would be considered a placebo treatment since this portion of the plant does not contain the active ingredient.

Each subject in the experiment has been selected on the basis of her extreme fear of snakes as measured by the distance she maintains between herself and a live snake in an aquarium. Only those patients who will not approach nearer than 10 feet in a preliminary test are used in the study.

In the actual experiment each subject is given a cookie to eat which contains one of the three substances. Ten minutes later each subject is tested a second time for approach to the feared object. The distance she maintains between the snake and herself in this second test is the dependent variable. The data are:

Group Stems	Group Flowers	Group LSD
10	6	11
8	5	12
9	4	10

Group Stems	Group Flowers	Group LSD
7	2	10
5	1	9
3	0	9
42	18	61

The groups means are:

Group Stems

$$\overline{X} = \frac{\Sigma X}{N} = \frac{42}{6} = 7$$

Group Flowers

$$\overline{X} = \frac{18}{6} = 3$$

Group LSD

$$\overline{X} = \frac{61}{6} = 10.17$$

The total mean is $(42 + 18 + 61) \div 18 = 121 \div 18 = 6.72$.

Remember that we are interested in analyzing the variance in this chapter. What are the sources of variance in the data? To begin, we can immediately see that there is *variability within each group*. For example, in the Group Stems the mean is 7 but only one subject actually had this score with the rest of the group members deviating from the mean. We first considered the variability within a group back in the fifth chapter when we learned that it is based on the deviation between each score in a particular group and the mean of the group. This deviation is symbolized by $X - \overline{X}_g$, where $\overline{X}_g$ indicates the mean of each group.

Since the total mean ($\overline{X}_{tot}$) is 6.72, we can see that each of the group means deviates from it. We will call this source of variability in the data the *variability between groups*. The variability between groups is based on the deviation between each group mean and the total mean ($\overline{X}_g - \overline{X}_{tot}$).

Not only does each group mean deviate from the total mean, but also each score deviates from the total mean. This source of variability is called the *total variability* and is the sum of the variability between and within groups. Adding the expressions given for

variability within each group

variability between groups

total variability

the variability between and within groups we see that $(\overline{X}_g - \overline{X}_{tot}) + (X - \overline{X}_g) = X - \overline{X}_{tot} + \overline{X}_g - \overline{X}_g = X - \overline{X}_{tot}$. Thus, the total variability is based on the deviation between each score and the total mean $(X - \overline{X}_{tot})$.

In summary, we have seen that the total variability contained in two or more groups is the sum of the variability between each group and the variability within each group. The test of significance based on the analysis of variance considers which of the two sources of variability (between or within) contributes most to the total variability.

Let's suppose that we have selected three large samples from the *same* population. The distribution of scores based on measurement of some behavioral characteristic might resemble the graph shown in figure 9–1.

The variability between groups based on the deviation of each group mean from the total mean is small relative to the variability within each group. However, what about the situation where one or more of the samples is taken from *different* populations? Assuming that the variability within each group remains essentially the same as before, the variability between each group will be large relative to the within-group variability. A hypothetical illustration of this last point is shown in figure 9–2.

The test of significance based on the analysis of variance assesses the relative contribution of the two sources of variability,

Figure 9–1: Graph showing the degree of overlap of three samples drawn from the same population.

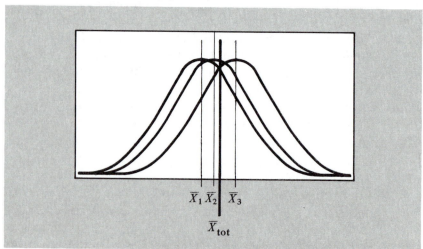

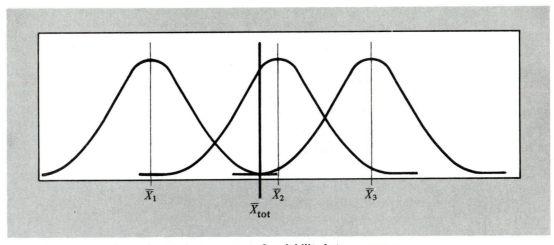

Figure 9–2: Graph illustrating the large amount of variability between groups when one or more of the groups come from different populations.

assuming that the samples all come from the same population. If this is true, then the ratio of the variability between groups to the variability within groups will be relatively small. However, if this is not true, then the ratio will be relatively large and we can conclude that the samples came from different populations. The question is, how do we measure the variability?

Part of the measure of variability involves what we call the *sum of squares,* which is very similar to a statistic we first encountered in chapter 5. We found in chapter 5 that the variance was the average squared deviation of each score from the mean or the sum of the squared deviations divided by the number of deviations or N. The defining formula for sample variance is $\Sigma(X - \overline{X})^2/N$. The numerator of sample variance is a sum of squares and is very similar to the sums of squares we are going to consider in this chapter.

Earlier I said that the total variability is based on the deviation between each score and the total mean. Thus, the *total sum of squares* is the sum of the squared deviation of each score about the total mean. The defining formula is:

total sum of squares

$$SS_{tot} = \Sigma(X - \overline{X}_{tot})^2$$

The similarity between the defining formula for the total sum of squares and the numerator of sample variance is striking.

Continuing, I said that the variability within each group is based on the deviation between each score in a group and the mean of the group. Thus, the *sum of squares within each group* is defined as the sum of the squared deviation of each score in a group from its group mean and the deviations are summed across groups. The defining formula is:

$$SS_w = \sum_g (X_g - \bar{X}_g)^2$$

Finally, we have the *sum of squares between groups* which is based on the deviation between each group mean and the total mean. The defining formula is:

$$SS_b = \sum_g N_g (\bar{X}_g - \bar{X}_{tot})^2$$

The equation for SS_b tells us to square the deviation between each group mean and the total mean, to multiply by the number of subjects in the particular group with which we are dealing, and to sum over groups.

As interesting as the defining formulas are, they are not the ones we will use to compute the sums of squares. Instead we will use computational or raw score formulas as before. To begin, the equation for the total sum of squares is:

$$SS_{tot} = \sum X^2 - \frac{(\sum X)^2}{N}$$

where X is a score and N is the total number of subjects in all groups combined. To calculate the total sum of squares, we first square each score and then add all these squared scores together ($\sum X^2$). Next we add all the scores, square this sum, and then divide by the total number of scores $[(\sum X)^2]/N$. Subtracting the last value from the first, we have the total sum of squares.

The computational formula for the within group sum of squares is:

$$SS_w = \sum_g \left[(\sum X_g^2) - \frac{(\sum X_g)^2}{N_g} \right]$$

This formula tells us to sum the squared scores within each group ($\sum X_g^2$), to subtract from the total the sum of the scores within a group squared and divided by the number of subjects within the group $[(\sum X_g)^2]/N_g$, and to sum the totals for each group.

The computational formula for the between group sum of squares is:

$$SS_b = \sum_g \left[\frac{(\Sigma X_g)^2}{N_g} \right] - \frac{(\Sigma X)^2}{N}$$

The formula tells us to first sum the scores within a group, square them, and divide by the number within the group $[(\Sigma X_g)^2]/N_g$. Next, sum the totals for each group $(\sum_g)$. From this total subtract the sum of all the scores squared divided by the total number of scores $[(\Sigma X)^2]/N$.

Computation of the Sums of Squares

Obviously the computation of the sums of squares even with the computational formulas is going to be quite tedious. There is one thing that we can do which will simplify the task considerably. The secret is to compute the sum of the scores in each of the groups or ΣX_g, then to compute the sum of the squared scores in each group or ΣX_g^2, and finally to note the number of subjects within each group or N_g. From these totals we can easily determine the sum of all the scores or ΣX, the sum of all the squared scores or ΣX^2, and the total N. Let's go back to our original example and compute the sums of squares.

Group Stems	Group Flowers	Group LSD
10	6	11
8	5	12
9	4	10
7	2	10
5	1	9
3	0	9
42	18	61

	ΣX_g	ΣX_g^2	N_g
Stems (X_1)	42	328	6
Flowers (X_2)	18	82	6
LSD (X_3)	61	624	6
	121	1037	18
	(ΣX)	(ΣX^2)	(N)

As you can see, I have obtained the sum of the scores for each group and this is shown below the label ΣX_g. For example, if we call Group Stems X_1, the sum of X_1 is found by adding $10 + 8 + \cdots + 3 = 42$. Similarly, $\Sigma X_2 = 18$ and $\Sigma X_3 = 61$.

To find the sum of the squared scores in each group, you square each of the scores in the group and add. For example, ΣX_1^2 is obtained by adding $10^2 + 8^2 + \cdots + 3^2 = 328$. Also, $\Sigma X_2^2 = 82$ and $\Sigma X_3^2 = 627$.

The totals are found by adding each column in the summary table and ΣX is found by summing $\Sigma X_1 + \Sigma X_2 + \Sigma X_3 = 42 + 18 + 61 = 121$. Similarly, ΣX^2 is found by adding $\Sigma X_1^2 + \Sigma X_2^2 + \Sigma X_3^2 = 328 + 82 + 627 = 1037$. The number of subjects in each group is 6 and the total $N = 18$. We are now ready to compute the sums of squares.

$$SS_{tot} = \Sigma X^2 - \frac{(\Sigma X)^2}{N}$$

$$= 1037 - \frac{(121)^2}{18} = 1037 - \frac{14641}{18} = 1037 - 813.39 = 223.61$$

$$SS_b = \Sigma_g \left[\frac{(\Sigma X_g)^2}{N_g} \right] - \frac{(\Sigma X)^2}{N} = \left[\frac{(\Sigma X_1)^2}{N_1} + \frac{(\Sigma X_2)^2}{N_2} + \frac{(\Sigma X_3)^2}{N_3} \right] - \frac{(\Sigma X)^2}{N}$$

$$= \left(\frac{42^2}{6} + \frac{18^2}{6} + \frac{61^2}{6} \right) - \frac{121^2}{18}$$

$$= \left(\frac{1764}{6} + \frac{324}{6} + \frac{3721}{6} \right) - \frac{14641}{18}$$

$$= (294 + 54 + 620.17) - 813.39 = 968.17 - 813.39 = 154.78$$

$$SS_w = \Sigma_g \left[(\Sigma X_g^2) - \frac{(\Sigma X_g)^2}{N_g} \right]$$

$$= \left[\Sigma X_1^2 - \frac{(\Sigma X_1)^2}{N_1} \right] + \left[\Sigma X_2^2 - \frac{(\Sigma X_2)^2}{N_2} \right] + \left[\Sigma X_3^2 - \frac{(\Sigma X_3)^2}{N_3} \right]$$

$$= \left(328 - \frac{42^2}{6} \right) + \left(82 - \frac{18^2}{6} \right) + \left(627 - \frac{61^2}{6} \right)$$

$$= \left(328 - \frac{1764}{6} \right) + \left(82 - \frac{324}{6} \right) + \left(627 - \frac{3721}{6} \right)$$

$$= (328 - 294) + (82 - 54) + (627 - 620.17) = 34 + 28 + 6.83$$

$$= 68.83$$

We have now determined the total sum of squares (223.61), the between group sum of squares (154.78), and the within group sum of squares (68.83). As a check on our computations, we can see if the between and within group sums total the SS_{tot}. Thus, we find that $154.78 + 68.83 = 223.61$.

Although the computations needed to derive the sums of squares appear to be quite involved and tedious, the amount of work involved is considerably lessened with the aid of the pocket calculator. The procedures involved will be demonstrated in a later section.

Now that we have the sums of squares, what do we do with them? Well, as I pointed out earlier, the formulas for the sums of squares are very similar to the numerator of the formula for sample variance. As you might anticipate we now need to define the denominator for each of the sums of squares so that we can determine a variance. It will greatly simplify proceedings at this point if the *source table* for analysis of variance is introduced.

Analysis of Variance Source Table

The analysis of variance source table, a place to summarize the values we have determined, takes the form illustrated below.

Analysis of Variance Source Table

Source	SS	df	MS	F
Between Groups				
Within Groups				
Total				

Examination of the source table quickly reveals some items that we have not yet discussed. First, note that there is a place for the sums of squares (between groups, within groups, and total). Then, we can see that there is a place for degrees of freedom *(df)* which we have not discussed for the analysis of variance test. There is also a column labeled MS, an abbreviation for mean square, which is discussed in the next paragraph. Finally, there is a heading at the end of the source table labeled *F*. In this area we put the number indicating the relative contribution of the two sources of variability. The size of *F* determines whether or not we conclude that the samples were drawn from the same population.

The mean square (MS) is really the variance we want to analyze. It is determined by dividing the sums of squares by the appropriate degrees of freedom. All we need to do, then, is to determine the *df* and the MS will be easy to calculate.

The between-groups *df* is equal to $K - 1$, where K is the number of groups we are comparing. For our specific example, $df_b = 2$ since we are comparing 3 groups and $K - 1 = 3 - 1 = 2$. The within-groups df equals $N - K$, which for our example is $18 - 3 = 15$. Finally, the total df equals $N - 1$ or $18 - 1 = 17$. Here again, the total is equal to the sum of the parts just as it was for the sum of squares. Thus, $df_{tot} = df_b + df_w$ or $N - 1 = (K - 1) + (N - K)$. On the right side of the equation, the Ks cancel and we are left with $N - 1 = N - 1$.

The final piece of information that we need in order to fill in the source table is F is the ratio of the MS_b to the MS_w or $F = MS_b/MS_w$. The completed source table for the problem we have been considering is shown below.

Analysis of Variance Source Table

Source	SS	df	MS	F
Between Groups	154.78	$K - 1 = 2$	$\dfrac{SS_b}{df_b} = \dfrac{154.78}{2} = 77.39$	$F = \dfrac{MS_b}{MS_w}$
Within Groups	68.83	$N - K = 15$	$\dfrac{SS_w}{df_w} = \dfrac{68.83}{15} = 4.59$	$= \dfrac{77.39}{4.59}$
Total	223.61	$N - 1 = 17$		$= 16.86$

At the end of the source table under the heading F, the F-ratio has been computed and it is 16.86. What does this mean? Were the groups drawn from different populations or did they come from the same population? As I said earlier, if the groups are actually drawn from the same population, then there should not be very much difference between the group means, and the variance between the groups should not be disproportionately large in relation to the variance within the groups. Thus, the value of F will be fairly small when the groups actually come from the same population. If, on the other hand, the F-ratio is large, the groups probably come from different populations with different means. The key question is: What constitutes large and small values of F?

The critical values of F that enable us to reject the null hypothesis at the 5% and the 1% levels are found in table C in appendix 1 a portion of which is shown in table 9–1.

Looking below the title of the table, we see the numbers 1 through 9 in a row with the heading "df associated with the numerator." To the left is a column of numbers from 1 to 120, not all of which are shown in either table 9-1 or in appendix table C of which

Table 9-1: *A portion of table C showing critical values for F. The entire table may be found in the appendix.*

df Associated with the Denominator		df Associated with the Numerator								
		1	2	3	4	5	6	7	8	9
1	5%	161	200	216	225	230	234	238	239	241
	1%	4052	5000	5403	5625	5764	5859	5928	5981	6022
2	5%	18.5	19.0	19.2	19.2	19.3	19.3	19.4	19.4	19.4
	1%	98.5	99.0	99.2	99.2	99.3	99.3	99.4	99.4	99.4
3	5%	10.1	9.55	9.28	9.12	9.01	8.97	8.89	8.85	8.81
	1%	34.1	30.8	29.5	28.7	28.2	27.9	27.7	27.5	27.3
4	5%	7.71	6.94	6.59	6.39	6.26	6.16	6.09	6.04	6.00
	1%	21.2	18.0	16.7	16.0	15.5	15.2	15.0	14.8	14.7
5	5%	6.61	5.79	5.41	5.19	5.05	4.95	4.88	4.82	4.77
	1%	16.3	13.3	12.1	11.4	11.0	10.7	10.5	10.3	10.2
6	5%	5.99	5.14	4.76	4.53	4.39	4.28	4.21	4.15	4.10
	1%	13.7	10.9	9.78	9.15	8.75	8.47	8.26	8.10	7.98
7	5%	5.59	4.74	4.35	4.12	3.97	3.87	3.79	3.73	3.68
	1%	12.2	9.55	8.45	7.85	7.46	7.19	6.99	6.84	6.72
8	5%	5.32	4.46	4.07	3.84	3.69	3.58	3.50	3.44	3.39
	1%	11.3	8.65	7.59	7.01	6.63	6.37	6.18	6.03	5.91
9	5%	5.12	4.26	3.86	3.63	3.48	3.37	3.29	3.23	3.18
	1%	10.6	8.02	6.99	6.42	6.06	5.80	5.61	5.47	5.35
10	5%	4.96	4.10	3.71	3.48	3.33	3.22	3.14	3.07	3.02
	1%	10.0	7.56	6.55	5.99	5.64	5.39	5.20	5.06	4.94
11	5%	4.84	3.98	3.59	3.36	3.20	3.09	3.01	2.95	2.90
	1%	9.65	7.21	6.22	5.67	5.32	5.07	4.89	4.74	4.63
12	5%	4.75	3.89	3.49	3.26	3.11	3.00	2.91	2.85	2.80
	1%	9.33	6.93	5.95	5.41	5.06	4.82	4.64	4.50	4.39
13	5%	4.67	3.81	3.41	3.18	3.03	2.92	2.83	2.77	2.71
	1%	9.07	6.70	5.74	5.21	4.86	4.62	4.44	4.30	4.19
14	5%	4.60	3.74	3.34	3.11	2.96	2.85	2.76	2.70	2.65
	1%	8.86	6.51	5.56	5.04	4.70	4.46	4.28	4.14	4.03
15	5%	4.54	3.68	3.29	3.06	2.90	2.79	2.71	2.64	2.59
	1%	8.68	6.36	5.42	4.89	4.56	4.32	4.14	4.00	3.89

Source: This table is adapted from Merrington, M., & Thompson, C. M., Tables of percentage points of the inverted beta *(F)* distribution, *Biometrika*, 1943, *33*, 73–88, with permission of the editor.

table 9-1 is a part. The heading over this column of numbers is "*df* associated with the denominator." The terms "numerator" and "denominator" refer to the relevant portions of the *F*-ratio. The *df* = 2 for the numerator of our specific example since the MS_b has this value for *df*. The *df* = 15 for the denominator of the *F*-ratio in the problem we have considered. Thus, to find the critical values for rejection of the null hypothesis for *F*, we read down the row of numbers in the left margin of the table until we come to the *df* associated with the denominator (15), and then across the columns of numbers to the column headed with the *df* associated with the numerator (2). For our specific example, the critical values are 3.68 at the 5% level and 6.36 at the 1% level. Since our calculated *F* of 16.86 is larger than either of the two critical values, we reject the null hypothesis that the groups came from the same population and conclude that the drugs tested had an effect on the behavioral avoidance test in our phobic patients.

The *F*-test does not tell us which of the possible group comparisons would actually be significant. All we know at this point is that there are significant differences somewhere within the data we have analyzed. We might, at this point, perform *t*-tests on the groups that, from looking at the means, we feel might be significantly different. However, remember that analysis of variance was introduced as an alternative to multiple *t*-tests, both because of the tediousness of the computations and because the more tests we perform on the same data, the more likely we are to get a spurious significant difference. Fortunately, as alternatives to performing multiple *t*-tests there are *post-anova* tests or tests that follow the analysis of variance; for example, the Scheffé test, the Tukey HSD test, the Newman-Keuls test, and the Duncan test. We will discuss the Tukey HSD test after we examine some other examples of computing *F*.

Summary of the Procedure for Calculating *F*

1. For each separate group determine the number of subjects or observations in the group (N_g). Then add all the scores in the group (ΣX_g). Finally, square each of the scores and add the squared scores in the group (ΣX_g^2).
2. Use the values calculated in step 1 to determine *N*, the sum of all the N_gs; ΣX, the sum of all the ΣX_gs; and ΣX^2, the sum of all the ΣX_g^2s.
3. Calculate the total sum of squares from the formula:

$$SS_{tot} = \Sigma X^2 - \frac{(\Sigma X)^2}{N}$$

4. Calculate the sum of squares between groups with the formula:

$$SS_b = \Sigma_g \left[\frac{(\Sigma X_g)^2}{N_g} \right] - \frac{(\Sigma X)^2}{N}$$

For three groups the equation is:

$$SS_b = \left[\frac{(\Sigma X_1)^2}{N_1} + \frac{(\Sigma X_2)^2}{N_2} + \frac{(\Sigma X_3)^2}{N_3} \right] - \frac{(\Sigma X)^2}{N}$$

If there are four groups, merely add another expression into the brackets based on X_4, etc.

5. Calculate the sum of squares within each group with the formula:

$$SS_w = \Sigma_g \left[(\Sigma X_g^2) - \frac{(\Sigma X_g)^2}{N_g} \right]$$

For three groups the equation expands to:

$$SS_w = \left[(\Sigma X_1^2) - \frac{(\Sigma X_1)^2}{N_1} \right] + \left[(\Sigma X_2^2) - \frac{(\Sigma X_2)^2}{N_2} \right]$$
$$+ \left[(\Sigma X_3^2) - \frac{(\Sigma X_3)^2}{N_3} \right]$$

If there are four groups, add another expression at the end with X_4, etc.

6. You may determine the SS_b or the SS_w by subtraction once SS_{tot} and one or the other of SS_b and SS_w have been calculated. That is, $SS_b = SS_{tot} - SS_w$ and $SS_w = SS_{tot} - SS_b$.

7. After the sums of squares have been determined, construct and fill in the analysis of variance source table:

Analysis of Variance Source Table

Source	SS	df	MS	F
Between Groups		$K - 1$	$SS_b \div df_b$	
Within Groups		$N - K$	$SS_w \div df_w$	$F = \dfrac{MS_b}{MS_w}$
Total		$N - 1$		

The degrees of freedom are given by the expressions listed under the heading "*df*," where K is the number of groups you are comparing and N is the total number of subjects or observations you have.

8. Once the source table is properly completed, determine F by dividing the MS_b by the MS_w. The degrees of freedom for the F-test are the df associated with the numerator of the F-ratio and the df associated with the denominator. Compare the computed value of F with the critical values of F in table C for the appropriate degrees of freedom. If the obtained F is larger than either of the values required for significance, reject the null hypothesis and conclude that the samples were drawn from different populations. Finding that the F-ratio is significant does not indicate exactly which of the groups differ, only that they do differ. Further testing is needed to determine exactly where the significant difference(s) lie.

Another Example of the Computation of F and Using the Calculator to Help Compute It

Suppose we have three groups of subjects each of which learns a list of nonsense syllables under different conditions. The first group learns the list in a normally lighted room; the second group learns the task in a darkened room lighted only by a small lamp placed near the memory drum; the third group learns the list in a room with flashing lights. We are interested in determining whether or not visual distraction affects the rate of learning of nonsense syllables. So, we record the number of repetitions of the list each subject requires prior to giving an errorless repetition. Initially, we intended to have the same N in each group but one of the subjects was unable to complete training and her data were discarded. The data are as follows:

Group X_1 (Normal Room)	Group X_2 (Dark Room)	Group X_3 (Flashing Lights)
5	3	10
7	4	11
6	5	20
10	10	13
15	7	10
11	6	8
8	2	7
7	4	12
	5	12
69	46	103

	ΣX_g	ΣX_g^2	N_g
Group X_1	69	669	8
Group X_2	46	280	9
Group X_3	103	1291	9
	218	2240	26
	(ΣX)	(ΣX^2)	(N)

The pocket calculator would be used in the computation of the summation of the scores for each group and, to illustrate, ΣX_1 would be determined as follows:

$$5 \; \fbox{+} \; 7 \; \fbox{+} \; 6 \; \fbox{+} \; 10 \; \fbox{+} \; 15 \; \fbox{+} \; 11 \; \fbox{+} \; 8 \; \fbox{+} \; 7 \; \fbox{=} \; 69$$

Additionally, the calculator will speed the determination of the sum of the squared scores in each group and, by way of illustration, the ΣX_1^2 could be determined with the following operations:

$$5 \; \fbox{$\times$}\fbox{$=$}\fbox{M+} \; 7 \; \fbox{$\times$}\fbox{$=$}\fbox{M+} \; 6 \; \fbox{$\times$}\fbox{$=$}\fbox{M+} \; 10 \; \fbox{$\times$}$$
$$\fbox{$=$}\fbox{M+} \; 15 \; \fbox{$\times$}\fbox{$=$}\fbox{M+} \; 11 \; \fbox{$\times$}$$
$$\fbox{$=$}\fbox{M+} \; 8 \; \fbox{$\times$}\fbox{$=$}\fbox{M+} \; 7 \; \fbox{$\times$}$$
$$\fbox{$=$}\fbox{M+}\fbox{M} \fbox{$=$} \; 669$$

What we have done is to square each score (5 $\fbox{$\times$}\fbox{$=$}$), add the result into memory ($\fbox{M+}$), and recall memory when all the scores have been treated in this fashion ($\fbox{M}\fbox{$=$}$).

So much for the simple part. Once we have determined the values for the sum of the scores from the various groups and have found the sums of the squared scores from the different groups, we are ready to plug these values into the equations for the sums of squares. Thus, for the total sum of squares we have:

$$SS_{tot} = \Sigma X^2 - \frac{(\Sigma X)^2}{N} = 2240 - \frac{(218)^2}{26}$$

The sequence of operations using the calculator is as follows:

$$2240 \; \fbox{M+} \; 218 \; \fbox{$\times$}\fbox{$=$}\fbox{$\div$} \; 26 \; \fbox{$=$}\fbox{M}\fbox{$-$}\fbox{M}\fbox{$=$} \; 412.15$$

Stated verbally what happened was that ΣX^2 was added into memory (2240 $\fbox{M+}$), ΣX was squared and divided by N (218 $\fbox{$\times$}\fbox{$=$}\fbox{$\div$}$ 26), the result was subtracted from memory ($\fbox{M}\fbox{$-$}$), and memory was recalled ($\fbox{M}\fbox{$=$}$ 412.15).

Continuing, we see that the

$$SS_b = \sum_g \left[\frac{(\Sigma X_g)^2}{N_g} \right] - \frac{(\Sigma X)^2}{N} = \left[\frac{(69)^2}{8} + \frac{(46)^2}{9} + \frac{(103)^2}{9} \right] - \frac{(218)^2}{26}$$

Using the calculator, the sequence of operations for finding SS_b is:

69 ⊗ ⊜ ⊘ 8 ⊜ Ⓜ ⊕ 46 ⊗ ⊜ ⊘ 9
⊜ Ⓜ + 103 ⊗ ⊜ ⊘ 9 ⊜ M ⊕ 218 ⊗
⊜ ⊘ 26 ⊜ Ⓜ ⊖ Ⓜ ⊜ 181.17

The sum of the scores in each group has been squared and divided by the N_g and the result added into memory (69 ⊗ ⊜ ⊘ 8 ⊜ Ⓜ ⊕); the total sum of scores has been squared and divided by the total N and the result subtracted from memory (218 ⊗ ⊜ ⊘ 26 ⊜ Ⓜ ⊖); and memory was recalled (Ⓜ ⊜ 181.17).

Having computed both the SS_{tot} and SS_b, we could at this point determine SS_w by subtraction. Thus, we would find that $SS_w = SS_{tot} - SS_b = 412.15 - 181.17 = 230.98$. Computation of SS_w using the calculator will now be demonstrated. The formula for SS_w is:

$$SS_w = \sum_g \left[(\Sigma X_g^2) - \frac{(\Sigma X_g)^2}{N_g} \right]$$

and filling in the relevant values we have

$$SS_w = \left[669 - \frac{(69)^2}{8} \right] + \left[280 - \frac{(46)^2}{9} \right] + \left[1291 - \frac{(103)^2}{9} \right]$$

Using the calculator, the sequence of operations for finding SS_w is:

669 Ⓜ ⊕ 69 ⊗ ⊜ ⊘ 8 ⊜ M ⊖ 280 Ⓜ ⊕ 46 ⊗
⊜ ⊘ 9 ⊜ M ⊖ 1291 Ⓜ ⊕ 103 ⊗
⊜ ⊘ 9 ⊜ M ⊖ Ⓜ ⊜ 230.99

As you can see, there is a slight difference in the value obtained with the calculator and the value found by subtraction. This is caused by rounding which occurred in the computation of the SS_{tot} and the SS_b.

Stated verbally, the procedure involves first adding the ΣX_g^2 into memory (for example, 669 Ⓜ ⊕). Next the ΣX_g is squared and divided by N_g (for example, 69 ⊗ ⊜ ⊘ 8 ⊜) and the result subtracted from memory ((M) (−)). After this has been done for each of the groups, memory is recalled ((M) (=) 230.99).

We have now determined each of the sums of squares and we can fill in the source table.

Source Table for Analysis of Variance

Source	SS	df	MS	F
Between Groups	181.17	$K - 1 = 2$	$\dfrac{181.17}{2} = 90.58$	
Within Groups	230.98	$N - K = 23$	$\dfrac{230.98}{23} = 10.04$	$F = \dfrac{90.58}{10.04} = 9.02$
Total	412.15	$N - 1 = 25$		

The final result is that $F = 9.02$ with the degrees of freedom associated with the numerator and with the denominator (2 and 23). With 2 and 23 degrees of freedom, the values required for significance from appendix table C are 3.42 at the 5% level and 5.66 at the 1% level. Since 9.02 is larger than either of the critical table values, we reject the null hypothesis that the samples came from the same population and conclude that visual distraction affects the rate of learning of nonsense syllables. Although the significant F value tells us nothing about where the significant differences lie, one glance at the data tells us that subjects in the darkened room in general made far fewer errors than the normal-room subjects who, in turn, were better than the subjects subjected to the flashing lights. If we decided to further test the data, we would definitely want to compare each of the experimental groups with the control group to determine whether or not the observed differences in repetitions to criterion are great enough for rejection of the null hypothesis.

Checking Your Progress

In an experiment designed to assess the effects of food deprivation on motivation, three groups of rats were subjected to the following treatments: one group was maintained under *ad libitum* conditions (food and water were always available), one group of rats received 15 grams of food per animal per day, and one group received 7.5 grams of food per day per rat. After one week on the feeding schedules, all animals were trained on a barpressing task and the number of responses each animal made in 30 minutes was recorded. The data are as follows:

Group Ad Libitum	Group 15 Grams	Group 7.5 Grams
45	100	125
50	85	200
110	73	98
38	110	100
55	125	108
60	51	155
42	105	160
85	100	85

The value obtained for F was 10.34, which for $df = 2, 21$ is significant ($p < .01$). If the F you obtain is very similar to the one I reported but not quite the same, the difference is probably due to differences in rounding.

Again we have found a significant F-ratio but do not know which of the possible comparisons is significant. The next section describes a technique that can be used to test for significant differences between groups after a significant F-ratio has been obtained.

Tukey's HSD Test

In previous sections I have mentioned that finding a significant F does not tell which group comparisons might actually differ significantly. A variety of techniques have been developed to make a posteriori (after the fact) comparisons. We will now discuss one of these, the Tukey HSD test. The Tukey HSD test was chosen both because it is often used by psychologists and because of the simplicity of the computation required.

Believe it or not, HSD stands for honestly significant differences (Tukey also developed an LSD test!). Although the HSD test can be used for more complex comparisons, we will use it for making all pairwise comparisons from the data when we have equal Ns per group. By pairwise I mean that all possible comparisons between groups are made by looking at one pair of groups at a time. For example, if you have three groups labeled A, B, and C, then you would compare Groups A and B, Groups A and C, and Groups B and C. You could not compare Group A with the combination of

Groups B and C, for example, since this would not be a pairwise comparison.

The technique is really very simple. The difference between two sample means is significant if it is greater than HSD which is found by the following equation:

$$HSD = q \sqrt{\frac{MS_w}{N_g}}.$$

where α is the level of significance, that is, either the .05 or the .01 level. The value of q is obtained from the distribution of the studentized range statistic found in appendix table D. (The studentized range statistic is sometimes used instead of the F-statistic for making group comparisons. It is generally a less powerful test than the F-test.) To determine the value of q from the table, we need to know two values, the df_w (degrees of freedom within groups) and K (the number of groups or treatments).

Let's look at a specific example. Earlier in the chapter we talked about some data from an experiment in which snake avoidance was measured after one of three different treatments. The group means were: Group Stems, $X_1 = 7$; Group Flowers, $X_2 = 3$; Group LSD, $X_3 = 10.17$. The analysis of variance source table is repeated below.

Analysis of Variance Source Table

Source	SS	df	MS	F
Between Groups	154.78	2	77.39	
Within Groups	68.83	15.	4.59	$F = 16.86$
Total	223.61	17		

The first step is to define all of the pairwise comparisons we are going to make and to find the difference in the means for each comparison. The pairwise comparisons we could make are as follows: Group Stems and Group Flowers, Group Stems and Group LSD, and Group Flowers and Group LSD. Subtracting, so that we obtain a positive difference for each comparison, we would have the following differences:

$$X_1 - X_2 = 7 - 3 = 4$$
$$X_3 - X_1 = 10.17 - 7 = 3.17$$
$$X_3 - X_2 = 10.17 - 3 = 7.17$$

Equivalently, we could have subtracted in the order originally specified (i.e., $\overline{X}_1 - \overline{X}_2$, $\overline{X}_1 - \overline{X}_3$, $\overline{X}_2 - \overline{X}_3$) and then used the absolute value of the differences in the comparison with HSD.

The next step is to determine HSD_a. Again, the formula for HSD_α is $HSD_\alpha = q_\alpha \sqrt{MS_w/N_g}$. The value of $q_{.05} = 3.67$ with 3 groups and $df_w = 15$. Also from appendix table D we see that the value of $q_{.01}$ is 4.84. Since $MS_w = 4.59$ from the summary table and $N_g = 6$, $HSD_{.05} = 3.67 \sqrt{4.59/6} = 3.67 \sqrt{0.765} = 3.67 \,(.87) = 3.19$. Similarly, $HSD_{.01} = 4.84 \,(.87) = 4.21$.

Now that values for HSD have been determined, we can compare them with the differences in means that were calculated earlier. The result is that two differences are larger than $HSD_{.05}$ and one is larger than $HSD_{.01}$. Thus, the difference between the means for Group Stems and Group Flowers was 4.0 which is larger than 3.19 or the value of HSD required for significance at the 5% level. Additionally, the difference of 7.17 between Groups Flowers and LSD is larger than the value of HSD required for significance at the 1% level or 4.21. Although not quite large enough for rejection of the null hypothesis, the difference between Groups Stems and LSD approached the critical value, 3.17 versus 3.19.

In summary, the F-test revealed that a significant difference(s) existed in the data. The Tukey HSD test suggested that the difference between the first and second groups (Stems and Flowers) was significant and that the difference between the second and third groups (Flowers and LSD) was significant.

Another example of the Tukey HSD procedure may be instructive. A study was performed to determine the effect of Mirex (a recently banned pesticide used to control the fire ant) upon the number of rat offspring surviving to weaning. Thus, three groups of pregnant female rats were given different amounts of Mirex in their food, and the data are the number of pups surviving to 21 days of age. For 15 females with litters culled to 10 pups each, the data are shown below.

No Mirex	Low Dose	High Dose
6	5	4
8	6	3
8	8	3
10	9	6
7	7	2

The problem is to determine whether or not there is a significant overall result, and, if so, determine which groups differ significantly. Without going through all the computations resulting in F (I suggest that you treat this example like another review exercise), the source table is shown below.

Analysis of Variance Source Table

Source	SS	df	MS	F
Between Groups	49.7	2	24.85	
Within Groups	28.0	12	2.33	$F = 24.85/2.33 = 10.67$
Total	77.7	14		$df = 2, 12$

The computed F-ratio of 10.67 is larger than the table values of F with 2 and 12 degrees of freedom (3.89, 6.93), and we reject the null hypothesis at the 1% level. Since a significant F has been found, the next step is to apply the Tukey HSD test. As developed earlier, the steps are:

1. Determine the mean for each of the treatment groups.
2. Determine the differences between means for each pairwise comparison.
3. Compute HSD for the 5% and 1% levels.
4. Compare the value determined for HSD with the difference in means. If the difference in means is larger than the value of HSD, the groups being compared are considered to be significantly different.

For the present example, we have the following:

1. $\bar{X}_1$ (Group No Mirex) $= 39 \div 5 = 7.8$
   $\bar{X}_2$ (Group Low Dose) $= 35 \div 5 = 7.0$
   $\bar{X}_3$ (Group High Dose) $= 18 \div 5 = 3.6$
2. $\bar{X}_1 - \bar{X}_2 = 7.8 - 7.0 = 0.8$
   $\bar{X}_1 - \bar{X}_3 = 7.8 - 3.6 = 4.2$
   $\bar{X}_2 - \bar{X}_3 = 7.0 - 3.6 = 3.4$
3. $HSD_{.05} = q_{.05} \sqrt{MS_w/N_g} = 3.77 \sqrt{2.33/5} = 3.77 (.68) = 2.56$
   $HSD_{.01} = 5.05 (.68) = 3.43$
4. The comparison between Group No Mirex and Group Low Dose is not significant since the difference in means (0.8) is less than $HSD_{.05}$ (2.56). The comparisons between Group No Mirex and

Group High Dose and between Groups Low Mirex and High Mirex are both significant since the difference in means is larger than the value of HSD for the 5% level. In fact, the comparison between Groups No Mirex and High Mirex resulted in a value that was larger than $HSD_{.01}$.

The conclusion from this study is that a high dose of mirex causes a decrease in the number of rat offspring surviving to weaning, while a low dose has little effect on the number of survivors.

Checking Your Progress

In a previous "Checking Your Progress" section, an experiment was described in which the motivation of three different groups of rats was compared after differing amounts of food deprivation. A significant F-ratio was obtained and the appropriate source table is shown below along with the other information necessary to perform the HSD test.

Analysis of Variance Source Table

Source	SS	df	MS	F
Between Groups	18639	2	9319.5	$F = \dfrac{9319.5}{901.55} = 10.34$
Within Groups	18932.63	21	901.55	$df = 2, 21$
Total	37571.63	23		

$$N_g = 8, \Sigma X_1 = 485, \Sigma X_2 = 749, \Sigma X_3 = 1031$$

The values for HSD were $HSD_{.05} = 38.02$ and $HSD_{.01} = 49.28$. Groups AL and 7.5 grams differed significantly with $p < .01$.

Summary

This chapter has dealt with a technique which allows us to perform a test of significance on the results from comparison of two or more levels of an independent variable. The test is called the *one-way analysis of variance* (ANOVA) and results in a value (F-ratio), which can be compared with table values. If the value of F that we compute is large enough, we can reject the null hypothesis and conclude that the groups were drawn from different populations. Further tests are then necessary to determine which groups actually differ significantly.

The determination of F begins with the calculation of the *sums of squares*. We first compute the *total sum of squares* from the formula:

$$SS_{tot} = \Sigma X^2 - \frac{(\Sigma X)^2}{N}$$

Further details on the computation of SS_{tot} are given in the chapter. The total sum of squares is divided into the *sum of squares between groups* and the *sum of squares within groups* which are determined from the following formulas:

$$SS_b = \sum_g \left[\frac{(\Sigma X_g)^2}{N_g} \right] - \frac{(\Sigma X)^2}{N}$$

and

$$SS_w = \sum_g \left[(\Sigma X_g^2) - \frac{(\Sigma X_g)^2)}{N_g} \right]$$

For further details on the computation of SS_b and SS_w, see the chapter.

The *mean square* (MS) is determined by dividing each sum of squares by the appropriate degrees of freedom. In the case of SS_b, $df = K - 1$, where K is the number of groups being compared. The df for SS_w is $N - K$ where N is the total number of subjects while the $df_{tot} = N - 1$.

The *F-ratio* is calculated by dividing the MS_b by the MS_w. Using the df associated with the numerator and the df associated with the denominator, the computed value of F can be compared with the table values required for significance at the 5% and the 1% levels. If the observed value is larger than the values in the table, the null hypothesis is rejected.

After a significant F has been obtained, further analysis of the data may be performed with the *Tukey HSD test*. The value of HSD is obtained from the following equation:

$$HSD = q_\alpha \sqrt{\frac{MS_w}{N_g}}$$

The value for q_α is obtained from appendix table D using the appropriate K (number of groups) and df_w. Differences between all pairs of group means are compared with $HSD_{.05}$ and $HSD_{.01}$ and if the differences are larger, the null hypothesis is rejected. The HSD test may be used to make all pairwise comparisons between group means when the N_g is the same for all groups.

Troubleshooting Your Computations

Using formulas as complex as those discussed in this chapter increases the possibility of computational error. Two obvious signs of trouble when you are calculating the sums of squares are a negative value for SS and the failure of the SS_b and SS_w to total SS_{tot}. If either of these occur, your best step generally speaking is to return to the raw data and check your initial totals. In other words, you should redetermine the ΣX_gs and the ΣX_g^2s. In the majority of cases, an error has been made at this point.

Assuming that your mistake is not in the original summing of the scores and of the squared scores, check your formulas. Then be sure that you have substituted the correct number for the appropriate symbol in the equations. If you have unequal N_gs, be sure that you have noted this in substituting in the formulas for SS_b and SS_w.

The most common error made in filling out the source table is to incorrectly determine the degrees of freedom. Remember that $df_b = K - 1$, where K is the number of groups you are comparing and that $df_w = N - K$. Also, $df_{tot} = df_b + df_w$ and the sum of df_b and df_w should equal $N - 1$.

The most common error made in calculating HSD is to use N instead of N_g in the expression $\sqrt{MS_w/N_g}$. Be careful not to do this. Also, remember that after you compute HSD, you compare it to the difference in means that you have determined. If the difference in means is larger than HSD, you reject the null hypothesis for that comparison and conclude that there is a significant difference between the means (that they were drawn from different populations).

Exercises

1. An experiment has been performed to evaluate the effects of method of teaching on performance as measured by a standardized exam. The three methods used in an introductory class were: a totally self-paced approach, a self-paced approach with optional lectures, and a traditional lecture approach. The scores on the standardized exam for the students in each class were as follows:

Totally Self-paced	Self-paced With Lectures	Traditional Lecture
67	97	98
83	95	49
95	90	75
97	89	76
53	88	78
75	75	83
76	84	81
82	91	92
85	87	90
72	63	65
74	77	65
71	84	94

Compare the teaching methods using the tools we have developed in this chapter. If a significant F is obtained, make all pairwise comparisons.

2. Five groups of rats were placed into boxes under five different temperature conditions. The amount of time spent running in activity wheels attached to the boxes was recorded over a five-day period. Compare the groups to see whether temperature affected activity. If a significant F is obtained, make all pairwise comparisons.

30°F	50°F	70°F	90°F	100°F
6	4	3	2	0
6	4	3	2	0
3	5	2	1	0
5	4	5	1	1
4	2	1	3	0
7	2	6	2	1

The scores for each subject represent the average hours per day spent running.

3. Forty college students who were members of a fraternity volunteered for an experiment to determine the effects of different amounts of alcohol on aggression as measured by the number of shocks administered to a rat being trained on a discrimination task. The students were randomly assigned to one of four different groups and given either 0, 1, 2, or 3 ounces of scotch to drink within a one-hour period. Two of the students in the 3-ounce group passed out prior to the end of the experiment and their data have been discarded. The number of shocks administered by the subjects in each of the four groups was as follows:

0 oz.	1 oz.	2 oz.	3 oz.	
10	·30	45	10	
10	25	50	5	
15	35	60	10	
20	20	70	13	
25	40	20	40	(Continued)

0 oz.	1 oz.	2 oz.	3 oz.
10	25	100	10
10	20	35	20
12	15	50	10
13	23	40	
13	35	30	

Determine whether or not the amount of alcohol consumed affected the degree of aggression exhibited by the subjects.

4. Several students were deprived of sleep for varying periods of time and their performance on a pursuit rotor task was measured. The object of the pursuit rotor task is to keep a stylus in contact with a spot on a rotating turntable. It is primarily a measure of hand-eye coordination and should be sensitive to the effects of sleep deprivation. The length of the deprivation and the amount of time during a one-minute test each student could keep the stylus in contact with the target are shown below. Determine whether or not the lack of sleep affected performance on the task. People scoring zero often fell asleep at the start of the session. If a significant F is obtained, make all pairwise comparisons.

0 Depr.	24 Hr. Depr.	48 Hr. Depr.	72 Hr. Depr.
30	10	5	5
45	10	10	3
15	5	5	5
20	15	5	0
30	20	0	0
35	10	20	6

5. An experiment is performed to see the effect of various types of brain damage on the reactivity to shock of rats. To do the study, 20 rats are selected from a large animal colony and are evenly and randomly assigned to one of four different treatment groups. The first group of animals receives control operations in which the brain is not damaged (Group OC); the second group receives a lesion to the septal area of the brain (Group SEP); the third group has complete removal of the olfactory bulbs (Group OB); and the fourth group sustains a lesion of the ventromedial hypothalamic area of the brain (Group VMH). Following a recovery period of one week, all rats are placed into a shock apparatus and given a small shock to the feet. The height of the animals' jump in centimeters constitutes the dependent variable. The data are as follows:

Group OC	Group SEP	Group OB	Group VMH
0	10	0	5
1	12	5	6
2	9	2	10
3	7	2	9
1	13	3	3

Perform an overall test of significance and if a significant F is obtained, do all pairwise comparisons.

6. Give two reasons why it is better not to use multiple t-tests for further analysis of data after a significant F-ratio has been obtained.

7. What was the name of the *a posteriori* test discussed? Why was it chosen?

8. An experiment has been done to determine the effect of alcohol on reaction time of adult males. Reaction time is measured in a simulated driver's seat and is measured from the moment a picture of a stop sign is presented until the subject applies force to a brake. Forty subjects are selected and randomly assigned to one of four treatment groups: Group 1, placebo; Group 2, 0.5 ounces of alcohol; Group 3, 1.0 ounces; Group 4, 2.0 ounces. Testing is conducted thirty minutes after the subject has ingested a drink containing the amount of alcohol specified by his group designation. The data are:

Reaction Time in Seconds

0 oz.	0.5 oz.	1.0 oz.	2.0 oz.
0.8	1.1	1.5	2.0
1.2	1.5	1.3	1.8
0.7	0.9	1.2	1.7
0.9	1.6	1.4	1.5
1.1	1.4	1.6	1.8
1.5	1.3	0.9	1.7
0.6	1.4	1.1	1.6
0.8	0.9	1.8	1.7
1.0	1.1	1.5	1.5
1.1	1.2	1.4	2.1

Determine whether or not there are group differences, and make all pairwise comparisons if a significant F-ratio is found.

9. In a state home for the mentally retarded, 24 children classified as either severely or moderately retarded are given nine days of training to identify the color red in a two-choice test. On the tenth day the number of correct responses in 10 trials is recorded for each of the children. Each has been randomly assigned to one of three treatment groups: one group receives no reward during the training period, one group receives verbal reinforcement for each correct response, and the third group is rewarded with candy for each correct response. The tenth day results are:

No Reward	Verbal Reward	Candy
5	8	9
3	6	10
4	7	8
6	9	9
5	5	10
6	8	9
4	7	9
3	6	10

Determine whether or not the different methods of reinforcement had any effect. If a significant F-ratio is found, make all pairwise comparisons.

10

Correlation and Regression

Introduction

Correlation, a term used often by most of us, is defined as the degree of relationship between two or more variables. In this chapter we will be discussing *linear correlation* or the degree to which a straight line best describes the relationship between two variables. The idea of a straight line or linear relationship between two variables will become more apparent when we discuss and graph scatter plots.

linear correlation

To illustrate what is meant by correlation, consider the variables height and weight. In general, the taller you are the more you weigh; we say that the two variables are highly correlated. In other words, they go together and are related to each other. Many of you will say at this point that you know an exception to the rule that height and weight are related to each other. You have a friend who is only 5 feet tall and weighs 237 pounds, or perhaps your friend, the exception, is 6 feet 6 inches tall and weighs 135 pounds. When I said that there was a correlation between height and weight, I didn't say that the correlation was perfect! As long as the relationship between two variables is not perfect, there will be exceptions.

Classes of Correlation

Although the degree of relationship between two variables may assume an infinite number of values, it is customary to speak of three different classes of correlation; that is, positive, negative, and zero. The example given of correlation between height and weight in the previous paragraph was an illustration of positive correlation. A *positive correlation* between variables exists when a high score on one variable is associated with a high score on the other or a low score is associated with a low score. In other words, positive correlation occurs when there is a direct relationship between the variables.

positive correlation

In addition to the height-weight example already mentioned, a positive correlation has been found between the rank of a female monkey in a colony and the subsequent ranking of her offspring. Thus, a female who ranks high in the dominance hierarchy of her troop will tend to rear offspring who assume high ranks in the hierarchy. By contrast, a low-ranking female will tend to have low-ranking offspring.

Another example of two variables that we hope are positively correlated is that of the number of hours spent studying some material and the score that one receives on an examination on the material. We would have to assume that the people studying the material are approximately equal in intelligence and that they are studying the same thing; but, given that this is true, the amount of time spent studying should be positively related to the results. Suppose that we have actually done a study of this and have obtained the following data from 10 students:

Student	Number of Hours Spent Studying	Score on Exam
A	28	95
B	25	95
C	3	58
D	10	75
E	0	44
F	15	83
G	20	91
H	24	87
I	7	65
J	8	70

scatter plot

One way to study the relationship between the two variables is to look at the *scatter plot* of the data. The *scatter plot* is a graph that plots pairs of scores with the scores on one of the variables plotted on the *x*-axis and the scores on the other variable plotted on the *y*-axis. In the case of the students' time spent studying versus the score made on some exam over the material that they were studying, we would have the scatter plot shown in figure 10–1.

In general, if the pattern of points on the scatter plot of some data falls pretty closely around a straight line slanting upward to the right, we are dealing with an example of positive correlation. Figure 10–1 shows that there is a strong linear relationship between the two variables, since a straight line connects almost all of the points. Additionally, the correlation is positive; that is, a high score on one variable (amount of time spent studying) is related to a high score on the other variable (a good grade on the exam). As you might suspect, we can calculate a statistic to represent the degree of linear relation-

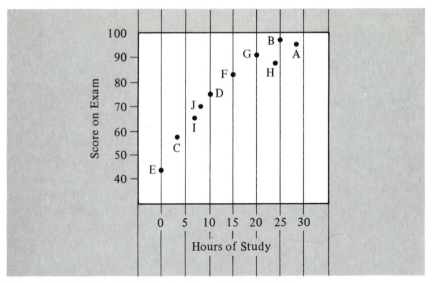

Figure 10–1: Scatter plot of the positive relationship between time spent studying and the score on an exam.

ship. But, we will save the calculation until we have talked about the other two classes of correlation, negative and zero.

A *negative correlation* is one in which a high score on one variable is associated with a low score on the other or vice versa. In other words, there is an inverse relationship between the two variables. An example of this might be the relationship between the IQ score of a professional boxer and the number of blows to the head he has sustained. We might expect to find that the greater the number of punches he had taken to the head, the lower his IQ score would be. Or, perhaps, we might find an inverse relationship between the number of years of formal education and the number of years a person had spent behind bars.

I have found in my research that for some types of brain damage there is a negative correlation between the amount of destruction to a given area of the brain and the amount of retention (recorded in terms of a percentage savings score) an animal shows on a previously learned task. A typical experiment involves training a group of animals on a simple discrimination task to a criterion of 90% or 95% correct responses in a day's training session consisting of maybe ten trials. After an animal has reached the criterion, it is given a brain lesion designed to destroy a particular structure of interest. After a suitable recovery period, each brain-damaged animal is retrained on the originally learned task, and the number of

negative correlation

errors made prior to reaching the criterion is again recorded. From the errors made in original learning and the errors made in relearning the task, a percentage savings score is computed from the simple equation:

$$\%SS = \frac{OL - RL}{OL} \times 100$$

For example, if an animal makes 10 errors in original learning and 3 errors in relearning, the percentage savings score would be $(10 - 3)/10 \times 100 = 7/10 \times 100 = 70\%$.

At any rate, after a group of animals has relearned the task, it is sacrificed and a determination is made of the percentage of the desired area that has been destroyed by the lesion. Thus, for each animal we would have two measures:

1. a retention score in terms of percentage savings, and
2. a score indicating the amount of damage to a particular structure in the brain.

To examine the scatter plot of negative correlation, let's consider the following data:

Animal No.	% Damage	% Savings
A	100	0
B	98	0
C	95	5
D	92	30
E	90	20
F	85	40
G	60	70
H	55	50
I	40	95
J	20	100

From the scatter plot of our example of negative correlation shown in figure 10–2, it is apparent that the points plotted form a reasonably close approximation of a straight line that slopes downward to the right.

zero correlation

The final category of correlation to be considered is that of *zero correlation*. Here there is no relationship between the variables; a high score is just as likely to be associated with a low score as it is

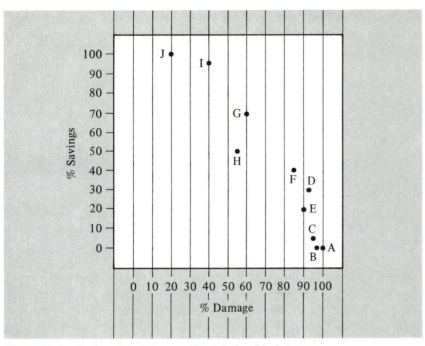

Figure 10–2: Scatter plot of the negative relationship between percentage of damage to a brain structure and the percentage of savings on a test of retention.

with a high score or even with a medium score. In other words, knowing a value for one variable would provide absolutely no information that would allow us to predict a value for the other variable. A classical example of zero correlation is the relationship between the number and location of bumps on the skull and the intelligence or special abilities of a person. But, of course, phrenologists made a living for a while from just such a presumed relationship.

We might mention some other examples of zero correlation. There is little evidence for a relationship between the length of the lines in the palm of your hand and your lifespan. Similarly, I have read that there is a zero correlation between smoking and your eventual height; that is, there is little evidence to support the old adage that smoking will stunt your growth. Going back to our discussion of negative correlation, often the result of such studies of brain damage and behavior end in findings of zero correlation.

To illustrate the scatter plot of zero correlation, suppose that a professor wants to see whether or not there is a relationship between the order in which students turn in test papers and their score on the test. As the students turn in their papers, the teacher adds a number to the top of each test indicating the order of completion. After the tests have been graded, the following data are noted:

Order of Completion	Score
1	95
2	57
3	90
4	70
5	75
6	65
7	60
8	85
9	87
10	75
11	76
12	72
13	93
14	85

The scatter plot of the data, shown in figure 10–3, reveals essentially a random pattern of points. In other words, the scores seem to be well "scattered," and don't seem to be well described by a straight line (or any other manner of line).

Before we leave the idea of classes of correlation; that is, positive, negative, and zero, I would like to point out that negative correlation is just as meaningful as positive. Knowing that a correlation is negative rather than positive just tells us that the relationship is inverse rather than direct. Actually, when we have a positive relationship between two variables, merely changing the way in which we measure one of the variables will change the relationship from direct to inverse!

To illustrate, an example that I gave of positive correlation involved the relationship between the amount of time spent studying and a score on an exam. Suppose that instead of recording the score on the exam as our *Y* variable, we had noted the number of errors made by each student. Now we would find that the more time a student spent studying, the fewer mistakes he or she would make and vice versa. In other words, we would now have an inverse relationship instead of a direct one. This simple example should illustrate to you that a negative correlation is just as meaningful as a positive one.

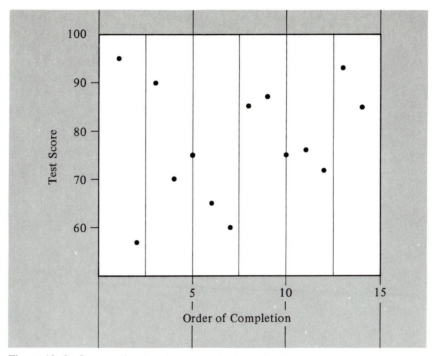

Figure 10–3: Scatter plot showing the lack of relationship between the order of completion of a test paper and the score on it.

Causation and Correlation

A final point about correlation that is often abused or ignored in the popular press is that high correlation does not necessarily mean that one variable *causes* the other. For example, we often hear reports that there is a high correlation between cigarette smoking and lung cancer. In other words, the more cigarettes you smoke, the more likely you are to develop cancer of the lungs (and many other dreadful diseases). Does this mean that cigarette smoking *causes* lung cancer? Not necessarily. It is possible that a virus causes the cancer and that the effect of smoking is to diminish the capacity of the lungs to resist invasion.

Another example of a correlation that doesn't necessarily mean causation is that between the incidence of viral ailments commonly called colds and the air temperature. That is, it is commonly accepted that cold weather is associated with a high incidence of colds. But, does the cold weather cause the colds? In part, the higher incidence of upper respiratory ailments in the winter may stem from the modifications in social behavior and higher levels of interpersonal contact during this period of time. Again, the point should be made that we should resist the temptation to conclude that one variable causes another when we find a high correlation between them. It is possible that one variable causes the other, but the high correlation between them doesn't prove it.

Pearson Product-Moment Correlation Coefficient

Pearson product-
moment correlation
coefficient

Now that we have talked about what is meant by correlation and about the three classes of it, it is time to consider ways to determine the degree of the relationship between the variables. The first way that we will consider is called the *Pearson product-moment correlation coefficient* or the *Pearson r*. The Pearson r is simply defined as the mean of the z-score products for X and Y pairs where X stands for one variable and Y stands for the other.

One very important thing to note about the Pearson r is that its range is from +1 to −1. A positive value for r is indicative of a positive relationship between the variables, while a negative value indicates an inverse relationship. If the value of r is close to zero, in either a positive or a negative direction, you probably have an example of the third class of correlation discussed, zero correlation.

To illustrate the computation of r from the defining formula and also to show how the Pearson r reflects the three classes of relationship, three simple problems will be examined. The formula for r based on the given definition (the mean of the z-score products for X and Y) is:

$$\text{Pearson } r = \frac{\Sigma z_X z_Y}{N}$$

where z_X and z_Y are the z-scores for the X and Y variables, respectively. The number of pairs of scores is indicated by N.

Suppose we have the following 5 pairs of scores:

X	Y
5	7
4	6
3	4
2	2
1	1

Obviously, we are dealing with a perfect direct relationship between the X and Y variables. That is, the high scores on the X variable are associated with the high scores on the Y variable and the low scores are associated with the low scores. How is this relationship reflected in the computation of r?

According to the formula for r, we must compute the z-score for each X and also the z-score for each Y. Then we will multiply the scores for each X and Y pair, sum the products, and divide by N. The computations are as follows:

X	X^2	Y	Y^2	z_X	z_Y	$z_X z_Y$
5	25	7	49	1.414	1.32	1.87
4	16	6	36	.71	.88	.62
3	9	4	16	0.00	0.00	0.00
2	4	2	4	−.71	−.88	.62
1	1	1	1	−1.414	−1.32	1.87
15	55	20	106			4.98

$$\bar{X} = \frac{\Sigma X}{N} = \frac{15}{5} = 3$$

$$SD_X = \sqrt{\frac{\Sigma X^2}{N} - \bar{X}^2} = \sqrt{\frac{55}{5} - 3^2} = \sqrt{11 - 9} = \sqrt{2} = 1.414$$

$$z_X = \frac{X - \bar{X}}{SD_X} \qquad z_5 = \frac{5 - 3}{1.414} = \frac{2}{1.414} = 1.414$$

The rest of the z_X values are computed in a similar manner.

$$\bar{Y} = \frac{\Sigma Y}{N} = \frac{20}{5} = 4$$

$$SD_Y = \sqrt{\frac{\Sigma Y^2}{N} - \bar{Y}^2} = \sqrt{\frac{106}{5} - 4^2} = \sqrt{21.2 - 16} = \sqrt{5.2}$$

$$= 2.28$$

$$z_Y = \frac{Y - \bar{Y}}{SD_Y} \qquad z_7 = \frac{7 - 4}{2.28} = \frac{3}{2.28} = 1.32$$

Again, the rest of the z_Y values are computed similarly. The Pearson r is computed as follows:

$$r = \frac{\Sigma z_X z_Y}{N} = \frac{4.98}{5} = +0.996$$

Thus, the mean of the z-score products is found to be +0.996, a value which reflects the strong positive relationship between the variables.

There are several things to note about the preceding calculations. First of all, they were very tedious and would be exceedingly time consuming if we were dealing with larger sample sizes and larger numbers. For this reason, we will soon introduce a computational or raw score formula.

Secondly, and more importantly, even though the means and standard deviations were different for the X and Y variables, because of the direct relationship between them the z-scores opposite each other were of the same sign. For this reason, when we multiplied each pair of z-scores, the result in each case was either zero or a value with a positive sign. Summing the products gave us a value close to N and the mean of the z-score products was found to be approximately +1. Let's look at the computation of r when we have a perfect inverse relationship. To simplify matters, we will use the same numbers as in the previous example with the order of the Y-scores reversed. The resulting distribution and z-scores would be:

X	Y	z_X	z_Y	$z_X z_Y$
5	1	1.414	−1.32	−1.87
4	2	0.71	−0.88	−0.62
3	4	0.00	0.00	0.00
2	6	−0.71	0.88	−0.62
1	7	−1.414	1.32	−1.87
				−4.98

$$r = \frac{\Sigma z_X z_Y}{N} = \frac{-4.98}{5} = -0.996$$

The major difference this time is that in each case except one a positive z-score is paired with a negative z-score so that the resulting product has a negative value. Again, the sum of the products has a value close to N in absolute value and the mean was found to be approximately −1.

Before considering the computational formula for r, let's look at an example to illustrate the class of correlation in which there is essentially no relationship between the variables. The same numbers will be used in the example as before except that the values for Y are arranged randomly. The resulting distribution and the z-scores would be:

X	Y	z_X	z_Y	$z_X z_Y$
5	1	1.414	−1.32	−1.87
4	7	0.71	1.32	0.94
3	4	0.00	0.00	0.00
2	6	−0.71	0.88	−0.62
1	2	−1.414	−0.88	1.24
				−0.31

$$r = \frac{\Sigma z_X z_Y}{N} = \frac{-0.31}{5} = -0.062$$

Although the value obtained for r is not exactly zero, it is certainly low enough that we would be inclined to view it as indicating no relationship between X and Y. Because there is neither a strong direct relationship nor a strong inverse relationship between the variables, the z-score products are sometimes positive and sometimes negative with the result that they tend to cancel one another when summed. Thus, the sum of the products is quite low relative to N, and the resulting mean is correspondingly low.

Now we can consider the computational formula which is derived from the defining formula. It is:

$$r = \frac{\Sigma XY - \dfrac{\Sigma X \Sigma Y}{N}}{\sqrt{\left[\Sigma X^2 - \dfrac{(\Sigma X)^2}{N}\right]\left[\Sigma Y^2 - \dfrac{(\Sigma Y)^2}{N}\right]}}$$

When confronted with a formula with the complexity of the computational formula for r, the first thing you should do is to sit back and look at it to see exactly what you are asked to compute. You will see that, taking the components individually, there is almost nothing here that you have not seen before. But, just to spell it out, you need to determine the values of the following terms in order to plug them into the formula: ΣXY, ΣX, ΣY, N, ΣX^2, ΣY^2. The only thing that you have not seen before is ΣXY which is found by multiplying each X by each Y and summing the result.

Let's recompute one of the examples introduced earlier to illus-

trate the use of the defining formula. This should illustrate the equiv-
alence of the two formulas and show that the computational formula
is easier to use.

X	Y	XY
5	7	35
4	6	24
3	4	12
2	2	4
1	1	1
		76

We had found in the previous computation that $\Sigma X = 15$, $\Sigma Y = 20$,
$\Sigma X^2 = 55$, $\Sigma Y^2 = 106$, and $N = 5$.

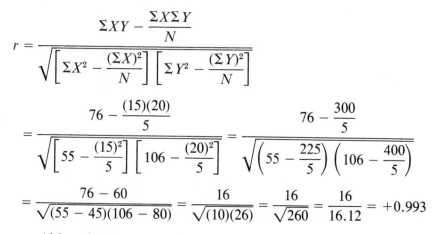

$$r = \frac{\Sigma XY - \dfrac{\Sigma X \Sigma Y}{N}}{\sqrt{\left[\Sigma X^2 - \dfrac{(\Sigma X)^2}{N}\right]\left[\Sigma Y^2 - \dfrac{(\Sigma Y)^2}{N}\right]}}$$

$$= \frac{76 - \dfrac{(15)(20)}{5}}{\sqrt{\left[55 - \dfrac{(15)^2}{5}\right]\left[106 - \dfrac{(20)^2}{5}\right]}} = \frac{76 - \dfrac{300}{5}}{\sqrt{\left(55 - \dfrac{225}{5}\right)\left(106 - \dfrac{400}{5}\right)}}$$

$$= \frac{76 - 60}{\sqrt{(55 - 45)(106 - 80)}} = \frac{16}{\sqrt{(10)(26)}} = \frac{16}{\sqrt{260}} = \frac{16}{16.12} = +0.993$$

Although the computation appears tedious when each step is
written out, using a pocket calculator makes it really quite simple.
The use of the calculator in the calculation of r will be illustrated in
the next section.

The value of r that we found with the computational formula is
quite similar to the value we found with the defining formula (.993
versus .996). Presumably the difference lies in the rounding that
occurred.

The Use of the Pocket Calculator in Computing r

Earlier we talked about the relationship between the number of
hours spent studying and a score on an exam, and we introduced the
following pairs of scores to illustrate the possible relationship.

Student	No. of Hours of Study, X	Score on Exam, Y
A	28	95
B	25	95
C	3	58
D	10	75
E	0	44
F	15	83
G	20	91
H	24	87
I	7	65
J	8	70

As before, we need to find ΣXY, ΣX, ΣY, N, ΣX^2, ΣY^2. Using the calculator ΣXY is found with the following sequence of operations:

ΣXY = 28 $\times$ 95 $=$ M $+$ 25 $\times$ 95 $=$ M $+$ 3 $\times$ 58
$=$ M $+$ 10 $\times$ 75 $=$ M $+$ 0 $\times$ 44
$=$ M $+$ 15 $\times$ 83 $=$ M $+$ 20 $\times$ 91
$=$ M $+$ 24 $\times$ 87 $=$ M $+$ 7 $\times$ 65
$=$ M $+$ 8 $\times$ 70 $=$ M $+$ M $=$ 12127

Expressed verbally, each X is multiplied by the appropriate Y and the product added into memory (e.g., 28 $\times$ 95 $=$ M $+$). When this has been done for each pair of scores, the total memory is recalled and the result is ΣXY (M $=$ 12127).

Next we need to find ΣX and ΣY. Since use of the memory function is unnecessary for their computation, only the final results will be given and they are $\Sigma X = 140$, $\Sigma Y = 763$. The value for N is 10 or the number of pairs of scores we have.

The calculator is a time-saving device when it comes to finding the sum of the squared scores as we found in earlier chapters. Thus, ΣX^2 is found by the following sequence of operations:

ΣX^2 = 28 $\times$ $=$ M $+$ 25 $\times$ $=$ M $+$ 3 $\times$
$=$ M $+$ 10 $\times$ $=$ M $+$ 0 $\times$
$=$ M $+$ 15 $\times$ $=$ M $+$ 20 $\times$
$=$ M $+$ 24 $\times$ $=$ M $+$ 7 $\times$
$=$ M $+$ 8 $\times$ $=$ M $+$ M $=$ 2832

Expressed verbally, each number is squared and added into memory. When each number has been treated in this fashion, memory is recalled. Since the sequence of operations for finding ΣY^2 is precisely the same as for ΣX^2, it will not be shown here. The result was $\Sigma Y^2 = 60839$. You might want to verify this for yourself.

To summarize, we have found that $\Sigma XY = 12127$, $\Sigma X = 140$, $\Sigma Y = 763$, $N = 10$, $\Sigma X^2 = 2832$, and $\Sigma Y^2 = 60839$. We are now ready to compute r:

$$r = \frac{\Sigma XY - \dfrac{\Sigma X \Sigma Y}{N}}{\sqrt{\left[\Sigma X^2 - \dfrac{(\Sigma X)^2}{N}\right]\left[\Sigma Y^2 - \dfrac{(\Sigma Y)^2}{N}\right]}}$$

$$= \frac{12127 - \dfrac{(140)(763)}{10}}{\sqrt{\left[2832 - \dfrac{(140)^2}{10}\right]\left[60839 - \dfrac{(763)^2}{10}\right]}}$$

Using the calculator to compute the numerator, we would have:

12127 (M+) 140 (×) 763 (=)(÷) 10 (=)(M−)(M=)
(=) 1445

In other words, we have added ΣXY into memory (12127 (M+)); found the product of ΣX and ΣY and divided the result by N (140 (×) 763 (=)(÷) 10 (=)); subtracted the result from the memory ((M−)); and recalled memory ((M=) 1445).

The first half of the denominator is found as follows:

2832 (M+) 140 (×)(=)(÷) 10 (=)(M−)(M=) 872

Thus, ΣX^2 is added into memory (2832 (M+)); ΣX is squared and divided by N and the result subtracted from memory (140 (×)(=)(÷)(10)(=)(M−)); and memory is recalled ((M=)872). The second half of the denominator is found in the same fashion and will not be detailed here. The result is 2622.1, which you may want to check.

At this point, we need to write down what we have: $r = 1445/\sqrt{(872)(2622.1)}$. Further simplification of the denominator is done as follows: 872 (×) 2622.1 (=)(√).The answer is 1512.1, which will appear after the operation $\sqrt{}$. Now we have $r = 1445/1512.1 = 0.96$.

To evaluate the correlation coefficient of $+0.96$, we must recall another piece of information about the Pearson r—that the range of r is from $+1$ to -1. Thus, the value of r that would express a perfect direct relationship between two variables is $+1$, while -1 would tell us that there was a perfect inverse relationship between the variables. Anything close to $r = 0$ would indicate no relationship between the variables. But, when we say close to zero, how close do we mean? To answer this question, we will have to talk about testing r for significance.

The Null Hypothesis and Testing r for Significance

To test r for significance, we first assume that there is no relationship in the population between the two variables. In other words, we make the assumption that in the population from which our sample was drawn the two variables are not related, i.e., that the population correlation coefficient, ρ or rho, is zero. This assumption of no relationship in the population is a form of the null hypothesis.

If it is true that the underlying population correlation coefficient is zero, what is the likelihood or probability of obtaining a sample correlation coefficient as deviant as the one we obtained? At this point, it may be helpful to consider an actual correlation coefficient based on a sample.

We found for our sample of students that the correlation between the time spent studying and the grade they made on the exam was $+0.96$. Again, what is the probability of obtaining a sample of size 10 with a correlation coefficient as deviant as .96 from a population in which the underlying variables are not related? Obviously, most of the samples of size 10 from a population with a zero coefficient would have coefficients pretty close to zero and only a relatively few samples would have values as extreme as the one we obtained. To actually determine the probability of our sample value, we would need to know the standard deviation of the distribution of sample coefficients or we would have to estimate it. But, as with the t-test, the determination of the actual probability is unnecessary.

Instead, we can refer to a table that contains correlation coefficients so deviant that they occur less than 5% or 1% of the time in samples of a given size drawn from a population with a zero coefficient. The table for this purpose is appendix table E and its title indicates that it contains values of r at the 5% and 1% levels of significance. In other words, if our sample value exceeds the values in the table for the appropriate degrees of freedom, we reject the null hypothesis and conclude that the sample was *not* drawn from a population with a zero correlation coefficient. If the null hypothesis is rejected, we say that a significant relationship exists between the variables in question.

Looking at the table, we see that the left column is labeled ''degrees of freedom'' or df. In the case of the correlation coefficient r, $df = N - 2$, where N is the number of pairs of scores. The two restrictions placed on r have to do with the fact that r measures the degree of linear relationship between X and Y. Both restrictions are required in fitting a straight line to a sample of score pairs.

In the example we have been considering, $N = 10$ and $df = N - 2 = 10 - 2 = 8$. Looking across from $df = 8$ in appendix table E, we see that the coefficient required for significance at the 5% level is .632. Since .96 is much larger in absolute value than .632, we can reject the null hypothesis at the 5% level and can conclude that a relationship probably exists between the two variables. What about the 1% level? Here again we find that the table value is smaller than the coefficient we observed (.765 vs. .96), and again we reject the null hypothesis. In summary, we have found by referring to a table of critical values for r that the probability of obtaining a correlation coefficient as large as the one we obtained when the population value is zero is less than 0.01. (We rejected the null hypothesis at the 1% level which is the same as saying that the probability is less than 0.01.)

Thus, we decide that, since the probability of our obtained sample value is so small given that the population correlation coefficient is really zero, it is only reasonable to conclude that the population coefficient is *not* zero and that a relationship exists between the variables ''study time'' and ''exam score.'' Since we rejected the null hypothesis at the 5% (or 1%) level, does this mean that the population coefficient is not zero? Unfortunately, the answer to this question is not an unequivocal yes. Rejecting the null hypothesis means that given the size of the correlation coefficient we obtained, it is very unlikely that such a coefficient would be obtained from a sample drawn from a population in which the underlying coefficient was zero. Note that I said very unlikely, not impossible. We could obtain a sample with a high correlation coefficient from a population in which there is actually no relationship between the variables, but the probability in our example was less than 0.01.

In summary, the procedure for testing the significance of a sample correlation coefficient is:

1. Set up the null hypothesis. Make the assumption that the sample was drawn from a population in which the two measured variables have no relationship, i.e., there is a zero correlation between the variables in the population ($H_0: \rho = 0$).
2. Choose a level for rejection of the null hypothesis. For most purposes, a reasonable level is the 5% level. If the obtained value of r is greater than the value required for rejection at the 1% level, then the lower probability may be reported; i.e., $p < .01$.
3. Determine the degrees of freedom for the test. For correlation this is based on the sample size in the following relationship: $df = N - 2$, where N is the number of pairs of measurements.
4. Using the value computed for the df, determine from table E the correlation coefficients necessary for rejecting the null hypothesis at the 5% and 1% levels. Compare the sample value with the table values to see whether or not, in terms of *absolute value,* the sample value is equal to or greater than the table values. If the sample value is less than the value required for significance at the 5% level, do not reject the null hypothesis. If it is equal to or greater than the value required for rejection at the 5% level but less than the value required at the 1% level, reject at the 5% level but not at the 1% level. If it is equal to or greater than the value at the 1% level, reject the null hypothesis at both levels.

Checking Your Progress

A psychologist has developed a new test of intelligence based on brain wave activity and wants to determine the reliability of the test. That is, he wants to see the degree to which the test yields the same score each time it is administered to a person. To measure its reliability, the test is given to 12 selected persons on two separate occasions with an intertest interval of three weeks. Scores on the test range from 1 to 25, and the data from the 12 individuals are shown below. Compute the correlation coefficient and test it for significance.

Subject No.	Score One	Score Two
1	3	5
2	22	17
3	19	21
4	18	16
5	15	17
6	10	8
7	11	12
8	13	15
9	7	9
10	6	4
11	20	22
12	18	10

The correct answer is $r = 0.85$ which is significant ($p < .01$). The conclusion is that the new test of intelligence has good reliability.

Linear Regression Equation: The Use of r in Predicting Y Given X

As one of its most useful functions, the correlation coefficient helps us predict a value of one variable if we know a value of the other. In other words, there is a formula that allows us to predict how some-one will score on variable Y if we know how they did on variable X. For example, in a previous problem we found a high correlation between the amount of time spent studying some material and the score a person made on an examination over the material. Given this information and an equation for prediction, we could estimate examination performance from a knowledge of the time a student spent studying.

regression equation   The development of an instrument for prediction, called a *regression equation,* is based on the definition given earlier of linear correlation. Correlation was defined as the degree of *linear* relationship between the variables, in other words, the degree to which the relationship can be described by a straight line. The *regression equation* is nothing more than the equation for the straight line that best describes the relationship between the variables. It is:

$$Y = \left(\frac{r\mathrm{SD}_Y}{\mathrm{SD}_X}\right)X - \left(\frac{r\mathrm{SD}_Y}{\mathrm{SD}_X}\right)\overline{X} + \overline{Y}$$

Although arranged differently, all the terms in the regression equation are familiar ones. To solve it we will need to know r, SD_X, SD_Y, $\overline{X}$, and $\overline{Y}$.

To begin, let's calculate the regression equation for the example of the study time and examination score. We found that $r = 0.96$, $\Sigma X = 140$, $\Sigma Y = 763$, $\Sigma X^2 = 2832$, $\Sigma Y^2 = 60839$, and $N = 10$. From these figures we can compute all the other information needed to compute the regression equation.

$$\overline{X} = \frac{\Sigma X}{N} = \frac{140}{10} = 14$$

$$\overline{Y} = \frac{763}{10} = 76.3$$

$$SD_X = \sqrt{\frac{\Sigma X^2}{N} - \overline{X}^2} = \sqrt{\frac{2832}{10} - 14^2} = \sqrt{283.2 - 196} = \sqrt{87.2}$$

$$= 9.34$$

$$SD_Y = \sqrt{\frac{60839}{10} - 76.3^2} = \sqrt{6083.9 - 5821.69} = \sqrt{262.21} = 16.19$$

$$\overline{Y} = \left(\frac{rSD_Y}{SD_X}\right)X - \left(\frac{rSD_Y}{SD_X}\right)\overline{X} + \overline{Y}$$

$$= \left(\frac{.96 \cdot 16.19}{9.34}\right)X - \left(\frac{.96 \cdot 16.19}{9.34}\right)14 + 76.3$$

$$= \left(\frac{15.54}{9.34}\right)X - \left(\frac{15.54}{9.34}\right)14 + 76.3$$

$$= (1.66)X - (1.66)14 + 76.3$$

$$= (1.66)X - 23.24 + 76.3$$

$$= (1.66)X + 53.06$$

Although the computations and manipulations are fairly straightforward, there is one particular point at which many students go awry. In the step immediately prior to the final answer, the last two terms are -23.24 and $+76.3$. Written in this fashion, it is obvious that the sum of the two is 53.06. However, there is a tendency to treat the last two terms as though there were a parentheses around them, i.e., $-(23.24 + 76.3)$. If this were true, the answer would be -99.54; but, since it is not true, such an answer is incorrect. Be careful on this step and think about what you are doing.

Now we can use the regression equation $Y = (1.66)X + 53.06$ to predict a score on one variable given some value on the other. For example, a student tells us that he has studied for 8 hours for the exam. What would we predict that he would make on the exam?

Substituting 8 for X would give us:

$$Y = (1.66)X + 53.06 = (1.66)8 + 53.06 = 13.28 + 53.06 = 66.34$$

Thus, we would predict that a student studying eight hours would make a score of about 66 on the exam. In the data from which the regression equation was computed, there was a student who had studied 8 hours with a score on the exam of 70. Why is there the discrepancy between the actual score and the predicted score? The reason is that the correlation between the two variables was not perfect. Hence, any particular prediction that we might make will probably not be perfect but will err somewhat. Of course, the higher the correlation that we have, the better our ability will be to predict a score on one variable given the other.

To help illustrate what has been done, the scatter plot of the sample data is shown in figure 10–4. On it, the line generated by the regression equation is drawn. Note the discrepancy between the line generated by the equation and the actual points.

Figure 10–4: Scatter plot of the relationship between time spent studying and the score on an exam. The line generated by the regression equation is shown.

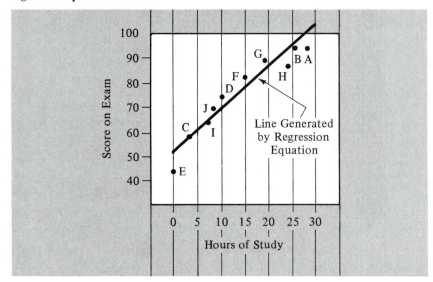

In reality, it wouldn't make much sense to determine a regression equation from some data just so that we could use it to predict scores that we already had. Rather, we would use our equation to predict the performance of individuals who have not yet been assessed on both behavioral measures. The example in the next section amplifies this point.

Suppose that we find that there is a correlation of $+.90$ between IQ scores and grade point averages (GPA) at a particular university. Further let us assume that the administration of the university has decided to strengthen their program and one way to do this is to admit only students that are likely to excel in academic work. Their definition of outstanding work is a grade point average of 2.8 (on a 4-point scale) or better. What is the minimum IQ score that they should allow in order to accomplish their goal; i.e., exclude students that are likely to earn GPAs of less than 2.8?

The problem is to determine the regression equation based on the correlation between IQ and GPA, and then find the IQ score that would lead to a GPA of at least 2.8. In order to calculate the regression equation, we need more data. Let's assume that the mean IQ score on the test the administrators are using is 100 and that the standard deviation for the test is 16. Further, the mean GPA at the time the correlation was determined was 2.60 with a standard deviation of 0.60. Given this information and designating IQ as the X variable and GPA the Y variable, the regression equation would be as follows:

$$Y = \left(\frac{r\mathrm{SD}_Y}{\mathrm{SD}_X}\right)X - \left(\frac{r\mathrm{SD}_Y}{\mathrm{SD}_X}\right)\overline{X} + \overline{Y}$$

$$= \left(\frac{.9 \cdot .6}{16}\right)X - \left(\frac{.9 \cdot .6}{16}\right)100 + 2.6$$

$$= (.034)X - (.034)100 + 2.6 = (.034)X - 3.4 + 2.6$$

$$= (.034)X - 0.8$$

We now have the regression equation $Y = (.034)X - 0.8$ and are in a position to answer the original question; that is, what IQ score would lead to a GPA of 2.8? Here we have been given a Y-score (GPA) and want to use it to determine an X (IQ score). Using the regression equation, we would have:

$$Y = (.034)X - 0.8$$
$$2.8 = (.034)X - 0.8$$
$$2.8 + 0.8 = (.034)X$$
$$(.034)X = 2.8 + 0.8$$
$$(.034)X = 3.6$$
$$X = \frac{3.6}{.034}$$
$$= 105.9, \text{ or about } 106$$

Therefore, to accomplish their goals our fictitious administrators might decide to reject any applicants with IQ scores below 106.

Another question that we might ask is: "What GPA would we expect from an individual with an IQ score of 135?" The correct answer is 3.79.

Checking Your Progress

In a study of alcoholics, a significant correlation between blood-alcohol concentration and the score on a 50-item test of recent memory function has been found. The average blood-alcohol concentration in the persons studied was 0.01% with a SD of 0.004, while the average number of items correctly answered on the recent memory test was 35 with a SD of 6. Assuming that the correlation is $-.83$, find the regression equation and predict the score of a person with a blood-alcohol concentration of 0.015. The correct answers are $Y = (-1245)X + 47.45$ for the regression equation and $Y = 28.78$ or about 29 for the number of correct responses on the recent memory test.

Spearman Rank Order Correlation Coefficient

The *Spearman rank order correlation coefficient* (r_S) was originally derived as an easy-to-compute alternative to the Pearson r. In addition to being computationally simpler, it is useful when the level of measurement for one or both of the two variables under consideration does not meet the requirements for the use of the Pearson r.

The Pearson r requires at least *interval scale* measurement, whereas the Spearman coefficient does not. With interval scale measurement we can precisely identify the length of the interval between measurements. For example, if we measure the length of two pieces of wood with a ruler, we might find that one was 50 cm long while the other was 100 cm. In this case we could say that one board (100 cm) was twice as long as the other (50 cm) and that the difference in their lengths (the interval between them) is exactly 50 cm. Similarly, we might measure the weight of two rats after some treatment and find that one weighs 300 gm while the other weighs 200 gm, with the interval between them being precisely 100 gm.

Sometimes, however, the crudeness of our measurement prevents us from being able to precisely specify the length of the interval between measurements. For example, in my research I often have occasion to rate the handling characteristics of rats after some form of brain damage. The rating scale has 5 different components. The animals are rated on reactivity to the presentation of a pencil in front of their snouts, reactivity to a tap on the flank with a pencil, ease of capture from a cage, ease of handling when the captured animal is held on a glove, and the amount of vocalization during the entire test. On each of the components the animal receives a score from 0 to 3 depending on its response to the test, and each animal is given a daily total based on the sum of the scores on the 5 components. Suppose that on a given day one animal receives a total rating of 10 while another receives a total of 5. Can we say that the first animal was twice as irritable or hard to handle as the second? The answer is no, we cannot say that one was *exactly* twice as hard to handle as the other. That is, we cannot precisely specify the length of the intervals between measurements because our "measuring stick" is too crude. About all that we can say is that the first animal was harder to handle than the second, that is, we can *rank* the animals in terms of relative ease or difficulty of handling.

Another example may be instructive. Suppose that one student in your class is designated as a "judge" and is given the assignment of rating each of the students in the class in terms of physical attractiveness. On the rating scale used by the "judge" each student is given a number from 1 to 10. The "judge" gives one student a score of 8, while another receives a score of 2. Can we say that the student with the score of 8 is 4 times as attractive as the student with the score of 2? Of course not. Again, all that we can say with any reasonable assuredness is that the person with the score of 8 ranks higher than the person with the score of 2.

Even though numbers may be used, rating people on such psychological variables as authoritativeness, subjectivity, masculinity, or compulsiveness is really a crude measure of the variable in question. It should only be used to determine a ranking of the individual relative to other individuals. Incidentally, this ranking of scores, as opposed to being able to specify the interval between them, results from a level of measurement known as the *ordinal scale*. That is, in   ordinal scale ordinal scale measurement, the precise interval between scores cannot be specified, and a ranking or ordering of the scores is the best that can be accomplished.

When we have interval scale measurement, we can use either the Pearson r or Spearman r_S to compute a correlation coefficient, although the Pearson r is better because it takes into account more of the data. On the other hand, when we have ordinal scale measurement, we cannot use the Pearson r but will have to rely on the Spearman r_S.

Let's consider a problem in which the Spearman r_S would be more appropriate. An experimenter wants to see if anxiety level is related to pain in people. A group of 10 persons is first given a rating scale instrument to determine their levels of anxiety. Based on their responses to the items on the scale, each person is given a number from 0 to 10 as a summary rating of anxiety level. Later each person is given a pain sensitivity test in which the amount of a painful stimulus needed to elicit a response is noted. The scores are:

Subject No.	X (Anxiety Rating)	Y (Pain Stimulus)
1	10.0	2.5
2	9.3	1.1
3	9.1	2.5
4	7.5	5.3
5	6.2	2.5
6	5.0	7.0
7	5.0	8.1
8	3.6	6.5
9	2.5	9.5
10	1.1	9.4

The formula for r_S is:

$$r_S = 1 - \frac{6\Sigma d^2}{N(N^2 - 1)}$$

where d is the difference between the ranks of individuals on the two variables and N is the number of pairs of observations as it was in the case of r. Looking at the formula we can see that the only thing that we are going to have to determine prior to the calculation of r_S is the value of Σd^2. To do this we first *rank* the scores on each of the two variables from the highest to the lowest, take the difference between the ranks, square it, and then sum the squared differences. Let's try the procedure on the example shown above.

Subject No.	X	Rank on X	Y	Rank on Y	d	d^2
1	10.0	1.0	2.5	8	−7.0	49.00
2	9.3	2.0	1.1	10	−8.0	64.00
3	9.1	3.0	2.5	8	−5.0	25.00
4	7.5	4.0	5.3	5	−2.0	4.00
5	6.2	5.0	2.5	8	−3.0	9.00
6	5.0	6.5	7.0	4	2.5	6.25
7	5.0	6.5	8.1	3	3.5	12.25
8	3.6	8.0	6.5	5	3.0	9.00
9	2.5	9.0	9.5	1	8.0	64.00
10	1.1	10.0	9.4	2	8.0	64.00
						306.50

As you can see each subject was assigned a rank on each of the two variables, for each pair of ranks the rank on the Y variable was subtracted from the rank on variable X, each of the differences was squared, and the numbers in the column labeled d^2 were summed to get Σd^2. All of this is relatively straightforward except perhaps for the assigning of the ranks to the scores on the variables.

To assign the ranks, start with the highest score (10.0 on the X variable) and give that score the rank of 1. Since the next highest score is 9.3, give this score the rank of 2. Continue this procedure until all the subjects have been assigned a rank on the X variable. In the case of ties (when two or more subjects receive the same score on a variable), each subject is given the average rank. For example, on the X variable subjects 6 and 7 both received ratings on the anxiety scale of 5.0. Because of their relative position in the distribution, they would have been assigned the ranks of 6 and 7. Since they are really tied for the two positions we assign each of them the average of the two ranks $[(6 + 7) \div 2 = 13 \div 2 = 6.5]$. Similarly, subjects 1, 3, and 5 are tied on the Y variable. Because of their relative position in the distribution, they would have received the ranks of 7, 8, and 9. But, because they are tied they are given the average of 7, 8, and 9 $[(7 + 8 + 9) \div 3 = 24 \div 3 = 8]$.

Now the calculation of r_S becomes a matter of plugging the relevant numbers into the equation.

$$r_S = 1 - \frac{6\Sigma d^2}{N(N^2 - 1)} = 1 - \frac{6(306.5)}{10(10^2 - 1)}$$

$$= 1 - \frac{1839}{10(a00 - 1)} = 1 - \frac{1839}{10(99)} = 1 - \frac{1839}{990}$$

$$= 1 - 1.86 = -0.86$$

The value of r_S that we obtained (-0.86) indicates a fairly sizable inverse relationship between a person's rating on an anxiety scale and the same person's score on reactivity to painful stimulus. That is, the higher the rating on the anxiety scale, the lower is the amount of stimulus necessary to elicit a response. But, is the value of r_S that we observed large enough for us to conclude that there is a significant relationship between the *ranks* of the variables in the population?

The null hypothesis for the significance test of r_S is that no relationship exists between the ranks of the two variables in the population from which the sample was drawn. To test r_S all we have to do is to compare its value with critical values in appendix table F for the appropriate sample size. For the example above, our sample size was 10. Looking at table F we find that the values of r_S at the 5% and 1% levels of significance for samples of size 10 are .648 and .794, respectively. Our obtained r_S was -0.86, which is .86 in absolute value and is larger than the value required for rejection of the null hypothesis at the 1% level. Therefore, we reject the null hypothesis and conclude that anxiety level is related to pain sensitivity.

Let's consider another example to illustrate how easy it is to compute r_S. Suppose we have rated a group of 12 students on the extent of their fat deposits with a scale that assigns a value of 0 to a person who is 50% under the average weight for his age and bone structure and a score of 7 to a person who is at least 50% over his desired body weight. In addition, the same people have been rated in terms of an introvert-extrovert scale, giving a score of 0 to an extremely withdrawn person (introvert) and a score of 5 to a person who is very outgoing (extrovert). We would like to determine by means of a correlation coefficient whether or not there is any truth to the myth of the jolly fat person. The data are as follows:

Student	Rating of Obesity (0–7)	Introvert-Extrovert (0–5)
A	6.3	4.3
B	6.5	4.3
C	5.7	3.9
D	0.6	1.3
E	3.4	4.8
F	3.4	3.3
G	1.8	1.7
H	4.6	3.6

Student	Rating of Obesity (0–7)	Introvert-Extrovert (0–5)
I	1.8	2.5
J	1.8	2.2
K	5.9	1.1
L	6.7	4.7

The first step is to rank the scores on the X variable and on the Y variable from the highest to the lowest. Looking at the X variable we see that the highest score is 6.7, so we assign this person a rank of 1. The next highest is a score of 6.5, which gets a rank of 2, and so forth. As we rank the scores on the X variable we see that there are some tied scores and that we must assign the average rank to each of the tied scores. For example, the scores that would be assigned the ranks of 7 and 8 are both 3.4. The average rank in this case is $7 + 8 \div 2$ or 7.5. In addition, ranks 9, 10, and 11 should go to the three scores of 1.8. Since the 1.8s are tied, we assign the average rank or $(9 + 10 + 11) \div 3$ which is 10. Finally, the score of 0.6 is assigned the rank of 12.

Scores on the Y variable range from a high of 4.8 which receives a rank of 1 to a low of 1.1 which gets a rank of 12. The only tie comes in ranks 3 and 4 where we have two students scoring 4.3. Each receives the average rank or 3.5.

After ranking each person on the two variables, find the difference between the ranks and square and sum each of the differences. The result is:

Student	X	Rank on X	Y	Rank on Y	d	d^2
A	6.3	3.0	4.3	3.5	−0.5	0.25
B	6.5	2.0	4.3	3.5	−1.5	2.25
C	5.7	5.0	3.9	5.0	0.0	0.00
D	0.6	12.0	1.3	11.0	1.0	1.00
E	3.4	7.5	4.8	1.0	6.5	42.25
F	3.4	7.5	3.3	7.0	0.5	0.25
G	1.8	10.0	1.7	10.0	0.0	0.00
H	4.6	6.0	3.6	6.0	0.0	0.00
I	1.8	10.0	2.5	8.0	2.0	4.00
J	1.8	10.0	2.2	9.0	1.0	1.00
K	5.9	4.0	1.1	12.0	−8.0	64.00
L	6.7	1.0	4.7	2.0	−1.0	1.00
						116.00

Having determined that $\Sigma d^2 = 116$, we are ready to apply the formula for r_S.

$$r_S = 1 - \frac{6\Sigma d^2}{N(N^2 - 1)} = 1 - \frac{6(116)}{12(12^2 - 1)} = 1 - \frac{696}{12(144 - 1)}$$

$$= 1 - \frac{696}{12(143)} = 1 - \frac{696}{1716} = 1 - 0.406 = +0.594$$

Inserting the value we computed for Σd^2 into the formula for r_S, we find the correlation coefficient to be +0.594. We can test this value for significance by referring to appendix table F as before. With an N of 12, a coefficient of .591 is required for significance at the 5% level. Since our observed coefficient of .594 is larger than the table value, we reject the null hypothesis and conclude that a rating on degree of obesity is related to a rating on a scale of introversion-extroversion.

Checking Your Progress

Two female students have been asked to independently rank the pictures of 8 male college students in terms of attractiveness. The rankings are:

Male Student	Judge A	Judge B
1	3.5	4
2	2	1
3	3.5	2.5
4	1	2.5
5	7	5
6	5	6
7	6	7
8	8	8

Determine the correlation between the rankings and test it for significance. Note that the data are given in the form of *rankings*. In other words, the males have already been ranked from highest to lowest and it is unnecessary to rank them again. The correct answer for r_S is 0.875 ($p < .05$).

Summary

Two different techniques for determining the degree of relationship between two variables have been detailed. The first was the *Pearson product-moment correlation coefficient* or the Pearson r. The definition of r is that it is the mean of the z-score products for the X and Y variables. The computational or raw score formula for the Pearson r is:

$$r = \frac{\Sigma XY - \dfrac{\Sigma X \Sigma Y}{N}}{\sqrt{\left[\Sigma X^2 - \dfrac{(\Sigma X)^2}{N} \right]\left[\Sigma Y^2 - \dfrac{(\Sigma Y)^2}{N} \right]}}$$

The obtained correlation coefficient can be compared to values given in appendix table E to determine whether or not there is a significant relationship between the two variables. The test of significance involves the assumption that there is no relationship between the variables in the population ($H_0 : \rho = 0$). The null hypothesis is rejected at either the 5% or the 1% level if the sample coefficient is equal to or larger in absolute value than the appropriate values in appendix table E. The degrees of freedom for the test of r for significance are $N - 2$, where N is the number of pairs of scores.

After r is obtained, it can be used to compute the *linear regression equation,* which is really the equation for the straight line that best fits the data from the sample. This equation is used to make predictions about a score on one variable if we know a score on the other. The formula is:

$$Y = \left(\frac{r\text{SD}_Y}{\text{SD}_X} \right) X - \left(\frac{r\text{SD}_Y}{\text{SD}_X} \right) \overline{X} + \overline{Y}$$

A second type of correlation coefficient was introduced. Based on the difference in the ranks of the X and Y variables, the *Spearman rank order correlation coefficient* is useful when the level of measurement of one or both of the variables is of the ordinal scale type.

The formula for the Spearman r_S is:

$$r_S = 1 - \frac{6\Sigma d^2}{N(N^2 - 1)}$$

After computing r_S it can be tested for significance by comparing it to values in appendix table F for the sample size that we have observed.

Troubleshooting Your Computations

When computing either type of correlation coefficient discussed in this chapter, there is a built-in check for the accuracy of your computations. That is, always remember that the range of r and r_S is from $+1$ to -1. If you obtain an answer outside this range (which sometimes happens when you make some kind of error), then it is incorrect and you need to reexamine both your formula and *all* calculations.

There are two frequently made errors in the computation of r_S. The first is forgetting to rank the scores on the X and Y variables when it is appropriate to do this. Remember the name of the statistic—the *Spearman rank order correlation coefficient*. In other words, it is the coefficient based on the relationship between the ranks and you must obtain the ranks before any computations can be made.

Another common mistake in computing r_S involves the application of the equation. You must remember that the first term in the equation, 1, is separate from the fraction, $6\Sigma d^2/N(N^2 - 1)$, and that the fraction is subtracted from it. It can easily happen that the 1 inadvertently becomes part of the numerator of the fraction which is incorrect. Additionally, don't become so involved in the computation of the fraction that you report it as r_S forgetting to subtract it from 1.

One main problem area in the computation of the regression equation is in the handling of the last two terms in the equation, $-(r\mathrm{SD}_Y/\mathrm{SD}_X)\overline{X} + \overline{Y}$. If your r is positive, simplification of the terms will result in something in the form $-A + B$. These two numbers should be added algebraically.

Remember that r_S must be used when you have ordinal scale data, that is, the precise intervals between the scores cannot be specified, and ranking or ordering of the scores is appropriate. When the data have been collected using an interval scale, then the use of r is indicated.

In testing r for significance, remember to use table E and $df = N - 2$. If you have determined r_S and want to test it for significance, then appendix table F is used and the critical values are reported in relation to N rather than df.

Exercises

1. Given the following data: $\Sigma XY = 1555.2$, $\Sigma X^2 = 1308$, $\Sigma Y^2 = 1920$, $\Sigma X = 120$, $\Sigma Y = 144$, $N = 12$,
   (a) Calculate r and test it for significance.
   (b) Calculate the regression equation.
   (c) Find Y when $X = 13$.
   (d) Find X when $Y = 6$.
2. A significant correlation between number of cigarettes smoked and life expectancy has been found. Given the following data, determine the life expectancy of a man who smokes 80 cigarettes per day: $r = -0.40$, mean number of cigarettes per day $= 20$ with a standard deviation of 4, mean life expectancy of smokers $= 60$ years with a standard deviation of 5 years.
3. An experiment has been performed to see if there is any truth to the obnoxious television commercials concerning the offensiveness of bad breath. Ten students have been surreptitiously rated on the degree of offensiveness of their breath on a scale from 0 to 10, reserving 10 for persons with extremely bad breath. They have also been given a self-administered scale to determine the quality and quantity of their contact with the opposite sex. Scores on this last scale range from 0 to 5, with a 5 being given to a person who constantly dates all the most popular people on campus. The data are:

Person No.	Halitosis Scale	Popularity
1	9	1
2	7	2
3	3	4
4	1	5
5	0	5
6	2	4
7	4	3
8	10	0
9	7	4
10	6	2

Determine the degree of relationship between the variables and test it for significance.
4. In some studies that I have performed involving the handling characteristics of rats after certain types of brain damage, I have had students use a rating scale to determine a handling score for each animal. To ensure that the student was performing the rating accurately, I independently rated the same animals at the same time as the student and then determined the correlation between the rankings. Some data of this sort are provided below. Determine r_S and test it for significance.

Rat No.	Thorne's Rating	Student's Rating
1	14	12
2	3	3
3	0	1
4	12	10
5	8	11
6	8	7
7	3	1
8	3	3
9	5	4
10	7	5

5. A study has been done to see whether or not there is a relationship between height and salary in adult males in a particular company. Thus, 15 males were measured to find their height and were then asked to tell their annual salary. The subjects were approximately equivalent in terms of time with the company and in terms of education. The results were as follows:

Male No.	Height in Inches	Salary in Thousands of Dollars
1	79	25.2
2	63	15.7
3	65	17.1
4	67	17.5
5	75	23.5
6	70	19.5
7	70	18.2
8	69	17.2
9	71	20.0
10	74	21.8
11	73	25.4
12	70	20.3
13	68	16.5
14	67	15.5
15	61	14.3

If a significant r is found, construct the regression equation and predict the salary of an employee who was 66 inches tall.

6. For what purpose is the regression equation used? Why is the prediction usually not perfect?

7. Rank the following correlation coefficients in terms of degree of relationship: +0.08, +0.95, +0.57, −0.98, −0.37, +0.85.

8. A professor has devised a new personality test and he wants to assess its reliability. To do this he divides the test items in half and administers one half to 12 people. A week later he administers the other half to the same people. Determine the correlation between the two halves of the test.

Person No.	First Half	Second Half
1	34	37
2	25	22
3	15	15
4	17	16
5	20	19
6	23	25
7	24	22
8	31	30
9	18	14
10	10	8
11	7	10
12	16	20

9. Eight pairs of identical twins are found and their IQ scores are determined. From the data below, what is the correlation between the scores? Is it significant?

Pair	Twin A	Twin B
1	106	115
2	127	117
3	85	89
4	73	61
5	102	98
6	85	100
7	97	98
8	110	108

10. Eight pairs of fraternal twins have their IQ scores measured. From the data, what is the correlation between the scores. Is it significant?

Pair	Twin A	Twin B
1	101	110
2	153	110
3	115	107
4	97	105
5	75	68
6	120	126
7	110	112
8	105	100

Chi Square and Fisher Exact Probability

Introduction

In chapters 8 and 9 we talked about methods for comparing the results from two or more different samples. The level of measurement necessary for the use of the t-test and for the F-test is interval scale data or data in which the intervals between scores have meaning and can be precisely stated. In chapter 10 the Spearman rank order correlation coefficient was introduced as a means of dealing with the data generated by an ordinal scale or data that can be ranked from top to bottom but the precise interval between each score cannot be stated. A less sophisticated scale than either of the two that have already been identified is the nominal scale.

A *nominal scale* is just what the title implies, that is, it is a scale in name only. With the nominal scale we cannot specify the interval between values nor the ranking or ordering of the values. All that we can do is to record frequencies of occurrence; that is, how many subjects happen to fall under a particular label or name.   nominal scale

An example of the use of the nominal scale might be the naming of particular automobiles. As an illustration, the cars passing a streetcorner might be divided into the categories, Chevrolet, Ford, Buick, and Dodge, and the number of vehicles falling into each of the categories would constitute data. Similarly, the designations male and female are nominal categories. Since people seem to have a penchant for naming things, other examples of nominal categories are all too obvious. The point is that nominal categories are names only and cannot be used for even ranking the items that fall within them.

Suppose that an experimenter has administered a survey of common fears to a group of male and female students. He has arbitrarily decided that a score of 1 to 10 on the scale indicates a low number of fears, 11 to 20 indicates a medium number of fears, and 21 to 30 indicates that the subject has a high number of fears. For the group of students he finds that 10 females fall into the low category, 15 fall into the medium category, and 25, with scores of 21 to 30, are in the high category. On the other hand, the results for the males are just the opposite: 25 males in the low category, 15 in the medium category, and 10 in the high category. For convenience, the data have been summarized below.

	Low Fear	Medium Fear	High Fear	Total
Males	25	15	10	50
Females	10	15	25	50
Total	35	30	35	100

As you can see, some differences exist in the frequencies of males and females falling under the three categories of low, medium, and high fear. Are the differences great enough so that the experimenter can conclude that females are more likely to have a large number of fears than males? In other words, our experimenter would like to do a test of significance on the data he has generated to see if the differences in frequencies are meaningful or whether they are likely to exist just by chance. None of the tests discussed up to this point is appropriate for such data, so it is time to introduce the chi-square test.

The Chi-Square Test of Significance

Chi-square test

Much of the data that I have collected over the past several years has been the sort that would be analyzed by means of the *chi-square test*, symbolized by χ^2 (pronounced ki-square, with a long i). I would like to use some of my data to introduce the use of this test. In a study that I did in 1973, a large number of rats had their olfactory bulbs removed, while an equal number was subjected to sham operations. After a period of recovery, all animals were tested for the presence of predatory aggression. The results of the experiment have been put into the table below which is called a 2×2 table because it has two rows and two columns.

	Predators	Nonpredators	Total
Sham Operated	6	74	80
OB Removed	25	55	80
Total	31	129	160

If the operation had no effect we would expect to find equal numbers of predators and nonpredators in each group. However, there are more predators in the brain-damaged group than in the sham-operated group. The question is: Is the difference great enough for us to conclude that there is a significant difference between the groups and that the olfactory bulb removal did, in fact, increase the number of predatory rats?

The formula for the test is very simple:

$$\chi^2 = \Sigma \frac{(O - E)^2}{E}$$

where O stands for the *observed* frequency and E stands for the *expected* frequency. So, we just determine the expected frequency for each cell of the 2×2 table, subtract it from the observed frequency in the cell, square the result and divide it by the expected frequency, and add together the results from each cell to get χ^2. How do we determine the expected frequency or E?

Again, if the operation had no effect we would expect to observe equal numbers of predators in the two groups. Since a total of 31 predators were observed in both groups combined, half (15.5) of these should have been observed in each of the two groups if the operation was without effect. Similarly, of the total of 129 nonpredators observed, half (64.5) would have been expected in each group.

Another way these expected values can be determined is to multiply the row total for a given cell by the column total for the same cell and divide the result by the overall total. Since the expected frequencies for a given row or column must sum to the row or column total, for a 2×2 table we only have to calculate one of the Es since we can determine the others by subtraction. Using our specific example with the predator and nonpredator rats, we see that the expected frequency for the sham-operated predators is the row total (80) times the column total (31) divided by the overall total or 160. Thus, we have $(80 \cdot 31) \div 160 = 2480 \div 160 = 15.5$. There is no need to determine the rest of the expected values by the same procedure, since it can be done with less effort by subtraction. The expected frequency for the sham-operated nonpredators is $80 - 15.5 = 64.5$. Similarly, E for the OB predators is $31 - 15.5 = 15.5$; for the OB nonpredators E is $80 - 15.5 = 64.5$. With the expected values in parentheses, the original 2×2 table now becomes:

	Predators	*Nonpredators*	*Total*
Sham Operated	(15.5) 6	(64.5) 74	80
OB Removed	(15.5) 25	(64.5) 55	80
Total	31	129	160

Having determined the expected frequencies, we are now ready to compute χ^2.

$$\chi^2 = \Sigma \frac{(O - E)^2}{E} = \frac{(6 - 15.5)^2}{15.5} + \frac{(74 - 64.5)^2}{64.5} + \frac{(25 - 15.5)^2}{15.5}$$

$$+ \frac{(55 - 64.5)^2}{64.5}$$

$$= \frac{(-9.5)^2}{15.5} + \frac{(9.5)^2}{64.5} + \frac{(9.5)^2}{15.5} + \frac{(-9.5)^2}{64.5}$$

$$= \frac{90.25}{15.5} + \frac{90.25}{64.5} + \frac{90.25}{15.5} + \frac{90.25}{64.5}$$

$$= 5.82 + 1.40 + 5.82 + 1.40 = 14.44$$

For each cell in the 2 × 2 table, the difference between the observed frequency and the expected frequency is squared and divided by the expected frequency. The results for each cell are then summed to give χ^2 which in this case was found to be 14.44.

To determine whether or not the χ^2 we obtained is significant, we must refer to appendix table G. The title of table G tells us that it contains values of chi square at the 5% and 1% levels of significance. As before, we see that we need to determine the degrees of freedom in order to use the table. Recall that *df* was defined as the number of values that are free to vary after certain restrictions are placed on the data. For chi square the restriction that we place on the data is that the row and column totals are fixed.

Now, how many expected frequencies did we actually have to compute? The answer is only one, since the others were obtained by subtraction. Thus, the *df* for a 2 × 2 table will always be 1, since this is the number of values free to vary with the row and column totals fixed. A formula to determine the *df* for χ^2 is $df = (R - 1)(C - 1)$ where R stands for the number of rows and C for the number of columns. In the example we have computed both R and C were 2 and $df = (2 - 1)(2 - 1) = 1 \cdot 1 = 1$. With $df = 1$ the value required for significance at the 5% level is 3.84 and at the 1% level is 6.64. Since 14.44 is larger than either of the critical values, we conclude that the groups differ significantly and that OB damage causes an increase in predatory behavior in rats.

Checking Your Progress

To study the effects of alcohol on distance perception, 30 men drank a rum and cola (two ounces of rum) while 30 drank a rum-flavored cola. After 30 minutes all men were asked to estimate the distance between themselves and an object. The results were categorized into the number of men who overestimated the distance versus the number who underestimated. In the alcohol group, 23 men underestimated the distance while 14 underestimated it in the no-alcohol group. Determine χ^2 for this fictitious example and test it for significance.

The answer is 5.71, which for $df = 1$ is significant at the 5% level. The conclusion is that alcohol affects distance perception.

Restrictions on χ^2

Before we continue with further examples of the use and computation of χ^2, we need to discuss some restrictions that have been placed on it.

The first restriction states that *chi square can be used only with frequency data*. Any data can be converted to frequency data merely by dividing the data into some logical categories and counting the number of scores that occur in each category. For example, in my studies of the predatory response of the rat, I am often interested in the latency with which the response occurs. That is, I am interested in the time interval between initiation of the test and when the predatory response occurs. Let's assume that in a particular study I have observed 100 rats and have noted their predatory latencies as follows:

Latency in Seconds	f	Latency in Seconds	f
1100	2	555	4
1050	3	500	3
1025	4	400	2
1005	1	385	2
1002	3	350	1

(Continued)

Latency in Seconds	f	Latency in Seconds	f
955	3	325	1
925	2	300	2
890	3	295	3
875	5	285	4
800	3	250	3
755	6	245	3
730	4	240	6
725	2	120	5
700	2	110	3
655	1	100	4
630	2	90	2
600	2	80	2
		30	2

Given that all the tests were 20 minutes in length, I might be interested in determining whether or not the predatory behavior tends to be rather evenly spread throughout the test or whether the majority of animals exhibit it within certain time periods. To do this, I might divide the data into some logically consistent time intervals or some intervals that make sense on the basis of previous research. The main idea here is to decide on the intervals prior to examining the data or at least to decide on the basis of some reasonable criteria. Otherwise there is the danger that the intervals will be chosen to maximize the possibility of a desired result.

At any rate, suppose I have divided the data into four equal intervals; i.e., 1–300 seconds, 301–600 seconds, 601–900 seconds, and 901–1200 seconds. I can now determine the number of scores occurring in each interval of time and apply the χ^2 test to the resulting data to test the assumption that the frequencies are evenly distributed across the intervals. The data would be as follows:

Time Interval	1–300	301–600	601–900	901–1200	Total
Frequency within interval	(25) 39	(25) 15	(25) 28	(25) 18	100

Since the assumption has been made that there is an equal distribution of frequencies in each of the different time intervals, the expected frequency for each interval is 25 ($100 \div 4 = 25$) and this value is shown in parentheses in each interval. Computation of χ^2 proceeds as follows:

$$\chi^2 = \Sigma \frac{(O - E)^2}{E} = \frac{(39 - 25)^2}{25} + \frac{(15 - 25)^2}{25} + \frac{(28 - 25)^2}{25}$$

$$+ \frac{(18 - 25)^2}{25}$$

$$= \frac{14^2 + (-10)^2 + 3^2 + (-7)^2}{25}$$

$$= \frac{196 + 100 + 9 + 49}{25} = \frac{354}{25} = 14.16$$

For this example, the *df* is 3 since there were four intervals and the sum of the frequencies was fixed. Thus, the values free to vary are 3 since the values in the first three intervals could have been any numbers less than 100 while the value of the fourth interval would be determined by the frequencies in the first three intervals.

The table of frequency values shown above would be called a 1 × 4 contingency table since there is 1 row and 4 columns. The formula for *df* introduced earlier [$df = (R - 1)(C - 1)$] cannot be used for the type of contingency table in which there is only one row of scores since the outcome would always be zero for *df* ($R - 1$ would always be equal to $1 - 1 = 0$). Thus, in a contingency table with only one row of numbers, *df* will be equal to the number of columns minus one, i.e., $C - 1$.

According to appendix table G, the values required for significance at the 5% and 1% levels with $df = 3$ are 7.82 and 11.34, respectively. Since our computed value of 14.16 is larger than the table values, we conclude that the assumption of equal distribution of frequencies across the intervals was false and that animals are more likely to exhibit predatory behavior at certain times after the beginning of the test than at others.

Since there is a possibility that I have obscured the original point that I was trying to make with the example, let me repeat it. We can only use χ^2 with frequency data. However, it is possible to convert whatever data we have into frequency data by selecting different categories and counting the number of scores that fall into each one. The primary danger with doing this is that χ^2 is a less sensitive test than others that we might apply.

The second restriction that must be placed on chi square is that *the individual events or observations that constitute the data must be independent of each other*. This would not be true, for example, if we asked each subject multiple questions and then treated each of the responses as though they were independent of each other. Similarly, if we were dealing with wife-husband pairs, we should not expect their responses to be independent of each other.

The third restriction states that *we must have in the data both the frequency of occurrence and the frequency of nonoccurrence if we are recording whether or not an event occurs*. For example, if I have tested 20 rats for predatory behavior after brain damage and 20 rats after sham operations, I could not compare the number of predators in each group without also considering the nonpredators. This restriction is necessary in order for the sums of the observed and expected frequencies to be the same.

The fourth restriction placed on χ^2 is that *no expected frequency should be less than 5*. The reason for this is that the distribution of χ^2 may have different values than those shown in table G if any expected frequencies are less than 5. There are ways to get around this rule, however.

First, the rule may be relaxed a bit if we have more than 4 cells and only a few of them have expected frequencies less than 5. Second, if we have a 2 × 2 table and expected frequencies less than 5, we may use another test called the *Fisher exact probability test* (to be discussed later in the chapter). Finally, we can do what we probably should have done anyway and that is to test more subjects so that our observed and expected frequencies are larger.

The fifth restriction states that *when we have a small number of categories (that is, df = 1) and the expected frequency is less than 10 but more than 5 in one or more of the cells, a correction factor should be applied*. The correction is called a correction for continuity and is needed because the table values of χ^2 are based on continuous distributions. In an earlier chapter we found that a continuous variable was one whose measurement resulted in numbers without gaps between them, i.e., the numbers could take on any value including fractional values.

Since frequencies from which χ^2 is calculated vary in discrete fashion, χ^2 itself tends to vary in the same manner. This becomes a problem especially when *df* and the expected frequencies are very small, and it necessitates the use of the correction factor as a partial compensation.

The procedure is really very simple and involves the subtraction of 0.5 from the absolute value of each $O - E$. Applying this correction factor the formula for χ^2 becomes:

$$\chi^2 = \Sigma \frac{(|O - E| - 0.5)^2}{E}$$

Again, we would only have to apply the correction factor when we have either a 2×2 table or a 1×2 table and expected frequencies between 5 and 10. An example of a problem in which the correction factor has been applied is given in the next section.

χ^2 With Correction

A professor wants to determine whether or not his department should keep the requirement of college algebra as a prerequisite for the course entitled Introductory Psychological Statistics. Accordingly he allows some students to register for the course on a pass-fail basis whether or not they have had the prerequisite. Of the 35 students in the class, 20 have had the algebra course and 15 have not. At the end of the semester, the professor determines the number of students passing or failing the course in relation to whether or not they had had algebra. The results are summarized as follows:

	Pass	*Fail*	*Total*
Algebra	(13.14) 17	(6.86) 3	20
No Algebra	(9.86) 6	(5.14) 9	15
Total	23	12	35

As you can see, we have a 2×2 table and three of the cells have expected frequencies less than 10 but more than 5 as shown in parentheses. Thus, the situation calls for the correction factor. The χ^2 is computed as follows:

$$\chi^2 = \Sigma \frac{(|O - E| - 0.5)^2}{E} = \frac{(|17 - 13.14| - 0.5)^2}{13.14}$$

$$+ \frac{(|6 - 9.86| - 0.5)^2}{9.86} + \frac{(|3 - 6.86| - 0.5)^2}{6.86} + \frac{(|9 - 5.14| - 0.5)^2}{5.14}$$

$$= \frac{(|3.86| - 0.5)^2}{13.14} + \frac{(|-3.86| - 0.5)^2}{9.86} + \frac{(|-3.86| - 0.5)^2}{6.86}$$

$$+ \frac{(|3.86| - 0.5)^2}{5.14}$$

$$= \frac{(3.86 - 0.5)^2}{13.14} + \frac{(3.86 - 0.5)^2}{9.86} + \frac{(3.86 - 0.5)^2}{6.86} + \frac{(3.86 - 0.5)^2}{5.14}$$

$$= \frac{3.36^2}{13.14} + \frac{3.36^2}{9.86} + \frac{3.36^2}{6.86} + \frac{3.36^2}{5.14}$$

$$= \frac{11.29}{13.14} + \frac{11.29}{9.86} + \frac{11.29}{6.86} + \frac{11.29}{5.14}$$

$$= .86 + 1.14 + 1.65 + 2.20 = 5.85, \ df = 1$$

From appendix 1 table G the values of χ^2 required for significance with $df = 1$ are 3.84 at the 5% level and 6.64 at the 1% level. Since the value of χ^2 that we computed is larger than the value required for rejection of the null hypothesis at the 5% level, we reject it and conclude that whether or not the person has had algebra prior to taking statistics is important in determining whether or not the person will fail. Thus, the hypothetical professor would be wise to keep algebra as a prerequisite for statistics.

Checking Your Progress

In an experiment in social psychology, 28 students (13 females and 15 males) are asked to wait individually outside a closed door. While they are sitting outside the room waiting for their turn, a person of the opposite sex walks toward them carrying a large notebook filled with loose papers. Under the pretext of stumbling, the person drops the notebook spilling a large number of papers onto the floor. The experiment is designed to see whether or not there is a sex difference in willingness to aid a stranger of the opposite sex in distress.

Thus, of the 13 female experimental subjects, 10 helped the clumsy person pick up the loose papers while 3 continued to wait their turn in the experiment. Of the 15 males, only 5 went to the aid of the female confederate. Construct the appropriate 2 × 2 table and apply the χ^2 test with correction factor.

The correct answer for χ^2 is 3.75, which for $df = 1$ does not quite meet the value required for significance at the 5% level. However, the probabilities given in table G are from a two-tailed test. If we had predicted prior to collection of the data that females would show more willingness to help, a one-tailed test would have been appropriate. For a one-tailed test, the probabilities shown in appendix table G would be halved and the probability of 3.84 with $df = 1$

would be 0.025 instead of 0.05. The probability associated with a χ^2 of 3.75 would be slightly greater than 0.025 but still much less than 0.05 and the result would be significant at the 5% level with a one-tailed test.

Fisher Exact Probability Test

One of the restrictions on the use of χ^2 is that it is not appropriate when we are dealing with a 1×2 table or a 2×2 table in which the expected frequencies are less than 5. In the case of the 2×2 table, an alternative to χ^2 is the *Fisher exact probability test*. Actually the Fisher test can be used whenever we have a 2×2 table and will provide us with the exact probability of the result (and any less likely) that we obtain. It is, however, considered by many to be much more tedious to calculate than χ^2 and, because of this, is normally used only when there are expected frequencies less than 5.

Fisher exact probability test

In a 2×2 contingency table, we can label the cells as follows:

			Total
	A	B	A + B
	C	D	C + D
Total	A + C	B + D	A + B + C + D = N

The equation that can be used to compute the probability of a 2×2 table is:

$$P = \frac{(A + B)!\,(C + D)!\,(A + C)!\,(B + D)!}{N!\,A!\,B!\,C!\,D!},$$

where N! (pronounced N factorial) $= N(N - 1)(N - 2)(N - 3) \cdots [N - (N - 1)]$. For example, 5! would be $5(5 - 1)(5 - 2)(5 - 3)(5 - 4) = 5 \cdot 4 \cdot 3 \cdot 2 \cdot 1 = 120$. Also, 0! is by convention equal to 1.

Using the example from the last "Checking Your Progress" section, the 2×2 table would be as follows:

	Females	*Males*	*Total*
Helpers	10	5	15
Nonhelpers	3	10	13
Total	13	15	28

To determine the exact probability of the event that we have observed, we need to solve the equation

$$p = \frac{15!\ 13!\ 13!\ 15!}{28!\ 10!\ 5!\ 3!\ 10!}$$

It appears that the computation of p would be extraordinarily difficult because of the numbers involved. For example, $13! = 6227020800$ and this isn't even the largest factorial we have to determine. Can you imagine what $28!$ is? No wonder the symbol for factorial is an exclamation point.

Fortunately there is a shortcut. The shortcut is that we can cancel many of the terms in the denominator and numerator just as we would with a fraction such as $\frac{2}{4} = \frac{1}{2}$. Look at $13!$ This is really just $13 \cdot 12 \cdot 11 \cdot 10!$ and we can cancel out the $10!$ in the numerator and denominator leaving $13 \cdot 12 \cdot 11 \cdot$ in the numerator. Further examples of the canceling procedure are:

$$p = \frac{15\!\!/\ 13 \cdot 12 \cdot 11 \cdot 10\!\!/\ 13 \cdot 12 \cdot 11 \cdot 10\!\!/\ 15 \cdot 14 \cdot 13 \cdot 12 \cdot 11 \cdot 10 \cdot 9 \cdot 8 \cdot 7 \cdot 6 \cdot 5\!\!/}{28 \cdot 27 \cdot 26 \cdot 25 \cdot 24 \cdot 23 \cdot 22 \cdot 21 \cdot 20 \cdot 19 \cdot 18 \cdot 17 \cdot 16 \cdot 15\!\!/\ 10\!\!/\ 5\!\!/\ 3!\ 10\!\!/}$$

Once we have canceled all the large factorials, we can begin to cancel or divide all the appropriate terms in the numerator and denominator. Continuing, we have:

$$p = \frac{13 \cdot 12 \cdot 11 \cdot 13 \cdot 12 \cdot 11 \cdot \overset{5}{15} \cdot 14 \cdot 13 \cdot 12 \cdot 11 \cdot 10 \cdot 9 \cdot 8 \cdot 7 \cdot 6}{\underset{2}{28} \cdot \underset{9}{27} \cdot \underset{2}{26} \cdot 25 \cdot \underset{2}{24} \cdot 23 \cdot \underset{2}{22} \cdot \underset{3}{21} \cdot \underset{2}{20} \cdot 19 \cdot \underset{2}{18} \cdot 17 \cdot \underset{2}{16} \cdot 3 \cdot 2 \cdot 1}$$

Beginning at the left of the fraction, 13 goes into 26 twice so the 13 is canceled and a 2 is noted under the canceled 26. Continuing, 12 divides into 24 twice so both numbers are canceled and a 2 is again noted below the 24 in the denominator. The canceling continues until we can't find any more numbers to divide into each other. Collecting the terms from the above expression, we find that we can do some more canceling:

$$p = \frac{13 \cdot 12 \cdot 11 \cdot 5 \cdot 13 \cdot 12 \cdot 11}{2 \cdot \underset{3}{9} \cdot 2 \cdot \underset{5}{25} \cdot 2 \cdot 23 \cdot 2 \cdot 3 \cdot 2 \cdot 19 \cdot 2 \cdot 17 \cdot 2}$$

$$= \frac{13 \cdot 11 \cdot 13 \cdot 11}{2 \cdot 3 \cdot 5 \cdot 23 \cdot 19 \cdot 2 \cdot 17 \cdot 2}$$

$$= \frac{20449}{891480} = 0.0229$$

Personally I've always found the canceling procedure to be rather fun to do, but I can't deny that it is tedious. And, you must be extremely careful not to lose any of the numbers when you collect terms from one fraction to the next. At this point you may be saying to yourself that this test doesn't look so bad and you can't understand why anyone would prefer to calculate χ^2 when both are appropriate. Well, unfortunately there is one thing that I neglected to mention. We are not through yet!

We have found that the probability of the event that we observed was 0.0229. The Fisher exact probability test requires that we compute not only the probability of the observed event but also the probability or probabilities of any *less likely events*. Assuming that we always keep the same total number of subjects, what less likely events might we have observed? With the same marginal totals, the more extreme events are as follows:

11	4	15
2	11	13
13	15	28

12	3	15
1	12	13
13	15	28

13	2	15
0	13	13
13	15	28

As you can see, we have only scratched the surface since we still have three more probabilities to determine. The more extreme cases were obtained by keeping the marginal totals the same and lowering the value of the smallest observed value by one until a zero is obtained in the cell. For the original example, the cell with the smallest number of observations was C with a frequency of 3. To find the more extreme cases, the frequency in cell C was lowered by one each time creating a new set of values in the other cells. If one of the cells in the 2×2 table has a zero in it initially, then we only have to determine the value of one probability.

After we determine the value of our observed situation and any more extreme possibilities, we merely add them together and use this value to determine whether or not the event we observed was significant. That is, if the total probability is less than 0.05, then it is significant.

For some sample exercises involving the computation of the Fisher exact probability, calculate the probabilities for each of the extreme situations outlined above. The answers are 0.0028, 0.0002, and 0.000002. When these values are combined with the probability of occurrence for the observed situation, the total probability is $0.0229 + 0.0028 + 0.0002 + 0.000002 = 0.0259$. Since this value is much less than $p = 0.05$, we conclude that the observed result is significant and females are more likely to help than males in situations of this sort. The Fisher exact probability test is a one-tailed test. If we want to determine the probability with a two-tailed test, we merely have to double the probability we have obtained. In the example we have been considering, doubling gives a probability of 0.0518 which is slightly greater than 0.05 and is comparable to the result obtained initially with χ^2.

Let's try another example to illustrate the Fisher exact probability test. In a portion of an experiment that I reported earlier in the chapter, I was interested in determining whether or not damage to the olfactory bulbs in Sprague-Dawley rats (one of a number of different strains of domestic rat in common use in laboratories, an albino) would result in an increase in predatory aggression. Thus, I took 20 rats (half male and half female) and gave 10 of them lesions of the olfactory bulbs while 10 were given sham operations. After recovery, I tested all 20 animals for predatory behavior. The result is expressed in the following 2×2 table:

	Predators	*Nonpredators*	*Total*
Sham-Operated Rats	1	9	10
OB Lesions	5	5	10
Total	6	14	20

First of all, we should determine the smallest expected frequency so that we can see whether or not χ^2 is appropriate. In this case, the smallest Es are found in either cell A or cell C. They are found by multiplying the marginal totals and dividing by the overall total ($10 \cdot 6 = 60 \div 20 = 3$). Since the expected values are less than 5, the use of the Fisher test is required. The probability of the observed situation is computed by:

$$p = \frac{10! \ 10! \ 6! \ 14!}{20! \ 1! \ 9! \ 5! \ 5!} = \frac{10 \cdot \cancel{9!} \ 10! \ 6 \cdot \cancel{5!} \ \cancel{14!}}{20 \cdot 19 \cdot 18 \cdot 17 \cdot 16 \cdot 15 \cdot \cancel{14!} \ \cancel{9!} \ \cancel{5!} \ 5!}$$

$$= \frac{\overset{2}{\cancel{10}} \cdot \cancel{10} \cdot 9 \cdot \cancel{8} \cdot 7 \cdot 6 \cdot \cancel{5}\,\cancel{6}}{\underset{2}{\cancel{20}} \cdot 19 \cdot \underset{2}{\cancel{18}} \cdot 17 \cdot \underset{2}{\cancel{16}} \cdot \underset{3}{\cancel{15}}\,\cancel{5}} = \frac{\overset{3}{\cancel{2}} \cdot 7 \cdot 6 \cdot 6}{\cancel{2} \cdot 19 \cdot \cancel{2} \cdot 17 \cdot \cancel{2} \cdot \cancel{3}} = \frac{21}{323}$$

$$= 0.065$$

The result that we observed was not the most extreme result possible. We still need to compute one more probability, one in which the value in cell A is lowered to 0 with resulting changes in the other cells. But is it really necessary to compute the other probability value or can we make a decision about whether or not the result we observed is significant at this point?

It is not necessary to perform any further computations because the result we observed has a probability of 0.065 which is larger than 0.05. Any further probabilities will just make the final probability larger, and we have already determined that the probability of the observed event is larger than that required for significance.

We can conclude that OB lesions do not increase the incidence of predatory behavior in Sprague-Dawley rats. However, there was obviously a trend in the direction of an increase in predation. Because the N was so small in the study, before making a definitive conclusion it would be a good idea to look at some more subjects.

Checking Your Progress

In an experiment to test the effects of a certain type of brain lesion on the retention of a visual discrimination problem, the subjects were 17 rats of which 8 were unoperated controls while the remaining 9 received damage to the red nucleus. Only 1 of the control animals had a loss of retention while 6 of the brain-damaged group showed a loss. Construct a 2×2 table and determine whether or not the damage to the red nucleus affected retention. The correct answer is $p = 0.037$, and the difference is significant with a one-tailed test. Did you remember the extreme case?

Summary

In this chapter we have discussed a technique that can be used to determine whether or not two or more independent groups differ significantly when the data are in the form of a frequency count. The method is called the *chi square test* and is symbolized by χ^2. The formula for χ^2 is $\Sigma(O - E)^2/E$ where O is the observed frequency and E is the expected frequency. The expected frequency for a given cell is normally found by multiplying the row and column totals for the cell in a contingency table and dividing by the overall total or N.

Once the value of χ^2 has been calculated it can be compared with the values in appendix table G with the appropriate degrees of freedom [$df = (R - 1)(C - 1)$, where R is the number of rows and C is the number of columns in the contingency table]. In a 2×2 or 1×2 table, $df = 1$. If the obtained value is larger than the value in the table, then we conclude that there is a significant difference between the groups.

There are certain restrictions on the use of χ^2 that must be considered:

1. χ^2 can only be used with frequency data.
2. The individual events or observations that constitute the data must be independent of each other.
3. No expected frequency should be less than 5. This rule is often relaxed if there are more than 4 cells and only a few have expected frequencies less than 5. If, however, we have a 2×2 table and expected frequencies less than 5, the Fisher exact probability test can be applied.
4. The data from which we compute the χ^2 must contain both the frequency of occurrence and the frequency of nonoccurrence if both have been recorded.
5. When we have either a 2×2 or a 1×2 table and expected frequencies less than 10 but more than 5 in one or more of the cells, a correction factor must be applied to the calculation of χ^2. Applying the correction factor, the formula for χ^2 becomes $\chi^2 = \Sigma(|O - E| - 0.5)^2/E$.

The *Fisher exact probability test* was introduced as an alternative to χ^2 when we have a 2×2 table and expected frequencies less than 5. It is a one-tailed test but may be used as a two-tailed test by doubling the probability obtained.

The formula for Fisher exact probability is based on labeling of the 2×2 table as follows:

A	B	A + B
C	D	C + D
A + C	B + D	N

The formula for the probability of the observed event is:

$$p = \frac{(A + B)! \, (C + D)! \, (A + C)! \, (B + D)!}{N! \, A! \, B! \, C! \, D!}$$

where a number factorial is just the number multiplied by successively smaller numbers ending with 1. An example is $5! = 5 \cdot 4 \cdot 3 \cdot 2 \cdot 1 = 120$. Also, $0! = 1$.

One fact that makes the Fisher exact probability test so tedious to calculate is that it is necessary to compute both the probability of the observed event and any more extreme as well. The more extreme situations are determined by looking at the cell of the 2×2 table having the smallest observed frequency and lowering this value by one until a zero is obtained in the cell. If one cell contains a zero in the observed case, only one probability has to be determined.

To determine whether or not the event is significant, the probability of the observed situation is added to the probabilities of the less likely events and if the final total is less than 0.05, the difference is significant.

Troubleshooting Your Computations

The computations for chi square are simpler than for most of the other tests we have encountered and usually cause little trouble. However, one area of difficulty with the test stems from improper application. That is, you must be very aware of the restrictions placed on χ^2 at the time you are setting up the problem so that you will know whether to calculate χ^2, χ^2 with correction, or the Fisher exact probability test.

There are two major sources of error that I have noted in the computation of Fisher exact probability. One has to do with not fully understanding factorials. For example, I have frequently encountered students who think that $5!$ goes into $10!$ twice or that $6!$ goes into $12!$ twice, and so on. It would make the computations much simpler if this were true but it is not. Look at this simple example:

$$\frac{4!}{!2} = \frac{4 \cdot 3 \cdot 2 \cdot 1}{2 \cdot 1} = \frac{4 \cdot 3 \cdot \cancel{2} \cdot \cancel{1}}{\cancel{2} \cdot \cancel{1}} = 4 \cdot 3 = 12$$

Note that the 2's and the 1's cancel leaving 12, not 2, in the numerator.

The second source of error in the computation of Fisher exact probability comes from losing numbers from one set of canceling to the next. That is, it is easy to miss a number when gathering terms prior to writing a new fraction. The only advice I can give is to be careful.

Finally, don't forget to calculate the extreme probabilities if the lowest value in any of the cells of the 2 × 2 table is more than zero.

Exercises

1. There is some evidence for asymmetry in the size of the left and right hemispheres of the brain in humans. In a study of 100 brains, the left hemisphere was found to be larger in 60, the right hemisphere in 15, and 25 had left and right hemispheres that were equivalent in size. Perform a χ^2 test on the data to see whether or not there is evidence for asymmetry.

2. A test of verbal IQ has been given to 25 males and 20 females. The results, put into three categories, high, medium, and low, are as follows:

	High	Medium	Low	Total
Males	5	12	8	25
Females	13	4	3	20
Total	18	16	11	45

Perform a test of significance to see whether or not the frequencies are evenly distributed.

3. At a state university in the South, the student population is approximately one-third female and two-thirds male. Over a two-day period the sex of each student entering the Student Union Building is tallied with the following results: females, 452; males 1548. Determine whether males and females are as likely to enter the Union as would be predicted on the basis of their percentage in the student population.

4. A researcher observes the behavior of 25 randomly selected persons from a rural community and finds that 16 of them exhibit abnormal behavior. In a randomly selected group of 25 persons from a more urban region, he finds that 7 have behavior classified as abnormal. Do the two groups differ significantly?

5. In a study of intraspecific aggression (aggression directed toward other members of the same species), an experimenter finds that 7 of 9 animals tested in Species A exhibit aggression while only 3 of 10 are aggressive in Species B. Do the two species differ significantly in terms of intraspecific aggression?

6. In a survey conducted in a rural community, people of different religious affiliation were asked whether they had voted for a Republican or for a Democrat in the last presidential election. The results are shown below:

	Baptist	Catholic	Methodist	Episcopal
Republican	27	24	10	2
Democrat	9	15	33	14

Determine whether or not religious affiliation had anything to do with the way people voted.

7. What are the restrictions on χ^2? When should the Fisher exact probability test be used?

8. In a study of book-carrying style 200 high school males and females (100 of each) have been categorized. The results are shown below.

	Side Carry	Front Carry	Both Hands	Hip Carry
Females	15	35	15	35
Males	80	20	0	0

Determine whether or not males and females differ significantly in terms of book-carrying style.

8. In a small introductory psychology class, 23 students (15 males, 8 females) have been given the following problem:

> Imagine a glass half filled with water. Suppose it is tilted through an angle of 30°. What angle does the surface of the water make with respect to the horizontal?

The responses, classified as either correct or incorrect, are:

	Correct	Incorrect
Males	12	3
Females	0	8

Use the appropriate test to determine whether males and females differ in their responses to this problem.

10. In a study of the effectiveness of an antipsychotic drug, patients treated with it were compared to patients receiving a placebo. In terms of the number relapsing, 698 of 1068 patients relapsed after taking the placebo while 639 of 2127 patients relapsed after the antipsychotic drug. Was the antipsychotic effective in preventing relapse?

Nonparametric Techniques

Introduction

In chapters 7, 8, and 9 we considered two important hypothesis testing procedures, the t- and F-tests. These tests are sometimes called *parametric tests* because they involve tests upon and assumptions about population parameters (e.g., μ and σ). In addition, the tests require that we make certain assumptions about the population or populations from which we are sampling, although we have not spent a great deal of time discussing these assumptions.

parametric tests

From chapter 8, for example, the assumptions underlying the t-test of significance were that the populations from which we have sampled are normally distributed and that the variances are equal. Although even moderate violation of the assumptions often makes little difference in the outcome of the statistical test, there are times when the violation of the assumptions would be so great that the use of tests based upon them would be unwarranted.

For this reason a number of tests have been developed in which the assumptions do not have to be made concerning the shape of the distribution in the population from which our samples are drawn. Because these assumptions are not required, the tests are sometimes called *distribution-free* tests. In addition, we will not be testing hypotheses about the population parameters and for this reason the tests are labeled *nonparametric tests*.

nonparametric tests

Thus, one major application of the nonparametric tests involves situations in which the assumptions for parametric tests, such as t and F, seem likely to be severely violated. In addition, there are a number of other times when the use of a nonparametric test might be warranted. For example, the nonparametric tests are generally less complex computationally than a corresponding parametric test. Thus, an experimenter may elect to use the nonparametric test even when the parametric technique would also be appropriate. Chapter 10 pointed out that the Spearman rank order correlation coefficient was originally devised as a simple method for obtaining a correlation coefficient, and it is certainly much easier to compute than the Pearson r.

Variables in question may have been measured with ordinal or nominal scales for which parametric tests are ordinarily not appropriate. For example, in chapter 10 the use of the Spearman r_S was suggested in situations in which ranking of the data was the best that we could do. Also, both of the techniques discussed in chapter 11, the χ^2 and Fisher exact probability test, are appropriate when the level of measurement is nominal. Thus, in addition to the nonparametric techniques we discussed earlier, the techniques to be discussed in this chapter are appropriate when the level of measurement is less than that required by the t- and F-tests.

Although the nonparametric techniques are easier to compute than the corresponding parametric tests, when both would be appropriate, the parametric test is recommended because the power of the parametric tests is generally greater than that of the nonparametric tests. That is, all things being equal, we will be more likely to reject the null hypothesis with a parametric than with a nonparametric test. In situations favoring the nonparametric technique such as a badly skewed population or an ordinal or nominal level of measurement, there may be no parametric alternative.

Mann-Whitney U Test

The Mann-Whitney (M-W) test is considered to be a powerful alternative to the t-test in two major instances:

1. The level of measurement is ordinal scale, and the best we can do with the numbers is to rank them from highest to lowest.
2. The assumption of normality in the population from which the samples were drawn cannot be made.

It can also be applied when the level of measurement is interval scale and when other assumptions of the t-test are met. However, unless the M-W test is being applied as a time-saving device, the t-test is preferable in situations where both tests are appropriate.

The assumptions required by the Mann-Whitney test are that the samples are independent, there is an underlying continuous scale of measurement, and that the measurement scale we have used is at least ordinal; that is, at least a ranking of the scores is possible. The hypothesis tested is that the populations from which the samples are drawn are identical.

The rationale for the test is based on the null hypothesis being tested. That is, assuming that the populations being sampled are identical, if we rank the combined observations from our two samples, we would expect to find the scores from the two samples rather evenly mixed in our combined ranking. On the other hand, if the scores are not evenly mixed in the combined ranking (e.g., most of the scores from one sample have lower ranks than the scores in the other sample), then they probably come from different populations. The test is based on a determination of how evenly mixed the scores are from the two samples.

Let's consider a type of problem for which the Mann-Whitney test would be appropriate. An investigator goes into a large state mental institution in order to study long-term retention in two types of schizophrenic. Two groups are selected for comparison, one consisting of seven simple schizophrenics and the other consisting of eight paranoid schizophrenics. All subjects are taught a list of nonsense syllables and retrained on the list one week later. A percentage savings score is computed for each patient. Any patient requiring more than twice as many trials to relearn the list as were needed to learn it originally is assigned a score of −100% and testing is discontinued. The savings scores are as follows:

Simple Schizophrenic	Paranoid Schizophrenic
50	90
35	75
10	65
−20	55
−50	50
−100	−10
−100	−30
	−100

There are at least two reasons for not applying the *t*-test to the data presented above. First, a parametric test is inappropriate—we should not even compute the mean of each of the samples, since several of the subjects were terminated in the study prior to relearning the list of nonsense syllables. In chapter 4, we said that $\overline{X}$ should not be calculated when there are arbitrary cutoff points in the data.

Secondly, the sample sizes are very small and oddly distributed. They are so oddly distributed, in fact, that it would be difficult to justify the assumption of normality in the population from which they were drawn.

At any rate, the Mann-Whitney test will be applied. The formula for the Mann-Whitney U is:

$$U = N_1 N_2 + \frac{N_1(N_1 + 1)}{2} - R_1$$

where R_1 is the sum of the ranks of the scores in the first group. The procedure for computing and testing U for significance is as follows:

1. The scores from both groups are ranked from the lowest to the highest. (The smallest score receives the rank of 1). The scores of the combined groups are ranked in contrast to the procedure for the Spearman rank order correlation coefficient in which the scores on the two variables were ranked separately. As before, the tied scores are given the average of the tied ranks.
2. The ranks for the first sample are summed and called R_1.
3. Once R_1 is obtained, U is computed.
4. After computing U, the formula $U' = N_1 N_2 - U$ is solved. The *lower* value, either U or U', is used for the test of significance.
5. The null hypothesis is that the two samples are drawn from identical populations. The alternative to this is that the two populations are different.
6. U or U' is compared to values in one of two tables depending upon the size of the samples. (The use of the tables will be outlined when we have a value of U to test.)

Going back to the example of the long-term memory experiment, let's compute U and test it for significance. The first step is to rank the two sets of scores.

SS	Rank	PS	Rank
40	10	90	15
35	9	75	14
10	8	65	13
−20	6	55	12
−50	4	50	11
−100	2	−10	7
−100	2	−30	5
		−100	2
	$R_1 = 41$		$R_2 = 79$

As you can see, the scores have been ranked algebraically with the largest negative score having the lowest rank. Thus, there are 3 scores of -100 which are tied for the ranks of 1, 2, and 3. They are assigned the average of the tied ranks $[(1 + 2 + 3) \div 3 = 6 \div 3 = 2]$. Continuing, the score of -50 is assigned the rank of 4, -30 the rank of 5, and this continues until the highest score is ranked. After the combined scores in the two groups have been ranked, the sum of the ranks for the first group is found and is called R_1. We are now ready to compute U, using the values $N_1 = 7$, $N_2 = 8$, and $R_1 = 41$.

$$U = N_1 N_2 + \frac{N_1(N_1 + 1)}{2} - R_1$$

$$= 7 \cdot 8 + \frac{7(7 + 1)}{2} - 41 = 56 + \frac{7 \cdot 8}{2} - 41 = 56 + \frac{56}{2} - 41$$

$$= 56 + 28 - 41 = 84 - 41 = 43$$

$$U' = N_1 N_2 - U = 7 \cdot 8 - 43 = 56 - 43$$

$$= 13 \text{ (the smaller of } U \text{ and } U')$$

When the larger of our two samples is size 8 or less, we will refer to appendix table H for the test of significance. Table H is unusual in that it consists of six separate tables depending upon the size of the larger of our two samples. The title of the table tells us that it contains probabilities associated with particular values of U (or U'). Thus, if we find that the probability associated with our computed value of U is less than or equal to 0.05, we reject the null hypothesis and conclude that our two samples were drawn from populations with different distributions; that is, that our samples differ significantly.

In the problem that we have been considering, we found that $U' = 13$ and our samples were of size $N_1 = 7$ and $N_2 = 8$. Looking in the appropriate portion of appendix table H for samples of size $N_2 = 8$ and $N_1 = 7$, we find that the probability associated with $U = 13$ is .047 for a one-tailed test. Since .047 is less than .05, we reject the null hypothesis and conclude that the two groups differ significantly.

As you can see, appendix table H can only be used for groups of size eight or less. What do we do for larger samples? For samples with Ns up to and including 20 subjects, we can use table I to determine whether or not the U or U' we have obtained is significant. Let's consider another example with larger sample sizes.

To study the effects of lesions of the septal area of the brain on a type of aggression in rats, a physiological psychologist subjected 22 animals to brain surgery: 12 received destruction aimed at the septal area of the brain while 10 were given sham operations. Following a suitable recovery period, the handling characteristics of all animals were rated once daily for five days using a scale from 0 to 15. The total five- day scores for each animal are shown below.

Group SO	Group SEP
21	63
15	57
10	55
9	54
8	49
7	48
6	45
5	43
4	42
4	20
	14
	11

Again, the first step is to rank the scores for the combined groups. After this has been done, the sum of the ranks is found and U can be computed.

Group SO	Rank	Group SEP	Rank
21	13	63	22
15	11	57	21
10	8	55	20
9	7	54	19
8	6	49	18
7	5	48	17
6	4	45	16
5	3	43	15
4	1.5	42	14
4	1.5	20	12
	$R_1 = 60$	14	10
		11	9
			$R_2 = 193$

$$U = N_1 N_2 + \frac{N_1(N_1 + 1)}{2} - R_1 = 10 \cdot 12 + \frac{10(10 + 1)}{2} - 60$$

$$= 120 + \frac{10 \cdot 11}{2} - 60 = 120 + \frac{110}{2} - 60 = 120 + 55 - 60$$

$$= 175 - 60 = 115$$

Since $U' = N_1 N_2 - U = 120 - 115 = 5$ and U' is smaller than U, U' is the value that we will compare to the table value. We can also calculate U' directly by making some slight modifications in the original equation:

$$U' = N_1 N_2 + \frac{N_2(N_2 + 1)}{2} - R_2$$

Solving this equation we find:

$$U' = 10 \cdot 12 + \frac{12(12 + 1)}{2} - 193 = 120 + \frac{12 \cdot 13}{2} - 193$$

$$= 120 + \frac{156}{2} - 193$$

$$= 120 + 78 - 193 = 198 - 193 = 5$$

As you can see, this procedure would be a useful check on the accuracy of our original computations.

We can see that table I contains critical values of U (or U') for a two-tailed test with $\alpha = .05$. If our computed value of U or U' is equal to or *less* than the value in the table for the appropriate sample sizes, we reject the null hypothesis. Note that our value for U or U' must be *less* than the table value, not more as in the other cases we have considered, in order for us to reject H_0 and conclude that there is a significant difference between the groups.

For the experiment we have been considering, $N_1 = 10$ and $N_2 = 12$. The critical value of U or U' from appendix table I is 29. Obviously our computed value of 5 is much less than 29 and we reject the null hypothesis. The conclusion is that septal lesions significantly increase irritability in the rat.

The Mann-Whitney U test may also be used for comparing groups that are larger than size $N = 20$. The procedure is the same except that after U has been computed it is converted to a z-score using the equation:

$$z = \frac{U - N_1 N_2 / 2}{\sqrt{\dfrac{(N_1)(N_2)(N_1 + N_2 + 1)}{12}}}$$

If the z-score obtained is equal to or larger than 1.96, the null hypothesis is rejected. Since the M-W test is most useful for small samples, further examples illustrating its use with large samples will not be shown in this text.

Checking Your Progress

An investigator wants to see if sex is involved in self ratings on a scale of assertiveness. Eighteeen students, 10 males and 8 females, rate themselves on a twenty-item scale of assertiveness. The ratings are:

Female	Male
15	16
14	3
12	10
17	5
13	15
10	18
5	14
4	11
	9
	10

Using the M-W U test, compare males and females on the assertiveness ratings. The answer is $U = 38.5$ which is not significant.

Wilcoxon Matched-Pairs Signed-Ranks Test

In chapter 8, both the t-tests for independent and for dependent samples were discussed. In this chapter the Mann-Whitney test has been presented as a nonparametric alternative to the t-test for inde-

pendent samples. The *Wilcoxon test* will be discussed here as a corresponding alternative to the *t*-test for dependent or related samples.

For example, suppose we want to test the effectiveness of an
analgesic agent (Kilpain) on a pain other than headache. The experiment is conducted as described in chapter 8 except that, instead of
measuring the length of time that each subject can tolerate the
immersion, we have each subject rate the subjective quality of his or
her pain on a scale from 0 to 20 after the hand has been immersed in
icewater for a set period of time. The results are as follows:

Subject	Placebo	Kilpain
A	15	10
B	17	15
C	10	11
D	8	8
E	14	13
F	13	7
G	10	5
H	8	5

As you can see, we have eight subjects and each has been
tested with both the Kilpain and the placebo resulting in eight pairs
of scores. Our level of measurement is ordinal and we will use the
Wilcoxon test.

The assumptions of the test are that the subjects must be randomly and independently selected, the scale of measurement must
be at least ordinal, and we must be able to rank order the difference
scores. The null hypothesis is that the distributions of the populations under each condition are identical.

The computation of the test is very simple. We first find the
difference between each pair of scores. Pairs with zero differences
are discarded. Next, the difference scores are rank ordered in terms
of absolute magnitude while the appropriate sign is retained. Finally,
we sum the ranks with the less frequently occurring sign and this
value is compared with table values in a test of significance.

If the distributions of the populations under each condition are
identical, there will usually be about the same number of positive
and negative differences and the sums of the ranks for the positive
and negative differences will not differ to any great extent. However, if the population distributions are not the same, then we could
expect to see many more differences of one sign than the other.

Thus, the smaller the sum of the less frequently occurring ranks, the more likely that the population distributions under each condition are different.

But, enough of the rationale for the test. Let's go back to the problem and work through the computations.

Subject	Placebo	Kilpain	d	Rank of d	Rank with Less Frequent Sign
A	15	10	5	5.5	
B	17	15	2	3.0	
C	10	11	−1	−1.5	1.5
D	8	8	0		
E	14	13	1	1.5	
F	13	7	6	7.0	
G	10	5	5	5.5	
H	8	5	3	4.0	
					$T = 1.5$

The differences (d) have been found and the absolute values ranked. Ranking is carried out as before giving the smallest difference the first rank and continuing until all of the differences have been ranked. Tied scores are given the average rank; for example, in absolute value two differences had a magnitude of 1 and each received the average of ranks 1 and 2, or 1.5. In the last column, the ranks with the less frequent sign are entered. In our example, only one negative difference occurred and the rank of this difference, 1.5, appears. Finally, the ranks (rank in this case) with the less frequent sign are summed and called T. Thus, our obtained $T = 1.5$. For comparative purposes the sum of the positive ranks is 26.5.

The obtained T of 1.5 is compared with the appropriate values in appendix table J. The title of the table tells us that it contains critical values of T. Thus, for $N = 7$, a T of 2 or *less* is required for rejection of the null hypothesis at the 5% level with a two-tailed test. Incidentally, although we had eight pairs of scores originally, differences were found between only seven of them and the pair having no difference was discarded. Since our obtained T was 1.5, the null hypothesis is rejected.

Let's consider another example to illustrate the use of the Wilcoxon test. An experimental psychologist has decided to use each animal as its own control in an experiment to test the effects of marijuana on dominance behavior. Ten monkeys are given a score representing dominance in a two-monkey test. High scores reflect greater dominance. The scores before and after marijuana are:

Monkey	Before	After	d	Rank of d	Rank with Less Frequent Sign
A	27	29	−2	−3	3
B	22	14	8	8	
C	5	5	0		
D	9	7	2	3	
E	17	18	−1	−1	1
F	35	21	14	9	
G	14	7	7	7	
H	3	5	−2	−3	3
I	8	5	3	5	
J	7	3	4	6	
					$T = 7$

The difference is found for each pair of scores and then the differences are ranked without regard to sign. Monkey C did not change and its data are discarded. Finally, the ranks with the less frequent sign are summed giving a T of 7. In appendix table J with $N = 9$, we see that a T of 6 or less is required for rejection at the 5% level of significance with a two-tailed test. We conclude that our observed result is not different enough from chance to enable us to reject the null hypothesis.

With samples greater than 25, appendix table J cannot be used. However, as is true with a number of other test statistics, with large samples the distribution of T is approximately normal. The relevant formula for z is:

$$z = \frac{T - N(N + 1)/4}{\sqrt{\dfrac{N(N + 1)(2N + 1)}{24}}}$$

If the value computed for z is 1.96 or larger, the null hypothesis is rejected at the 5% level (two-tailed test).

Checking Your Progress

An experiment has been performed to study the effects of movie violence on expressed attitudes toward violence. Each member of twelve pairs of identical twins has been randomly assigned to one of two treatment conditions. One member of each pair watches scenes from the movie "Straw Dogs" depicting extreme violence while the other member watches nonviolent scenes from the same movie. Each subject is then given a self-rating scale designed to elicit attitudes about the expression of violence. High scores represent a low threshold for the expression of violence. The results are:

Twins No.	Group Violent	Group Nonviolent
1	23	15
2	13	15
3	15	12
4	17	17
5	19	15
6	23	19
7	25	19
8	10	10
9	16	17
10	8	5
11	7	2
12	12	11

Test the null hypothesis. The answer is $T = 4.5$ which has a $p < .02$ for a two-tailed test.

Kruskal-Wallis One-Way Analysis of Variance

Kruskal-Wallis one-way analysis of variance by ranks

The *Kruskal-Wallis one-way analysis of variance by ranks* is a very useful technique for comparing more than two groups when we have at least ordinal scale measurement and the assumptions of the one-way analysis of variance test cannot be met. In other words, it is used in situations similar to those we discussed favoring the M-W U test except that more than two independent groups are compared.

The K-W test is actually an extension of the M-W test and again requires that we rank the scores from the combined groups. The null hypothesis tested is that the samples have identical population distributions. If the distributions from which we draw our samples are identical, the sums of the ranks of each sample should be similar. Very different sums would indicate that the samples came from different populations and would enable rejection of the null hypothesis. Let's consider a problem of the type for which the K-W test would be appropriate.

An administrator of a mental health facility wants to find which of his three therapists is doing the best job or if all are equal in ability. In order to determine this, after treatment five patients from each therapist are given a scale on which they rate the quality of their treatment. The ratings are:

Therapist A	Therapist B	Therapist C
26	17	30
23	15	25
19	14	20
17	12	18
15	10	16

Obviously there are some differences in the ratings given to the three therapists, but are the differences great enough for us to conclude that the samples come from different populations? The K-W test is appropriate because of the level of measurement used, that is, the ratings of therapist performance constitute an ordinal level of measurement.

The formula for the K-W test is:

$$H = \frac{12}{N(N + 1)} \sum \frac{R_i^2}{N_i} - 3(N + 1)$$

where N_i = the number of observations in a particular sample

N = the total number of observations in all samples combined

R_i = the sum of the ranks for a particular sample

The large summation sign simply means that we will sum the squared ranks divided by the N in a group over all groups. With sample sizes greater than 5, H is distributed approximately as χ^2 and we can use the table for χ^2 (appendix table G) with $df = K - 1$ (K = the number of samples) to evaluate H. However, with 3 groups and 5 or fewer subjects in each group, the distribution of H is sufficiently deviant from χ^2 so that we cannot use its distribution. With small samples and $K = 3$, appendix table K will be used to evaluate H.

Let's go back to the example presented earlier and find H. As with the M-W test, the first step is to rank the combined scores from the lowest to the highest and then sum the ranks for each sample:

Therapist A	Rank	Therapist B	Rank	Therapist C	Rank
26	14	17	7.5	30	15
23	12	15	4.5	25	13
19	10	14	3	20	11
17	7.5	12	2	18	9
15	4.5	10	1	16	6
	$R_1 = 48$		$R_2 = 18$		$R_3 = 54$

The lowest rating in the combined groups was 10 and this is assigned a rank of 1. The same therapist also received a rating of 12 and this is given the rank of 2. The ranking is continued until the highest score, 30, is reached and this receives a rank of 15. As before, tied scores receive the average of the tied ranks. Finally, the sum of the ranks for each therapist is found and R_1 (the sum of the ranks of Therapist A) is 48, $R_2 = 18$, and $R_3 = 54$. It is now time to compute H.

$$H = \frac{12}{N(N + 1)} \Sigma \frac{R_i^2}{N_i} - 3(N + 1)$$

$$= \frac{12}{15(15 + 1)} \left(\frac{48^2}{5} + \frac{18^2}{5} + \frac{54^2}{5} \right) - 3(15 + 1)$$

$$= \frac{12}{15 \cdot 16} \left(\frac{2304}{5} + \frac{324}{5} + \frac{2916}{5} \right) - 3(16)$$

$$= \frac{12}{240} (460.8 + 64.8 + 583.2) - 48$$

$$= 0.05 (1108.8) - 48 = 55.44 - 48 = 7.44$$

Since we had 3 samples and none was larger than $N = 5$, we will use appendix table K to evaluate our computed H of 7.44. The title of table K tells us that it contains probabilities associated with values of H that might be computed. The values of H and the probabilities associated with them are listed for each possible combination of sample sizes through $N_i = 5$ for each of 3 samples.

For our particular problem, $N_i = 5$ and consulting the appropriate portion of the table, we see that an $H = 5.7800$ has a probability of .049 while an $H = 7.9800$ has a probability of .010. The H that we computed is larger than 5.7800 but slightly smaller than 7.9800 and therefore has a probability less than .049 but greater than

.010. Since it is less than .05, we reject the null hypothesis and conclude that the samples came from different populations.

Let's try another example to illustrate the case where the $N_i s$ are larger than 5. In a recent study I was interested in comparing the effects of several biochemical treatments on the handling characteristics of rats. To investigate this, 4 groups of 8 animals each were given the following treatments: Group C animals were fed a liquid diet of Similac; Group E rats were fed a liquid diet containing ethanol (a form of alcohol); Group M animals were given a liquid diet containing a quantity of methomyl, which is a pesticide; Group M-E animals received a diet containing both ethanol and methomyl. The handling characteristics were rated on 5 occasions during a two-week period and a total rating was found for each animal. The ratings were:

Group C	Group M	Group E	Group M-E
13	14	12	10
12	7	11	8
11	7	10	8
10	7	8	6
7	6	6	6
6	5	5	5
6	5	5	5
4	2	4	1

As before, the first step is to rank the combined scores. Once this has been done, find the sum of the ranks for each sample and compute H. The actual computations are as follows:

Group C	Rank	Group M	Rank	Group E	Rank	Group M-E	Rank
13	31.0	14	32.0	12	29.5	10	25.0
12	29.5	7	18.5	11	27.5	8	22.0
11	27.5	7	18.5	10	25.0	8	22.0
10	25.0	7	18.5	8	22.0	6	13.5
7	18.5	6	13.5	6	13.5	6	13.5
6	13.5	5	7.5	5	7.5	5	7.5
6	13.5	5	7.5	5	7.5	5	7.5
4	3.5	2	2.0	4	3.5	1	1.0
	162.0		118.0		136.0		112.0

$$H = \frac{12}{N(N+1)} \Sigma \frac{R_i^2}{N_i} - 3(N+1)$$

$$= \frac{12}{32(32+1)} \left(\frac{162^2}{8} + \frac{118^2}{8} + \frac{136^2}{8} + \frac{112^2}{8} \right) - 3(32+1)$$

$$= \frac{12}{1056} (3280.5 + 1740.5 + 2312 + 1568) - 99$$

$$= .01136 (8901) - 99 = 101.12 - 99 = 2.12.$$

Did you note there were quite a few tied scores in the ranking of the scores? Actually, the value of H is affected by the presence of ties and, for this reason, there is a procedure to correct for them. However, the correction is very minor and it would be worth applying only in a situation where the H value obtained was slightly below that required for significance. For the problem we have been considering, the H value corrected for ties is 2.16 even though there were 8 sets of tied scores including almost all of the 32 scores in the three samples. Because of the negligible difference, then, the correction procedure will not be presented. (For further details of the correction procedure, consult Siegel, S., *Nonparametric Statistics for the Behavioral Sciences,* McGraw-Hill, 1956).

Since we had 4 groups and N_is greater than 5, we will compare our obtained value of H (2.12 or 2.16) with the critical values for χ^2 in appendix table G. With 4 groups, $df = K - 1 = 4 - 1 = 3$ and the critical values are 7.82 and 11.34 at the 5% and 1% levels. Our H value, either corrected or uncorrected, is much less than either critical value and we cannot reject the null hypothesis.

Checking Your Progress

According to criteria established by Sheldon's somatotype theory of personality, 21 students have been designated as either endomorphs (large body type, fat), mesomorphs (athletic body build), or ectomorphs (skinny, slight body build). The students have then been rated by their classmates in terms of the amount of class participation and the score for each student is the sum of the student's ratings. The scores are:

Endomorphs	Mesomorphs	Ectomorphs
25	28	14
24	27	12
23	26	10
20	18	7
19	15	5
18	15	5
15	14	
	12	

Compute H and test it for significance. The answer is $H = 11.49$, $p < .01$.

One final note should be made about the K-W test. What happens when a significant H value is obtained? Does this tell us which group comparisons would be significant? The answer is no, just as it was with the analysis of variance. In this case, individual comparisons can be made with the M-W U test.

To illustrate, let's reconsider the first example discussed concerning the therapists at a mental health facility. Suppose the administrator wanted to compare the ratings obtained by Therapists A and B. Computation of the M-W test is shown as follows:

Therapist A	Rank	Therapist B	Rank
26	10.0	17	6.5
23	9.0	15	4.5
19	8.0	14	3.0
17	6.5	12	2.0
15	4.5	10	1.0
	38.0		17.0

$$U = N_1 N_2 + \frac{N_1(N_1 + 1)}{2} - R_1 = 5 \cdot 5 + \frac{5(5 + 1)}{2} - 38$$

$$= 25 + 15 - 38 = 40 - 38 = 2$$

$$U' = N_1 N_2 - U = 25 - 2 = 23$$

The smaller of U and U' is $U = 2$ and this is the value to be tested for significance. Reference to table H reveals that the probability associated with a $U = 2$ is .016. Since .016 is less than .05, we can reject the null hypothesis for the comparison between Therapists A and B. For further practice, compare Therapists A and C and Therapists B and C. (The answers are $U' = 10$, $p = .345$ for the comparison between Therapists A and C and $U' = 1$, $p = .008$ for the comparison between Therapists B and C.)

Summary

The techniques studied in this chapter, the *Mann-Whitney U test*, the *Wilcoxon matched-pairs signed-ranks test*, and the *Kruskal-Wallis H test*, are valuable alternatives to the *t*-test and the one-way analysis of variance. Instead of being based on a comparison of the means of independent samples or on a comparison of the variances, the M-W and the K-W tests compare the ranks of the sample scores while the Wilcoxon test involves the ranks of difference scores. As such, they are called nonparametric tests and are primarily used for comparing data generated by an ordinal scale, that is, rank order data.

The M-W test is used to compare two independent samples. The procedure is as follows:

1. Rank the scores from the combined samples from the lowest to the highest, giving the lowest score the rank of 1. Give tied scores the average of the tied ranks.
2. Find the sum of the ranks for each sample.
3. Compute the statistic U using the formula:

$$U = N_1 N_2 + \frac{N_1(N_1 + 1)}{2} - R_1$$

where N_1 is the number of observations in the first sample, N_2 is the number of observations in the second sample, and R_1 is the sum of the ranks in the first sample.
4. Compute U' from the equation: $U' = N_1 N_2 - U$. Use the smaller of U or U' in the significance test.
5. Compare the smaller of U or U' with table values from table I if the larger of the two samples has more than 8 subjects. If U or U' is smaller than the value in table I for the appropriate sample sizes, reject the null hypothesis. When the larger of the two samples has 8 or fewer observations, use table H to test the value of U or U' for significance. In this case an exact probability of the observed U or U' is found and if it is less than .05, the difference between the samples is significant.

6. For samples larger than $N = 20$, convert U to a z-score using the formula:

$$z = \frac{U - \dfrac{N_1 N_2}{2}}{\sqrt{\dfrac{(N_1)(N_2)(N_1 + N_2 + 1)}{2}}}$$

If the z-score is equal to or larger than 1.96, reject the null hypothesis.

The Wilcoxon test is useful as an alternative to the t-test for dependent samples when the assumptions for t cannot be met. The difference between pairs of scores is found and ranked without regard to sign. The sum of the ranks with less frequently occurring sign is found and if N is 25 or less the resulting T is compared with values in table J. If T is equal to or *less* than critical values in the table, the null hypothesis is rejected. For samples larger than 25 the distribution of T is approximately normal and z is computed from the equation:

$$z = \frac{T - N(N + 1)/4}{\sqrt{\dfrac{N(N + 1)(2N + 1)}{24}}}$$

If the z-score is 1.96 or larger, H_0 is rejected at the 5% level.

The K-W test is an extension of the M-W test when there are 3 or more samples to be compared. As with the M-W test, the combined scores from the groups are first ranked and then the sum of the ranks for each sample is found. A statistic H is computed from the formula:

$$H = \frac{12}{N(N + 1)} \Sigma \frac{R_i^2}{N_i} - 3(N + 1)$$

where N_i is the number of observations for a particular sample, N = the total number of observations for the combined groups, R_i is the sum of the ranks for a particular sample.

With sample sizes larger than 5 and/or more than 3 groups, H is distributed approximately as Chi square and table G can be used to evaluate the H with $df = K - 1$ where K is the number of samples. With 3 samples of size 5 or less, table K is used to evaluate H. Table K gives exact probabilities for particular values of H and if the probability of our computed H is less than .05, the null hypothesis is rejected.

Troubleshooting Your Computations

Although the techniques discussed in this chapter are fairly simple to compute, there are some possible problem areas and warnings that something has gone awry in your proceedings. For example, both the K-W test and the M-W test require ranking of the combined scores in the groups from the lowest to the highest. The rank of the highest score should be equal to N unless the highest scores are tied. If the highest score doesn't receive a rank equal to N, you should go back to the beginning of the ranking procedure and be sure that you haven't skipped a rank somewhere along the way.

The value that you obtain for either U or H should be a positive number. If it is not, go back and check the sum of the ranks to be sure that you have not made an error here.

If you are using the M-W U test, be sure to compute U' as well as U and be sure to use the smaller of the two values in the significance test. Also when using appendix table I be sure to remember that the value of U or U' is significant if it is *less* than the appropriate table value, not greater as in the other tests we have considered.

When using the Wilcoxon test be sure to discard all zero differences. Also the difference scores are ranked in terms of absolute value, that is, without regard to sign. The obtained T must be equal to or *less* than the table values to be significant.

Exercises

1. Ten monkeys, 5 isolate-reared (without a mother) and 5 normally reared, have been observed over a 10-day period in a group play area. The number of self-directed behaviors has been scored for each animal during a 20-minute daily test session. The summed scores for each animal are shown below.

Isolate-Reared	Normally-Reared
255	173
241	150
213	142
185	131
151	75

Compute the M-W U and test it for significance.

2. A large number of male students are given the masculinity portion of a masculinity-femininity test and from the results of the test, 3 groups are formed. They are: Group MM, 8 males scoring 2 standard deviation units above the mean in terms of masculinity; Group MN, 10 males scoring within one standard deviation unit of the mean on the scale; Group MF, 6 males scoring 2 standard deviation units below the mean. Each subject is asked to rate his attitudes toward homosexuality with a high score indicating very positive attitudes and a low score indicating very negative attitudes. The ratings are:

Group MM	Group MN	Group MF
18	14	19
7	12	17
6	10	15
6	9	15
5	8	13
3	8	9
2	7	
1	7	
	6	
	5	

Using the K-W test, determine whether or not the samples differ significantly.
3. Perform all pairwise comparisons for problem 2 using the M-W test.
4. A personality test called the Myers-Briggs test has been administered to a large number of persons. On the basis of this test, a number of persons have been designated as either thinking or feeling types and have been given a questionnaire concerning attitudes toward extrasensory perception. Each person receives a score on the questionnaire reflecting the degree of his or her belief in ESP. The scores are:

Group Thinking	Group Feeling
8	20
7	18
7	15
5	15
3	14
1	12
0	6
0	5
	4
	1

Compare the groups using the M-W test.
5. An experiment has been performed in which the handling characteristics of rats have been rated following several different types of brain damage. The results were:

Group OC	Group SEP	Group OB	Group VMH
12	45	20	37
10	43	13	35
9	42	11	28
9	41	8	27
8	36	6	20
7	25	5	13
3	23	4	10
2	15	1	
	10		

Determine whether or not the differences are significant.

6. Perform all pairwise comparisons for problem 5 using the M-W U test.
7. What does it mean to call a test nonparametric? Name a nonparametric test other than the three discussed in this chapter.
8. In situations where both parametric and nonparametric tests could be used, why is the parametric test preferable?
9. Using the Myers-Briggs test mentioned in problem 4, a large number of students classified as feeling types have been identified. From this group, 14 persons expressing strong belief in ESP on a questionnaire have been shown a film presenting a very negative view of the validity of ESP. Before and after scores on the ESP questionnaire are:

Student No.	Before the Film	After the Film
1	20	22
2	18	13
3	15	15
4	15	18
5	17	16
6	16	14
7	14	10
8	25	28
9	10	10
10	12	13
11	17	23
12	15	11
13	13	17
14	10	10

Test the null hypothesis that no change in attitude resulted from viewing the film.

10. An identical procedure has been followed as in problem 9 except that 13 thinking types have been selected for low belief in ESP. The students are shown a biased film presenting ESP in a favorable light. Before and after scores on the ESP questionnaire are:

Student No.	Before the Film	After the Film
1	7	7
2	5	8
3	0	5
4	3	7
5	2	4
6	1	3
7	4	10
8	4	12
9	5	4
10	7	4
11	8	8
12	5	15
13	2	11

Test the null hypothesis.

Appendix

Table A. Percentage of total area under the normal curve between the mean and any z-score

z	.00	.01	.02	.03	.04	.05	.06	.07	.08	.09
0.0	00.00	00.40	00.80	01.20	01.60	01.99	02.39	02.79	03.19	03.59
0.1	03.98	04.38	04.78	05.17	05.57	05.96	06.36	06.75	07.14	07.53
0.2	07.93	08.32	08.71	09.10	09.48	09.87	10.26	10.64	11.03	11.41
0.3	11.79	12.17	12.55	12.93	13.31	13.68	14.06	14.43	14.80	15.17
0.4	15.54	15.91	16.28	16.64	17.00	17.36	17.72	18.08	18.44	18.79
0.5	19.15	19.50	19.85	20.19	20.54	20.88	21.23	21.57	21.90	22.24
0.6	22.57	22.91	23.24	23.57	23.89	24.22	24.54	24.86	25.17	25.49
0.7	25.80	26.11	26.42	26.73	27.04	27.34	27.64	27.94	28.23	28.52
0.8	28.81	29.10	29.39	29.67	29.95	30.23	30.51	30.78	31.06	31.33
0.9	31.59	31.86	32.12	32.38	32.64	32.90	33.15	33.40	33.65	33.89
1.0	34.13	34.38	34.61	34.85	35.08	35.31	35.54	35.77	35.99	36.21
1.1	36.43	36.65	36.86	37.08	37.29	37.49	37.70	37.90	38.10	38.30
1.2	38.49	38.69	38.88	39.07	39.25	39.44	39.62	39.80	39.97	40.15
1.3	40.32	40.49	40.66	40.82	40.99	41.15	41.31	41.47	41.62	41.77
1.4	41.92	42.07	42.22	42.36	42.51	42.65	42.79	42.92	43.06	43.19
1.5	43.32	43.45	43.57	43.70	43.83	43.94	44.06	44.18	44.29	44.41
1.6	44.52	44.63	44.74	44.84	44.95	45.05	45.15	45.25	45.35	45.45
1.7	45.54	45.64	45.73	45.82	45.91	45.99	46.08	46.16	46.25	46.33
1.8	46.41	46.49	46.56	46.64	46.71	46.78	46.86	46.93	46.99	47.06
1.9	47.13	47.19	47.26	47.32	47.38	47.44	47.50	47.56	47.61	47.67
2.0	47.72	47.78	47.83	47.88	47.93	47.98	48.03	48.08	48.12	48.17
2.1	48.21	48.26	48.30	48.34	48.38	48.42	48.46	48.50	48.54	48.57
2.2	48.61	48.64	48.68	48.71	48.75	48.78	48.81	48.84	48.87	48.90
2.3	48.93	48.96	48.98	49.01	49.04	49.06	49.09	49.11	49.13	49.16
2.4	49.18	49.20	49.22	49.25	49.27	49.29	49.31	49.32	49.34	49.36
2.5	49.38	49.40	49.41	49.43	49.45	49.46	49.48	49.49	49.51	49.52
2.6	49.53	49.55	49.56	49.57	49.59	49.60	49.61	49.62	49.63	49.64
2.7	49.65	49.66	49.67	49.68	49.69	49.70	49.71	49.72	49.73	49.74
2.8	49.74	49.75	49.76	49.77	49.77	49.78	49.79	49.79	49.80	49.81
2.9	49.81	49.82	49.82	49.83	49.84	49.84	49.85	49.85	49.86	49.86
3.0	49.87									
3.5	49.98									
4.0	49.997									
5.0	49.99997									

Source: The original data for this table came from Karl Pearson (ed.), *Tables for Statisticians and Biometricians,* Vol. 1, 3rd ed., Table II, pp. 2–8, and are used with permission of Cambridge University Press. The adaptation of these data was taken from Lindquist, E. L., *A First Course in Statistics* (rev. ed.), Houghton Mifflin Co., copyright © 1942, and is shown here with permission of the publisher.

Table B. Critical values of t

$df = N - 1$ for one sample *t*-test and the *t*-test for dependent samples. $df = N_1 + N_2 - 2$ for two sample *t*-test.

	Level of significance for one-tailed test			
	5%	*2.5%*	*1%*	*.5%*
	Level of significance for two-tailed test			
df	*10%*	*5%*	*2%*	*1%*
1	6.3138	12.7062	31.8207	63.6574
2	2.9200	4.3027	6.9646	9.9248
3	2.3534	3.1824	4.5407	5.8409
4	2.1318	2.7764	3.7469	4.6041
5	2.0150	2.5706	3.3649	4.0322
6	1.9432	2.4469	3.1427	3.7074
7	1.8946	2.3646	2.9980	3.4995
8	1.8595	2.3060	2.8965	3.3554
9	1.8331	2.2622	2.8214	3.2498
10	1.8125	2.2281	2.7638	3.1693
11	1.7959	2.2010	2.7181	3.1058
12	1.7823	2.1788	2.6810	3.0545
13	1.7709	2.1604	2.6503	3.0123
14	1.7613	2.1448	2.6245	2.9768
15	1.7531	2.1315	2.6025	2.9467
16	1.7459	2.1199	2.5835	2.9208
17	1.7396	2.1098	2.5669	2.8982
18	1.7341	2.1009	2.5524	2.8784
19	1.7291	2.0930	2.5395	2.8609
20	1.7247	2.0860	2.5280	2.8453
21	1.7207	2.0796	2.5177	2.8314
22	1.7171	2.0739	2.5083	2.8188
23	1.7139	2.0687	2.4999	2.8073
24	1.7109	2.0639	2.4922	2.7969
25	1.7081	2.0595	2.4851	2.7874
26	1.7056	2.0555	2.4786	2.7787
27	1.7033	2.0518	2.4727	2.7707
28	1.7011	2.0484	2.4671	2.7633
29	1.6991	2.0452	2.4620	2.7564
30	1.6973	2.0423	2.4573	2.7500
35	1.6869	2.0301	2.4377	2.7238
40	1.6839	2.0211	2.4233	2.7045
45	1.6794	2.0141	2.4121	2.6896
50	1.6759	2.0086	2.4033	2.6778
60	1.6706	2.0003	2.3901	2.6603
70	1.6669	1.9944	2.3808	2.6479
80	1.6641	1.9901	2.3739	2.6387
90	1.6620	1.9867	2.3685	2.6316
100	1.6602	1.9840	2.3642	2.6259
110	1.6588	1.9818	2.3607	2.6213
120	1.6577	1.9799	2.3598	2.6174
∞	1.6449	1.9600	2.3263	2.5758

Source: This table is adapted from Owen, D. B., *Handbook of Statistical Tables*, Addison-Wesley, 1962, pp. 28–30, with permission of the author and publisher.

Table C. Critical values of F

df associated with the denominator		df associated with the numerator								
		1	2	3	4	5	6	7	8	9
1	5%	161	200	216	225	230	234	237	239	241
	1%	4052	5000	5403	5625	5764	5859	5928	5982	6022
2	5%	18.5	19.0	19.2	19.2	19.3	19.3	19.4	19.4	19.4
	1%	98.5	99.0	99.2	99.2	99.3	99.3	99.4	99.4	99.4
3	5%	10.1	9.55	9.28	9.12	9.01	8.94	8.89	8.85	8.81
	1%	34.1	30.8	29.5	28.7	28.2	27.9	27.7	27.5	27.3
4	5%	7.71	6.94	6.59	6.39	6.26	6.16	6.09	6.04	6.00
	1%	21.2	18.0	16.7	16.0	15.5	15.2	15.0	14.8	14.7
5	5%	6.61	5.79	5.41	5.19	5.05	4.95	4.88	4.82	4.77
	1%	16.3	13.3	12.1	11.4	11.0	10.7	10.5	10.3	10.2
6	5%	5.99	5.14	4.76	4.53	4.39	4.28	4.21	4.15	4.10
	1%	13.7	10.9	9.78	9.15	8.75	8.47	8.26	8.10	7.98
7	5%	5.59	4.74	4.35	4.12	3.97	3.87	3.79	3.73	3.68
	1%	12.2	9.55	8.45	7.85	7.46	7.19	6.99	6.84	6.72
8	5%	5.32	4.46	4.07	3.84	3.69	3.58	3.50	3.44	3.39
	1%	11.3	8.65	7.59	7.01	6.63	6.37	6.18	6.03	5.91
9	5%	5.12	4.26	3.86	3.63	3.48	3.37	3.29	3.23	3.18
	1%	10.6	8.02	6.99	6.42	6.06	5.80	5.61	5.47	5.35
10	5%	4.96	4.10	3.71	3.48	3.33	3.22	3.14	3.07	3.02
	1%	10.0	7.56	6.55	5.99	5.64	5.39	5.20	5.06	4.94
11	5%	4.84	3.98	3.59	3.36	3.20	3.09	3.01	2.95	2.90
	1%	9.65	7.21	6.22	5.67	5.32	5.07	4.89	4.74	4.63
12	5%	4.75	3.89	3.49	3.26	3.11	3.00	2.91	2.85	2.80
	1%	9.33	6.93	5.95	5.41	5.06	4.82	4.64	4.50	4.39
13	5%	4.67	3.81	3.41	3.18	3.03	2.92	2.83	2.77	2.71
	1%	9.07	6.70	5.74	5.21	4.86	4.62	4.44	4.30	4.19
14	5%	4.60	3.74	3.34	3.11	2.96	2.85	2.76	2.70	2.65
	1%	8.86	6.51	5.56	5.04	4.70	4.46	4.28	4.14	4.03
15	5%	4.54	3.68	3.29	3.06	2.90	2.79	2.71	2.64	2.59
	1%	8.68	6.36	5.42	4.89	4.56	4.32	4.14	4.00	3.89
16	5%	4.49	3.63	3.24	3.01	2.85	2.74	2.66	2.59	2.54
	1%	8.53	6.23	5.29	4.77	4.44	4.20	4.03	3.89	3.78
17	5%	4.45	3.59	3.20	2.96	2.81	2.70	2.61	2.55	2.49
	1%	8.40	6.11	5.18	4.67	4.34	4.10	3.93	3.79	3.68

Source: This table is adapted from Merrington, M., & Thompson, C. M., Tables of percentage points of the inverted beta (*F*) distribution, *Biometrika*, 1943, *33*, 73–88, with permission of the editor.

Table C. continued

df associated with the denominator		1	2	3	4	5	6	7	8	9
					df associated with the numerator					
18	5%	4.41	3.55	3.16	2.93	2.77	2.66	2.58	2.51	2.46
	1%	**8.29**	**6.01**	**5.09**	**4.58**	**4.25**	**4.01**	**3.84**	**3.71**	**3.60**
19	5%	4.38	3.52	3.13	2.90	2.74	2.63	2.54	2.48	2.42
	1%	**8.18**	**5.93**	**5.01**	**4.50**	**4.17**	**3.94**	**3.77**	**3.63**	**3.52**
20	5%	4.35	3.49	3.10	2.87	2.71	2.60	2.51	2.45	2.39
	1%	**8.10**	**5.85**	**4.94**	**4.43**	**4.10**	**3.87**	**3.70**	**3.56**	**3.46**
21	5%	4.32	3.47	3.07	2.84	2.68	2.57	2.49	2.42	2.37
	1%	**8.02**	**5.78**	**4.87**	**4.37**	**4.04**	**3.81**	**3.64**	**3.51**	**3.40**
22	5%	4.30	3.44	3.05	2.82	2.66	2.55	2.46	2.40	2.34
	1%	**7.95**	**5.72**	**4.82**	**4.31**	**3.99**	**3.76**	**3.59**	**3.45**	**3.35**
23	5%	4.28	3.42	3.03	2.80	2.64	2.53	2.44	2.37	2.32
	1%	**7.88**	**5.66**	**4.76**	**4.26**	**3.94**	**3.71**	**3.54**	**3.41**	**3.30**
24	5%	4.26	3.40	3.01	2.78	2.62	2.51	2.42	2.36	2.30
	1%	**7.82**	**5.61**	**4.72**	**4.22**	**3.90**	**3.67**	**3.50**	**3.36**	**3.26**
25	5%	4.24	3.39	2.29	2.76	2.60	2.49	2.40	2.34	2.28
	1%	**7.77**	**5.57**	**4.68**	**4.18**	**3.86**	**3.63**	**3.46**	**3.32**	**3.22**
26	5%	4.23	3.37	2.98	2.74	2.59	2.47	2.39	2.32	2.27
	1%	**7.72**	**5.53**	**4.64**	**4.14**	**3.82**	**3.59**	**3.42**	**3.29**	**3.18**
27	5%	4.21	3.35	2.96	2.73	2.57	2.46	2.37	2.31	2.25
	1%	**7.68**	**5.49**	**4.60**	**4.11**	**3.78**	**3.56**	**3.39**	**3.26**	**3.15**
28	5%	4.20	3.34	2.95	2.71	2.56	2.45	2.36	2.29	2.24
	1%	**7.64**	**5.45**	**4.57**	**4.07**	**3.75**	**3.53**	**3.36**	**3.23**	**3.12**
29	5%	4.18	3.33	2.93	2.70	2.55	2.43	2.35	2.28	2.22
	1%	**7.60**	**5.42**	**4.54**	**4.04**	**3.73**	**3.50**	**3.33**	**3.20**	**3.09**
30	5%	4.17	3.32	2.92	2.69	2.53	2.42	2.33	2.27	2.21
	1%	**7.56**	**5.39**	**4.51**	**4.02**	**3.70**	**3.47**	**3.30**	**3.17**	**3.07**
40	5%	4.08	3.23	2.84	2.61	2.45	2.34	2.25	2.18	2.12
	1%	**7.31**	**5.18**	**4.31**	**3.83**	**3.51**	**3.29**	**3.12**	**2.99**	**2.89**
60	5%	4.00	3.15	2.76	2.53	2.37	2.25	2.17	2.10	2.04
	1%	**7.08**	**4.98**	**4.13**	**3.65**	**3.34**	**3.12**	**2.95**	**2.82**	**2.72**
120	5%	3.92	3.07	2.68	2.45	2.29	2.18	2.09	2.02	1.96
	1%	**6.85**	**4.79**	**3.95**	**3.48**	**3.17**	**2.96**	**2.79**	**2.66**	**2.56**

Table D. Critical values of q_α

df_w	α	2	3	4	5	6	7	8	9	10
					k = Number of Means					
1	.05	17.97	26.98	32.82	37.08	40.41	43.12	45.40	47.36	49.07
	.01	90.03	135.00	164.30	185.60	202.20	215.80	227.20	237.00	245.60
2	.05	6.08	8.33	9.80	10.88	11.74	12.44	13.03	13.54	13.99
	.01	14.04	19.02	22.29	24.72	26.63	28.20	29.53	30.68	31.69
3	.05	4.50	5.91	6.82	7.50	8.04	8.48	8.85	9.18	9.46
	.01	8.26	10.62	12.17	13.33	14.24	15.00	15.64	16.20	16.69
4	.05	3.93	5.04	5.76	6.29	6.71	7.05	7.35	7.60	7.83
	.01	6.51	8.12	9.17	9.96	10.58	11.10	11.55	11.93	12.27
5	.05	3.64	4.60	5.22	5.67	6.03	6.33	6.58	6.80	6.99
	.01	5.70	6.98	7.80	8.42	8.91	9.32	9.67	9.97	10.24
6	.05	3.46	4.34	4.90	5.30	5.63	5.90	6.12	6.32	6.49
	.01	5.24	6.33	7.03	7.56	7.97	8.32	8.61	8.87	9.10
7	.05	3.34	4.16	4.68	5.06	5.36	5.61	5.82	6.00	6.16
	.01	4.95	5.92	6.54	7.01	7.37	7.68	7.94	8.17	8.37
8	.05	3.26	4.04	4.53	4.89	5.17	5.40	5.60	5.77	5.92
	.01	4.75	5.64	6.20	6.62	6.96	7.24	7.47	7.68	7.86
9	.05	3.20	3.95	4.41	4.76	5.02	5.24	5.43	5.59	5.74
	.01	4.60	5.43	5.96	6.35	6.66	6.91	7.13	7.33	7.49
10	.05	3.15	3.88	4.33	4.65	4.91	5.12	5.30	5.46	5.60
	.01	4.48	5.27	5.77	6.14	6.43	6.67	6.87	7.05	7.21
11	.05	3.11	3.82	4.26	4.57	4.82	5.03	5.20	5.35	5.49
	.01	4.39	5.15	5.62	5.97	6.25	6.48	6.67	6.84	6.99
12	.05	3.08	3.77	4.20	4.51	4.75	4.95	5.12	5.27	5.39
	.01	4.32	5.05	5.50	5.84	6.10	6.32	6.51	6.67	6.81
13	.05	3.06	3.73	4.15	4.45	4.69	4.88	5.05	5.19	5.32
	.01	4.26	4.96	5.40	5.73	5.98	6.19	6.37	6.53	6.67
14	.05	3.03	3.70	4.11	4.41	4.64	4.83	4.99	5.13	5.25
	.01	4.21	4.89	5.32	5.63	5.88	6.08	6.26	6.41	6.54
15	.05	3.01	3.67	4.08	4.37	4.59	4.78	4.94	5.08	5.20
	.01	4.17	4.84	5.25	5.56	5.80	5.99	6.16	6.31	6.44
16	.05	3.00	3.65	4.05	4.33	4.56	4.74	4.90	5.03	5.15
	.01	4.13	4.79	5.19	5.49	5.72	5.92	6.08	6.22	6.35
17	.05	2.98	3.63	4.02	4.30	4.52	4.70	4.86	4.99	5.11
	.01	4.10	4.74	5.14	5.43	5.66	5.85	6.01	6.15	6.27
18	.05	2.97	3.61	4.00	4.28	4.49	4.67	4.82	4.96	5.07
	.01	4.07	4.70	5.09	5.38	5.60	5.79	5.94	6.08	6.20
19	.05	2.96	3.59	3.98	4.25	4.47	4.65	4.79	4.92	5.04
	.01	4.05	4.67	5.05	5.33	5.55	5.73	5.89	6.02	6.14
20	.05	2.95	3.58	3.96	4.23	4.45	4.62	4.77	4.90	5.01
	.01	4.02	4.64	5.02	5.29	5.51	5.69	5.84	5.97	6.09
24	.05	2.92	3.53	3.90	4.17	4.37	4.54	4.68	4.81	4.92
	.01	3.96	4.55	4.91	5.17	5.37	5.54	5.69	5.81	5.92
30	.05	2.89	3.49	3.85	4.10	4.30	4.46	4.60	4.72	4.82
	.01	3.89	4.45	4.80	5.05	5.24	5.40	5.54	5.65	5.76
40	.05	2.86	3.44	3.79	4.04	4.23	4.39	4.52	4.63	4.73
	.01	3.82	4.37	4.70	4.93	5.11	5.26	5.39	5.50	5.60
60	.05	2.83	3.40	3.74	3.98	4.16	4.31	4.44	4.55	4.65
	.01	3.76	4.28	4.59	4.82	4.99	5.13	5.25	5.36	5.45
120	.05	2.80	3.36	3.68	3.92	4.10	4.24	4.36	4.47	4.56
	.01	3.70	4.20	4.50	4.71	4.87	5.01	5.12	5.21	5.30
∞	.05	2.77	3.31	3.63	3.86	4.03	4.17	4.29	4.39	4.47
	.01	3.64	4.12	4.40	4.60	4.76	4.88	4.99	5.08	5.16

Table E. Critical values of r

$df = N - 2$, where N is the number of pairs of scores.

Degrees of Freedom (df)	5%	1%	Degrees of Freedom (df)	5%	1%
1	.997	1.000	24	.388	.496
2	.950	.990	25	.381	.487
3	.878	.959	26	.374	.478
4	.811	.917	27	.367	.470
5	.754	.874	28	.361	.463
6	.707	.834	29	.355	.456
7	.666	.798	30	.349	.449
8	.632	.765	35	.325	.418
9	.602	.735	40	.304	.393
10	.576	.708	45	.288	.372
11	.553	.684	50	.273	.354
12	.532	.661	60	.250	.325
13	.514	.641	70	.232	.302
14	.497	.623	80	.217	.283
15	.482	.606	90	.205	.267
16	.468	.590	100	.195	.254
17	.456	.575	125	.174	.228
18	.444	.561	150	.159	.208
19	.433	.549	200	.138	.181
20	.423	.537	300	.113	.148
21	.413	.526	400	.098	.128
22	.404	.515	500	.088	.115
23	.396	.505	1000	.062	.081

Source: This table is adapted from Table VII of Fisher and Yates: *Statistical Tables for Biological, Agricultural and Medical Research,* published by Longman Group Ltd., London (previously published by Oliver & Boyd, Edinburgh), and by permission of the authors and publishers.

Table F. Critical values of r_s

N	5%	1%
5	1.000	—
6	.886	1.000
7	.786	.929
8	.738	.881
9	.683	.833
10	.648	.794
12	.591	.777
14	.544	.714
16	.506	.665
18	.475	.625
20	.450	.591
22	.428	.562
24	.409	.537
26	.392	.515
28	.377	.496
30	.364	.478

Source: This table is adapted from Olds, E. G., Distribution of sums of squares of rank differences for small samples, *Annals of Mathematical Statistics*, 1938, *9*, 133-148, and, the 5% significance levels for sums of squares of rank differences and a correction, *Annals of Mathematical Statistics*, 1949, *20*, 117-118, with permission of the editor.

Table G. Critical values of χ^2
$df = (R - 1)(C - 1)$, where R
is the number of rows and C is
the number of columns. For a
table with only one row,
$df = C - 1$.

Degrees of Freedom (df)	5%	1%
1	3.84	6.64
2	5.99	9.21
3	7.82	11.34
4	9.49	13.28
5	11.07	15.09
6	12.59	16.81
7	14.07	18.48
8	15.51	20.09
9	16.92	21.67
10	18.31	23.21
11	19.68	24.72
12	21.03	26.22
13	22.36	27.69
14	23.68	29.14
15	25.00	30.58
16	26.30	32.00
17	27.59	33.41
18	28.87	34.80
19	30.14	36.19
20	31.41	37.57
21	32.67	38.93
22	33.92	40.29
23	35.17	41.64
24	36.42	42.98
25	37.65	44.31
26	38.88	45.64
27	40.11	46.96
28	41.34	48.28
29	42.56	49.59
30	43.77	50.89

Source: This table is adapted from Table IV of Fisher and Yates: *Statistical Tables for Biological, Agricultural and Medical Research*, published by Longman Group Ltd., London (previously published by Oliver & Boyd, Edinburgh), and by permission of the authors and publishers.

Table H. Probabilities of observed values of U in the Mann-Whitney Test when the larger of the samples has N = 8 or less

$N_2 = 3$

U \ N_1	1	2	3
0	.250	.100	.050
1	.500	.200	.100
2	.750	.400	.200
3		.600	.350
4			.500
5			.650

$N_2 = 4$

U \ N_1	1	2	3	4
0	.200	.067	.028	.014
1	.400	.133	.057	.029
2	.600	.267	.114	.057
3		.400	.200	.100
4		.600	.314	.171
5			.429	.243
6			.571	.343
7				.443
8				.557

$N_2 = 5$

U \ N_1	1	2	3	4	5
0	.167	.047	.018	.008	.004
1	.333	.095	.036	.016	.008
2	.500	.190	.071	.032	.016
3	.667	.286	.125	.056	.028
4		.429	.196	.095	.048
5		.571	.286	.143	.075
6			.393	.206	.111
7			.500	.278	.155
8			.607	.365	.210
9				.452	.274
10				.548	.345
11					.421
12					.500
13					.579

$N_2 = 6$

U \ N_1	1	2	3	4	5	6
0	.143	.036	.012	.005	.002	.001
1	.286	.071	.024	.010	.004	.002
2	.428	.143	.048	.019	.009	.004
3	.571	.214	.083	.033	.015	.008
4		.321	.131	.057	.026	.013
5		.429	.190	.086	.041	.021
6		.571	.274	.129	.063	.032
7			.357	.176	.089	.047
8			.452	.238	.123	.066
9			.548	.305	.165	.090
10				.381	.214	.120
11				.457	.268	.155
12				.545	.331	.197
13					.396	.242
14					.465	.294
15					.535	.350
16						.409
17						.469
18						.531

Source: This table is adapted from Mann, H. B., & Whitney, D. R., On a test of whether one of two random variables is stochastically larger than the other, *Annals of Mathematical Statistics*, 1947, *18*, 52–54, with permission of the editor.

Table H. continued

$N_2 = 7$

N₂ \ N₁	1	2	3	4	5	6	7
0	.125	.028	.008	.003	.001	.001	.000
1	.250	.056	.017	.006	.003	.001	.001
2	.375	.111	.033	.012	.005	.002	.001
3	.500	.167	.058	.021	.009	.004	.002
4	.625	.250	.092	.036	.015	.007	.003
5		.333	.133	.055	.024	.011	.006
6		.444	.192	.082	.037	.017	.009
7		.556	.258	.115	.053	.026	.013
8			.333	.158	.074	.037	.019
9			.417	.206	.101	.051	.027
10			.500	.264	.134	.069	.036
11			.583	.324	.172	.090	.049
12				.394	.216	.117	.064
13				.464	.265	.147	.082
14				.538	.319	.183	.104
15					.378	.223	.130
16					.438	.267	.159
17					.500	.314	.191
18					.562	.365	.228
19						.418	.267
20						.473	.310
21						.527	.355
22							.402
23							.451
24							.500
25							.549

Table H. continued

$N_2 = 8$

U \ N₁	1	2	3	4	5	6	7	8
0	.111	.022	.006	.002	.001	.000	.000	.000
1	.222	.044	.012	.004	.002	.001	.000	.000
2	.333	.089	.024	.008	.003	.001	.001	.000
3	.444	.133	.042	.014	.005	.002	.001	.001
4	.556	.200	.067	.024	.009	.004	.002	.001
5		.267	.097	.036	.015	.006	.003	.001
6		.356	.139	.055	.023	.010	.005	.002
7		.444	.188	.077	.033	.015	.007	.003
8		.556	.248	.107	.047	.021	.010	.005
9			.315	.141	.064	.030	.014	.007
10			.387	.184	.085	.041	.020	.010
11			.461	.230	.111	.054	.027	.014
12			.539	.285	.142	.071	.036	.019
13				.341	.177	.091	.047	.025
14				.404	.217	.114	.060	.032
15				.467	.262	.141	.076	.041
16				.533	.311	.172	.095	.052
17					.362	.207	.116	.065
18					.416	.245	.140	.080
19					.472	.286	.168	.097
20					.528	.331	.198	.117
21						.377	.232	.139
22						.426	.268	.164
23						.475	.306	.191
24						.525	.347	.221
25							.389	.253
26							.433	.287
27							.478	.323
28							.522	.360
29								.399
30								.439
31								.480
32								.520

Table I. Critical values of U for samples of size N = 9 to 20

Critical Values of U for a One-tailed Test at $\alpha = .025$ or for a Two-tailed Test at $\alpha = .05$

U \ N_2	9	10	11	12	13	14	15	16	17	18	19	20
1												
2	0	0	0	1	1	1	1	1	2	2	2	2
3	2	3	3	4	4	5	5	6	6	7	7	8
4	4	5	6	7	8	9	10	11	11	12	13	13
5	7	8	9	11	12	13	14	15	17	18	19	20
6	10	11	13	14	16	17	19	21	22	24	25	27
7	12	14	16	18	20	22	24	26	28	30	32	34
8	15	17	19	22	24	26	29	31	34	36	38	41
9	17	20	23	26	28	31	34	37	39	42	45	48
10	20	23	26	29	33	36	39	42	45	48	52	55
11	23	26	30	33	37	40	44	47	51	55	58	62
12	26	29	33	37	41	45	49	53	57	61	65	69
13	28	33	37	41	45	50	54	59	63	67	72	76
14	31	36	40	45	50	55	59	64	67	74	78	83
15	34	39	44	49	54	59	64	70	75	80	85	90
16	37	42	47	53	59	64	70	75	81	86	92	98
17	39	45	51	57	63	67	75	81	87	93	99	105
18	42	48	55	61	67	74	80	86	93	99	106	112
19	45	52	58	65	72	78	85	92	99	106	113	119
20	48	55	62	69	76	83	90	98	105	112	119	127

Source: The original data for this table was adapted from Auble, D., Extended tables for the Mann-Whitney statistic, *Bulletin of the Institute of Educational Research at Indiana University,* 1953, and appears here with the permission of the publisher.

Table J. Critical values of T

N	Level of Significance for One-Tailed Test		
	.025	.01	.005
	Level of Significance for Two-Tailed Test		
	.05	.02	.01
6	0	—	—
7	2	0	—
8	4	2	0
9	6	3	2
10	8	5	3
11	11	7	5
12	14	10	7
13	17	13	10
14	21	16	13
15	25	20	16
16	30	24	20
17	35	28	23
18	40	33	28
19	46	38	32
20	52	43	38
21	59	49	43
22	66	56	49
23	73	62	55
24	81	69	61
25	89	77	68

Source: This table is adapted from Table I of Wilcoxon, F., *Some Rapid Approximate Statistical Procedures,* American Cyanamid Company, 1949, p. 13, with permission of the author and the publisher.

Table K. Probabilities of values as large as observed values of H when there are three groups and N = 5 or less in each group

Sample Sizes					Sample Sizes				
N_1	N_2	N_3	H	p	N_1	N_2	N_3	H	p
2	1	1	2.7000	.500	4	2	2	6.0000	.014
								5.3333	.033
2	2	1	3.6000	.200				5.1250	.052
								4.4583	.100
2	2	2	4.5714	.067				4.1667	.105
			3.7143	.200					
					4	3	1	5.8333	.021
3	1	1	3.2000	.300				5.2083	.050
								5.0000	.057
3	2	1	4.2857	.100				4.0556	.093
			3.8571	.133				3.8889	.129
3	2	2	5.3572	.029	4	3	2	6.4444	.008
			4.7143	.048				6.3000	.011
			4.5000	.067				5.4444	.046
			4.4643	.105				5.4000	.051
								4.5111	.098
3	3	1	5.1429	.043				4.4444	.102
			4.5714	.100					
			4.0000	.129	4	3	3	6.7455	.010
								6.7091	.013
3	3	2	6.2500	.011				5.7909	.046
			5.3611	.032				5.7273	0.50
			5.1389	.061				4.7091	.092
			4.5556	.100				4.7000	.101
			4.2500	.121					
					4	4	1	6.6667	.010
3	3	3	7.2000	.004				6.1667	.022
			6.4889	.011				4.9667	.048
			5.6889	.029				4.8667	.054
			5.6000	.050				4.1667	.082
			5.0667	.086				4.0667	.102
			4.6222	.100					
					4	4	2	7.0364	.006
4	1	1	3.5714	.200				6.8727	.011
								5.4545	.046
4	2	1	4.8214	.057				5.2364	.052
			4.5000	.076				4.5545	.098
			4.0179	.114				4.4455	.103

Source: This table was adapted from Kruskal, W. H., & Wallis, W. A., Use of ranks in one-criterion variance analysis, *Journal of the American Statistical Association*, 1952, *47*, 614–617, and includes corrections reported by the authors in Errata, *Journal of the American Statistical Association, 48* 910. The table appears with the permission of the publisher.

Table K. continued

Sample Sizes					Sample Sizes				
N_1	N_2	N_3	H	p	N_1	N_2	N_3	H	p
4	4	3	7.1439	.010	5	3	2	6.9091	.009
			7.1364	.011				6.8218	.010
			5.5985	.049				5.2509	.049
			5.5758	.051				5.1055	.052
			4.5455	.099				4.6509	.091
			4.4773	.102				4.4945	.101
4	4	4	7.6538	.008	5	3	3	7.0788	.009
			7.5385	.011				6.9818	.011
			5.6923	.049				5.6485	.049
			5.6538	.054				5.5152	.051
			4.6539	.097				4.5333	.097
			4.5001	.104				4.4121	.109
5	1	1	3,8571	.143	5	4	1	6.9545	.008
								6.8400	.011
5	2	1	5.2500	.036				4.9855	.044
			5.0000	.048				4.8600	.056
			4.4500	.071				3.9873	.098
			4.2000	.095				3.9600	.102
			4.0500	.119					
					5	4	2	7.2045	.009
5	2	2	6.5333	.008				7.1182	.010
			6.1333	.013				5.2727	.049
			5.1600	.034				5.2682	.050
			5.0400	.056				4.5409	.098
			4.3733	.090				4.5182	.101
			4.2933	.122					
					5	4	3	7.4449	.010
5	3	1	6.4000	.012				7.3949	.011
			4.9600	.048				5.6564	.049
			4.8711	.052				5.6308	.050
			4.0178	.095				4.5487	.099
			3.8400	.123				4.5231	.103

Table K. continued

Sample Sizes					Sample Sizes				
N_1	N_2	N_3	H	p	N_1	N_2	N_3	H	p
5	4	4	7.7604	.009	5	5	3	7.5780	.010
			7.7440	.011				7.5429	.010
			5.6571	.049				5.7055	.046
			5.6176	.050				5.6264	.051
			4.6187	.100				4.5451	.100
			4.5527	.102				4.5363	.102
5	5	1	7.3091	.009	5	5	4	7.8229	.010
			6.8364	.011				7.7914	.010
			5.1273	.046				5.6657	.049
			4.9091	.053				5.6429	.050
			4.1091	.086				4.5229	.099
			4.0364	.105				4.5200	.101
5	5	2	7.3385	.010	5	5	5	8.0000	.009
			7.2692	.010				7.9800	.010
			5.3385	.047				5.7800	.049
			5.2462	.051				5.6600	.051
			4.6231	.097				4.5600	.100
			4.5077	.100				4.5000	.102

Answers to Odd Numbered Exercises

It is possible that some of the answers that you get when you work the additional exercises beginning with chapter 4 will not be quite the same as the answers I obtained and am reporting here. In solving the problems I used a pocket calculator in the fashion that I have described in relevant portions of the text. Thus, if you do not use the memory function of your calculator, more frequent rounding decisions will be made and the final answer you obtain will reflect these rounding decisions. Now, I'm not saying that your answer is wrong; I'm merely warning you that you may have solved the problem correctly and your answer will not be quite the same as mine. Of course, if there is a great deal of discrepancy between your answer and mine, one of us is wrong.

Chapter 2

1. Frequency distribution:

X	f	X	f	X	f
50	2	35	1	20	2
48	1	34	1	18	2
47	1	33	2	16	2
45	1	29	2	15	1
44	1	28	1	14	2
40	2	27	1	13	2
38	2	25	2	12	1
37	1	23	1	11	1

Grouped frequency distribution:

$i = 5$

CI	f
46–50	4
41–45	2
36–40	5

(*Continued*)

CI	f
31–35	4
26–30	4
21–25	3
16–20	6
11–15	7

3. $i = 7$

CI	f
151–157	2
144–150	2
137–143	2
130–136	2
123–129	4
116–122	0
109–115	0
102–108	4
95–101	4

5. $i = 5$

CI			
Apparent Limits	Real Limits	Midpoints	f
65–69	64.5–69.5	67	1
60–64	59.5–64.5	62	1
55–59	54.5–59.5	57	2
50–54	49.5–54.5	52	2
45–49	44.5–49.5	47	4
40–44	39.5–44.5	42	6
35–39	34.5–39.5	37	6
30–34	29.5–34.5	32	5
25–29	24.5–29.5	27	3

7. $i = 5$

CI		
Apparent Limits	Real Limits	f
110–114	109.5–114.5	1
105–109	104.5–109.5	0
100–104	99.5–104.5	1
95–99	94.5–99.5	2
90–94	89.5–94.5	1
85–89	84.5–89.5	2
80–84	79.5–84.5	5
75–79	74.5–79.5	7
70–74	69.5–74.5	5
65–69	64.5–69.5	6

Chapter 3

1.

X	f
15	1
14	3
13	4
12	5
11	3
10	2

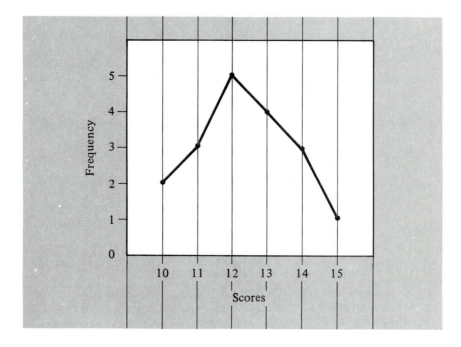

3. $i = 5$

	CI			
Apparent Limits	Real Limits	Midpoint	f	Cum f
94–98	93.5–98.5	96	12	49
89–93	88.5–93.5	91	21	37
84–88	83.5–88.5	86	6	16
79–83	78.5–83.5	81	3	10
74–78	73.5–78.5	76	3	7
69–73	68.5–73.5	71	1	4
64–68	63.5–68.5	66	1	3
59–63	58.5–63.5	61	0	2
54–58	53.5–58.5	56	2	2

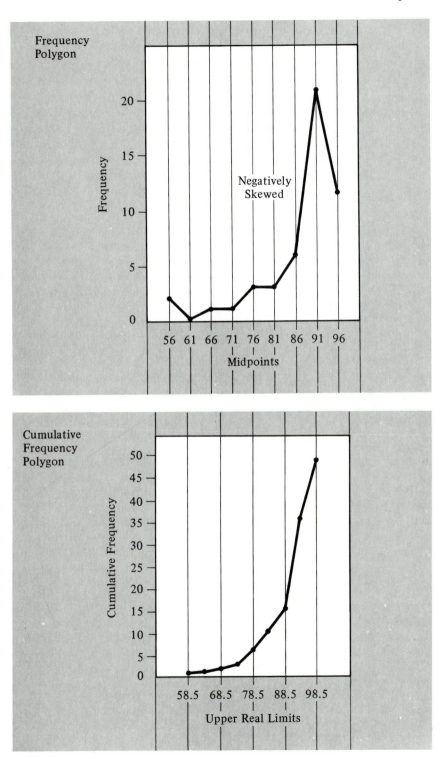

5.

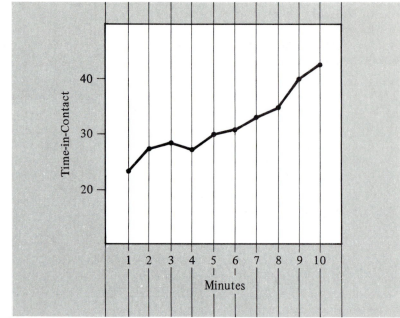

7.

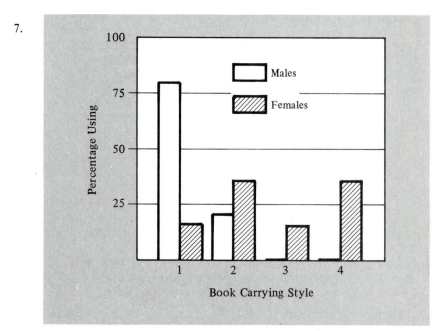

Chapter 4

1. $\bar{X} = -24.67\%$; Md $= -35$; Mo $= -100$; Md most appropriate measure; Positively skewed

3. (a) Md
   (b) Mo
   (c) $\bar{X}$

5. Group Rum-flavored cola. Mo $= 18$, Md $= 18$, $\bar{X} = 18.7$, $\bar{X}$ most appropriate
   Group Rum and cola. Mo $= 46$, Md $= 28.5$, $\bar{X} = 39.7$, Md most appropriate
   Group Rum and cola excluding subjects not achieving criterion: Mo $= 46$, Md $= 24$, $\bar{X} = 30.2$, $\bar{X}$ most appropriate

7. $\bar{X} = 7.79$, Md $= 8$, Mo $= 9$, Negatively skewed

9. $\bar{X} = 417.37$, Md $= 416.5$, Mo $= 423$

Chapter 5

1. SD $= 2$, $s = 2.01$, SD$^2 = 4$

3. SD $= 3$

5. $R = 8$, $\bar{X} = 5.14$, SD $= 1.88$, $s = 1.92$, $s^2 = 3.69$

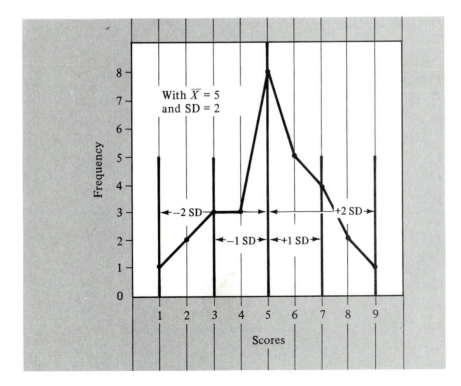

7. $SD^2 = 15.93$, $s^2 = 16.68$

9. $R = 20.8$, $SD = 6.22$, $s = 6.34$

11. σ^2, s, σ, SD, SD^2, s^2

Chapter 6

5. (a) 0.99, 97.72
   (b) 401
   (c) 5.56 or less, 11.44 or more
   (d) 23

7. (a) 99.66, 1.1
   (b) 46
   (c) 2
   (d) 171
   (e) 62.28 or less, 89.72 or more
       67.04 or less, 84.96 or more
   (f) 82.65
   (g) $p = 0.0051$

9. (a) 51
   (b) 827
   (c) $p = 0.015$
   (d) 70.1 inches
   (e) 73.94 inches

Chapter 7

1. (a) 7.19 to 12.81
   (b) 9.35 to 10.65

3. 95% confidence interval = 28.55 to 31.79
   99% confidence interval = 27.97 to 32.37

5. $t = -2.51$, $df = 9$, $p < .05$
   95% confidence interval = 91.48 to 99.12

9. $t = 3.62$, $df = 9$, $p < .01$

Chapter 8

1. $t = 2.26$, $df = 18$, $p < .05$
   Table values required: 5% = 2.1009, 1% = 2.8784

3. $t = 4.39$, $df = 38$, $p < .01$

5. $t = 2.91$, $df = 9$, $p < .05$

9. $t = -7.93$, $df = 5$, $p < .01$

Chapter 9

1. $F = 1.32$; $df = 2, 33$; not significant

3. $F = 14.80$; $df = 3, 34$; $p < .01$

5. $F = 17.65$; $df = 3, 16$; $p < .01$
   $HSD_{.05} = 3.91$, $HSD_{.01} = 5.01$
   The following group comparisons were significant with a $p < .01$: Groups OC
   and SEP, Groups OC and VMH, Groups SEP and OB. Groups OB and VMH
   differed also ($p < .05$).

9. $F = 37.33$; $df = 2, 21$; $p < .01$
   $HSD_{.05} = 1.39$, $HSD_{.01} = 1.80$
   All pairwise comparisons are significant ($p < .01$).

Chapter 10

1. (a) $r = 0.8$, $p < .01$
   (b) $Y = 1.07X + 1.3$
   (c) $Y = 15.21$
   (d) $X = 4.39$

3. $r_S = -.85$, $p < .01$

5. $r = .91$, $p < .01$
   $Y = .69X - 28.75$
   $Y = 16.8$

7. $-.98$, $.95$, $.85$, $.57$, $-.37$, $.08$ from most to least degree of relationship

9. $r = .86$, $p < .01$

Chapter 11

1. $\chi^2 = 33.53$, $df = 2$, $p < .01$

3. $\chi^2 = 103.98$, $df = 1$, $p < .01$

5. $p = .05124$, one-tailed test, not significant

9. $p = .0003$, one-tailed test, significant

Chapter 12

1. $U = 1$, $p = .008$

3. Group MM vs Group MN, $U = 16.5$, $p < .05$, two-tailed test
   Group MM vs Group MF, $U = 5$, $p = .006$
   Group MN vs Group MF, $U = 4.5$, $p < .05$, two-tailed test

5. $H = 19.54$, $df = 3$, $p < .01$

9. $T = 31$, not significant

Index